CONVEYANCING 2007

CONVEYANCING 2007

Kenneth G C Reid WS

Professor of Property Law in the University of Edinburgh

and

George L Gretton WS

Lord President Reid Professor of Law in the University of Edinburgh

with a contribution by Alan Barr of the University of Edinburgh

Avizandum Publishing Ltd
Edinburgh
2008

Published by
Avizandum Publishing Ltd
58 Candlemaker Row
Edinburgh EH1 2QE

First published 2008

ISBN 978-1-904968-25-2

British Library Cataloguing in Publication Data
A catalogue record for this book is available from the British Library.

Typeset by Waverley Typesetters, Fakenham
Printed and bound by Bell & Bain Ltd, Glasgow

CONTENTS

PREFACE

This is the ninth annual update of new developments in the law of conveyancing. As in previous years, it is divided into five parts. There is, first, a brief description of all cases which have been reported or have appeared on the Scottish Courts website (www.scotcourts.gov.uk) or have otherwise come to our attention since *Conveyancing 2006*. The next two parts summarise, respectively, statutory developments during 2007 and other material of interest to conveyancers. The fourth part is a detailed commentary on selected issues arising from the first three parts. Finally, in part V, there are two tables. The first, a cumulative table of appeals, is designed to facilitate moving from one annual volume to the next. The second is a table of cases digested in earlier volumes but reported, either for the first time or in an additional series, in 2007. This is for the convenience of future reference.

We do not seek to cover agricultural holdings, crofting, public sector tenancies (except the right-to-buy legislation), compulsory purchase or planning law. Otherwise our coverage is intended to be complete.

We gratefully acknowledge help received from Alan Barr, Duncan Campbell, John Glover, Roddy Paisley, David Sellar and Scott Wortley.

Kenneth G C Reid
George L Gretton
17 March 2008

TABLE OF STATUTES

TABLE OF ORDERS, RULES AND REGULATIONS

TABLE OF CASES

❦ PART I ❦
CASES

CASES

The full text of all opinions of the Court of Session and of many of the sheriff court is available on the Scottish Courts website: www.scotcourts.gov.uk.

Since 1 January 2005 all Court of Session opinions are numbered consecutively according to whether they are decisions of the Outer House or Inner House. Thus '[2007] CSOH 4' refers to the fourth Outer House decision of 2007, and '[2007] CSIH 15' refers to the fifteenth Inner House decision of 2007. This neutral method of citation is used throughout this volume.

COMMON PROPERTY

(1) MacLeod's Tr v MacLeod
2007 Hous LR 34, Sh Ct

This was an action of division and sale in respect of a matrimonial home by the trustee in sequestration on the estate of the husband, who co-owned with his wife. The wife defended on the basis of (i) s 40 of the Bankruptcy (Scotland) Act 1985 and (ii) art 8 of the European Convention on Human Rights read with art 1 of the First Protocol of the Convention.

Section 40 provides that the court can delay a sale of the debtor's property, or its division and sale if it is co-owned. In doing so, it must have regard to all the circumstances of the case, including:

(a) the needs and financial resources of the debtor's spouse or former spouse;
(b) the needs and financial resources of any child of the family;
(c) the interests of the creditors;
(d) the length of the period during which ... the family home was used as a residence by any of the persons referred to in paragraph (a) or (b) above.

In invoking this provision the defender pled that 'the defender and the debtor reside together at the property with ... their daughter, who is 18 years old, their daughter's partner, who is 22 years old, and their daughter and her partner's child, who is 22 months old'. There were further averments, including that the defender had a low income, that she helped look after her grandchild, and that one of her children suffered from depression. The sheriff (A V Noble) held that these averments were too lacking in specification to go to proof. For example, although the defender had averments about her income, she had no averments about whether she had any capital. Decree in favour of the pursuer was granted.

On the ECHR defence, the sheriff had this to say (para 13):

> There are sound reasons for enabling a *pro indiviso* proprietor who does not want to continue in co-ownership to require sale of the subjects: see *Upper Crathes Fishings Ltd v Bailey's Exrs* 1991 SC 30. It remains open to co-proprietors to deprive themselves contractually of that power, and in addition a *pro indiviso* proprietor might be personally barred from insisting on division and sale. Equitable considerations can arise in relation to the division of property, if it can be divided, or division of the proceeds. In relation to the situation where a family home is involved, further statutory provisions such as s 19 of the Matrimonial Homes (Family Protection) (Scotland) Act 1981 or, as in this case s 40 of the Bankruptcy (Scotland) Act 1985 come into play. In these circumstances the remedy of division and sale is Convention compliant.

See **Commentary** p 153.

TENEMENTS

(2) PS Properties (2) Ltd v Callaway Homes Ltd
[2007] CSOH 162, 2007 GWD 31-526

Circumstances in which an interim interdict was recalled, with the result that repairs to a common stair could go ahead. See **Commentary** p 140.

SERVITUDES

(3) Moncrieff v Jamieson
[2007] UKHL 42, 2007 SCLR 790, 2007 SLT 989

A servitude right of way was **held** to include, by implication, a right to park on the servient tenement. This affirms the decision of the sheriff (2004 SCLR 135; *Conveyancing 2003* Case (20)) and of the Inner House ([2005] CSIH 14, 2005 SC 281, 2005 SLT 225, 2005 SCLR 463; *Conveyancing 2005* Case (6)). See **Commentary** p 106.

(4) Latham v Hunt
2007 GWD 25-434, Sh Ct

Access to the pursuers' house was by means of a road which belonged to the defender. When the defender narrowed the road by placing rocks on both sides, and added speed humps, the pursuers sought, and obtained, an interdict against the defender from impeding, restricting or hindering access. This was the appeal, at which the defender (now appellant) represented himself. In rejecting the appeal, the sheriff principal (Sir Stephen S T Young QC) touched on two matters of general interest.

One was onus of proof. The sheriff principal said (para 12):

It is of course correct that the initial burden of proving that there has been an interference by the servient proprietor with a servitude right of access over his property rests upon the dominant proprietor. But, if such interference has been shown to have taken place, then it is up to the servient proprietor to demonstrate nonetheless that what he has done is required for the proper enjoyment of his property and is an immaterial interference with the rights of the dominant proprietor.

The other was the legality of speed humps. Cusine and Paisley had previously suggested that the decision in *Simpson v Head* (1990) *Unreported Property Cases from the Sheriff Courts* (eds R R M Paisley and D J Cusine) 237 'leaves it open to the servient proprietor to install road humps of lesser size which are not likely to cause' damage to vehicles: see D J Cusine and R R M Paisley, *Servitudes and Rights of Way* (1998) p 445 n 87. The sheriff principal thought that this formulation understated the rights of the dominant owner (para 15):

In my opinion it is not the law that, before it can be required to be removed from a road over which a servitude right of vehicular access exists, a speed hump must have caused, or be likely to cause, damage to vehicles passing over it. The true question here is whether the presence of the speed hump on the road constitutes an interference with the enjoyment by the dominant proprietor of his right of vehicular access which is more than merely immaterial.... In the present case the sheriff found in fact (see finding in fact 18) that the two speed humps which were last installed by the defender caused the driver and passengers in vehicles to be jolted and so caused discomfort. In addition the sheriff found that one of the original three speed humps also caused discomfort. In my opinion this was enough to entitle him to find in fact and in law as he did (see finding in fact and law 3) that the continued presence of these speed humps, in addition to those which had actually caused damage to passing vehicles, had unlawfully diminished the use or convenience of the pursuers' servitude right of access over the road.

(5) Peart v Legge
[2007] CSIH 70, 2007 SLT 982

Even though a servitude of way could only be exercised by first breaching a wall on the dominant tenement, it was **held** to not be *res merae facultatis*. Accordingly, it was extinguished by negative prescription where it had not been used for 20 years. See **Commentary** p 117. This reverses the decision of the sheriff principal reported at 2007 SCLR 86 (*Conveyancing 2006* Case (18)).

(6) Robertson v Network Rail Infrastructure Ltd
28 May 2007, Inverness Sheriff Court

The Railway Clauses Consolidation (Scotland) Act 1845 was designed to facilitate the construction of railway lines through private land. Section 60 provides that:

The company shall make and at all times thereafter maintain the following works for the accommodation of the owners and occupiers of lands adjoining the railway; (that is to say) Such and so many convenient gates, bridges, arches, culverts, and passages, over, under, or by the sides of or leading to or from the railway, as shall be necessary for the purpose of making good any interruptions caused by the railway to the use of the lands through which the railway shall be made; and such works shall be made forthwith after the part of the railway passing over such lands shall have been laid out or formed, or during the formation thereof.

Under this provision a level crossing was built to allow communication between two parts of a farm which were bisected by a railway line. When, in the 1990s, the two parts came to be owned separately, the owner of one part asked the railway company to replace the existing gate with a fence, and the level crossing was closed. In 2002 the two parts came once again into the same ownership, and the owner requested that the level crossing be reinstated. This was refused. In this litigation the owner sought decree ordaining the defenders 'to implement and fulfil their obligations to restore the works which formed the level crossing … within a period of 90 days from the date of decree and maintain thereafter in terms of s 60 of the Railways Clauses Consolidation (Scotland) Act 1845'.

A decision of the Court of Appeal on the parallel legislation for England and Wales was against the pursuer: *Midland Railway Co v Gribble* [1895] 2 Ch 827. The sheriff (Colin Scott Mackenzie) declined to follow it. On the one hand, in *Gribble* 'it seems to me as if there have been certain conclusions reached there which may depend upon certain peculiarities of English conveyancing and their common law which we in Scotland might not necessarily follow' (pp 27–28 of the transcript). On the other hand, the statute was clear (pp 28–29):

> The company and its successors, the defenders, are obliged in terms of the Act to 'make and at all times thereafter maintain'. That is, surely, not capable of interpretation as anything other than a right in perpetuity? There is nothing that I could see in the Act about such a right ever being extinguished for any reason whatsoever other than by supervening legislative process nor, short of the destruction of the subjects, does our common law so far as I can see give relief to the servient proprietor in the manner suggested in *Gribble*. Parliament alone gives a statutory right and Parliament alone can take it away.

Summary decree was granted in favour of the pursuer. Subsequently, the sheriff's interlocutor was partially reduced by the Court of Session, so as to allow an appeal on the merits (which would otherwise have been prevented by certain provisions in the 1845 Act). See *Network Rail Infrastructure Ptr* [2007] CSOH 169, 2008 SLT 25.

REAL BURDENS

(7) Barker v Lewis
2007 SLT (Sh Ct) 48

The owner of one of the houses in a five-house development started up a bed-and-breakfast business, contrary to the deed of conditions. Her neighbours sought interdict but this was refused on the ground that they had no interest to enforce. See **Commentary** p 74.

(8) Brown v Richardson
2007 GWD 28-490, Lands Tribunal

Burdens were imposed on a group of properties by a single feu charter. **Held:** that the properties were 'related' within the meaning of s 53 of the Title Conditions (Scotland) Act 2003. See **Commentary** p 77.

[Another aspect of this case is digested at (20).]

(9) Smith v Prior
2007 GWD 30-523, Lands Tribunal

A 1930s development was carried out by means of a series of separate feus. Doubt was expressed by the Lands Tribunal as to whether ss 52 or 53 of the Title Conditions (Scotland) Act 2003 applied. See **Commentary** p 79.

Some of the conditions were that certain activities were prohibited except with the superior's consent. As in *At.Home Nationwide Ltd v Morris* 2007 GWD 31-535 (see *Conveyancing 2006* pp 109–113), the Tribunal adopted the view, surely correctly, that the references to superiors fall so that one is left with an outright prohibition (p 18).

[Another aspect of this case is digested at (11).]

VARIATION ETC OF TITLE CONDITIONS BY LANDS TRIBUNAL

Many of the decisions which follow are unreported, but the full opinion in some can be found on the website of the Lands Tribunal: www.lands-tribunal-scotland.org.uk/title.html. For an analysis of the current state of the case law on the Lands Tribunal, see **Commentary** p 87.

(10) Smith v Elrick
2007 GWD 29-515, Lands Tribunal

In 1996 Fife Regional Council granted a feu disposition of a former farm steading comprising 1.9625 hectares. Among the burdens imposed was the following:

> [T]he feuar shall not be entitled to erect more than one additional house on the feu in addition to the existing farmhouse without the prior written consent of the Superiors....

The house was built and sold separately from the farmhouse. The applicant was the owner of that house. She had obtained planning permission to convert an existing barn into a house, and sought variation of the burden to the extent necessary to allow this to take place. The application was opposed by the owners of the farmhouse. The Tribunal granted the application, but subject to the imposition of two additional conditions, concerning windows, which were designed to protect the respondents' privacy.

As so often, the Tribunal founded mainly on factors (f), (b) and (c) in s 100 of the Title Conditions (Scotland) Act 2003, and in that order. Uncontroversially – but perhaps not very helpfully – the purpose of the burden (factor (f)) was found to be 'the protection of an area of natural beauty from over-development'. The burden itself, the Tribunal thought, was relatively ineffective. Although it prevented the erection of a new house, it did not prevent increased and intrusive use of the existing buildings – for example, subdivision of the applicant's house, or the use of the barn for a children's playroom or a teenager's den. Nor did it prevent the erection of buildings other than houses. Although, therefore, the properties were isolated and remote – qualities which were of value to the respondents – it could not be said that the burden was particularly effective in protecting the respondents' tranquillity. In other words – factor (b) – the benefit conferred was of a rather limited kind. By contrast, the burden impeded the applicant's enjoyment of her property to a considerable extent (factor (c)). Not only did it prevent her realising the financial gain which redevelopment would provide, but it limited the use of a building (ie the barn) which could no longer be used for its original purpose (there being no farm).

Although neither party had so argued, the Tribunal also gave weight to factor (j) (any other material factors), in respect that the new house was to be built wholly within the walls of an existing building. The impact of the change on the respondents would be correspondingly slight. The Tribunal did not 'consider that this development will have any significant effect on the amenity of the locality' (p 16).

(11) Smith v Prior
2007 GWD 30-523 (merits), 2 March 2007 (expenses), Lands Tribunal

This application concerned a 1930s development in the Murrayfield area of Edinburgh (Campbell Road and Cumlodden Avenue). The applicants wished to build a modest rear extension to their bungalow in Campbell Road but this was contrary to a no-building provision in the original feu charter of 1934. This was one of a series of feu charters, in similar terms, granted by the same superior in respect of a number of neighbouring feus. The houses were built by the feuars and varied in style. Although the position was unclear, the applicants took the cautious view that, despite the abolition of the feudal system, their neighbours might have enforcement rights by virtue of ss 52 and 53 of the Title Conditions (Scotland) Act 2003. Hence this application. It was opposed by three close neighbours.

Beginning as usual with the purpose of the burden (factor (f)), the Tribunal concluded that, read with the other burdens, it was 'to maintain the general amenity of the area and it was not conceived to protect the amenity of immediate neighbours' (p 20). More precisely (p 19):

It essentially contained building restrictions subject to consent, so it was a power of control over future development. Taken with the regulation of and control over the original building, the prohibition of sub-division and the use restriction, it would seem to reflect a purpose of protecting the residential character, low housing density and general amenity of the area as a whole. This was, however, protection in the superior's interest, not the interests of neighbours. The superior was a landowner in the course of selling off his land in lots or portions, thus replacing rents or other annual fruits of his use of the land with land sale prices and ongoing feuduties. These ongoing restrictive conditions would help to preserve a general amenity to the benefit of his remaining land and to preserve the security of his investment in feuduties. They would also enable him to preserve a stake in development values, because he would be able to extract payments for relaxations. There is, however, no indication in any part of the clause of any purpose of protecting the physical amenity of immediate neighbours as opposed to the general amenity of the area.

On the basis of earlier authority this should have led the Tribunal to take a very restricted view of factor (b) (extent of benefit). For in *Church of Scotland General Trs v McLaren* 2006 SLT (Lands Tr) 27 at para 39, the Tribunal had seemed to say that factor (b) must be read in the light of the purpose of the condition: see *Conveyancing 2005* p 108. If, in fulfilment of that purpose, the burden confers benefit, that is a matter which properly falls within factor (b); but if the burden confers only a benefit of a *different* kind, that benefit is disregarded for the purposes of factor (b). In the present case the benefit which was argued to accrue to the respondents was primarily amenity protection as immediate neighbours. The effect of the extension, it was said, was to affect light and to result in property being overlooked. On one view such considerations were disqualified as beyond the purpose of the condition. Nonetheless the Tribunal was willing to entertain them – perhaps because to do anything else would often make it difficult to give content to factor (b) in a case where the burdens had previously been enforceable only by the feudal superior.

In the event, the amenity arguments based on factor (b) were found to be slight – certainly as compared to the serious restraint on enjoyment of the burdened property caused by the condition (factor (c)). The age of the burden (factor (e)) was another factor in favour of discharge, particularly as, during the intervening 70 years, the introduction of proper planning controls, in 1947, had allowed general amenity to be controlled in a different way. But in any case (p 22):

> [T]o the extent that rights of control may produce sterility, there must come a time when, however attractive to its immediate neighbours, that should be at last relaxed. Holding the applicants to a prohibition on extension more than 70 years after it was imposed would seem to us to require quite strong justification.

In those circumstances the Tribunal varied the burden to the extent required in order to allow the building of the extension. An outright discharge was rejected (p 23):

We can see an argument for doing so [ie granting an outright discharge], namely that it has really some time ago fulfilled its original purpose, which is now generally fulfilled by the public planning regime. There may be few cases in which, planning permission having been granted, it should be reasonable for neighbours to insist in their right to veto. However, on the basis on which this case has been argued, Parliament has recently legislated either to create a new enforcement right or at least preserve one which existed. It does seem possible to envisage situations in which, in the particular circumstances, a development (perhaps of a building of some 'other description') might not be reasonable as against the immediate neighbours. If there is indeed here a 'common scheme' with 'related properties', the existence of a condition, even if it might be expected to be discharged or varied to accommodate many if not necessarily all developments for which there is planning consent, may at least encourage appropriate communication and discussion of plans, with a view in very many cases to sensible agreement being reached.

[Another aspect of this case is digested at (9).]

(12) Anderson v McKinnon
2007 GWD 29-513, Lands Tribunal

A modern housing estate in Uddingston was subject to a deed of conditions originally imposed by feudal superiors. Whether the owners of the 50 houses had mutual enforcement rights as co-feuars is not clear from the Tribunal's opinion, but at any rate such rights now existed by virtue of the Title Conditions (Scotland) Act 2003. The applicants wished to build a rear extension, which would be within 1.5 metres of the gable wall of a neighbouring house. (At present the gap was 4 metres). This was contrary to a burden in the deed of conditions. The application was opposed by the neighbour.

The application was granted. On the one hand, the burden materially impeded the enjoyment of the burdened property (factor (c)) (p 10):

> The applicants' motives for extending are not of importance. They are exercising a normal wish to enjoy their property by extending their house. It would be a considerable hardship to them if they were unable to do so.

On the other hand (pp 9–10):

> [W]e consider the benefit to the respondent in maintaining her right to refuse approval of the applicants' proposed extension to be quite slight [factor (b)] – some modest effect on a light source already not very strong, and some very slight effect on privacy in an area of fairly dense modern housing.

Factor (a) (change in circumstances) also favoured the applicants because quite a number of extensions had been built elsewhere in the estate.

On the purpose of the burden (factor (f)), the Tribunal's remarks have some resemblance to those in the previous case, although they appear to have led to no particular conclusion. The remarks are (p 11):

This title condition is in standard general terms which are related more to control over extensions and alterations, in the interests of the general amenity of the neighbourhood, than by the particular protection of neighbours. There is, for example, no provision in relation to further building at or close to the boundaries of the houses. There is a provision which was designed to facilitate supervision in the general interest of plans of further building, rather than a veto on the basis of individual interests. That is not to say, of course, that the benefit of neighbours is to be ignored.

As usual, the discharge was only to the extent necessary for the building of the extension. In the Tribunal's words (p 12), 'the 2003 Act having confirmed, or even given, the right of co-proprietors in property communities to enforce former feudal burdens, it would not be appropriate to discharge these completely where they may still have some application in the future'.

(13) Wilson v McNamee
2007 GWD 39-678, Lands Tribunal

The applicant owned a site in Hawthorn Walk, Cambuslang on which a hall was built. This was one of eight plots feued by a feu disposition of 1923. They all contained houses, but the applicant's plot also had a hall. The building of a hall on this plot was permitted, though not required, by the feu disposition on the basis that it 'be used only for religious purposes'. The hall had been used by the Assembly of Christian Brothers until 2003 when the congregation dwindled to one person. It had since been marketed and acquired by the applicant, who proposed to let it out as a children's nursery. But the condition stood in his way. His application to have it discharged was opposed by the owner of one of the other eight plots. Her house was round the corner, and was separated from the hall by another house.

The application was dealt with by written submissions and a site visit. The Tribunal granted the application.

The Tribunal thought that, since the building of the hall was only permissive, the purpose of the condition (Title Conditions (Scotland) Act 2003 factor (f)) was the amenity of the immediate area rather than the furtherance of religion (para 19). (Compare *Church of Scotland General Trustees v McLaren* 2006 SLT (Lands Tr) 27, discussed in *Conveyancing 2005* p 113.) But as amenity was already amply provided for by clause fifth of the deed (which included an anti-nuisance clause), which the applicant was not seeking to have discharged, the Tribunal – rather unexpectedly – regarded factor (f) 'as having no significant bearing on our decision'. The general decline in religion was a relevant change in circumstances (factor (a)), which favoured the applicant. And while the condition impeded 'significantly' the enjoyment of the hall (factor (c), para 21), it conferred 'little benefit' on the respondent, who lived round the corner, opposite a food take-away and near a pub (factor (b), para 22).

The Tribunal also discharged other parts of the same condition which restricted alterations and new buildings.

(14) Cattanach v Vine-Hall
3 October 2007, Lands Tribunal

In 1996 the owners of a house and garden ('Cairnlea') in Kirriemuir sold a double building plot, subject to a deed of conditions. The plots came to be separately owned. A house ('Whitemills') was built on the first plot, close to the boundary with the second, and with a window overlooking it. The applicants, owners of the second plot, obtained planning permission to build a substantial one-and-a-half-storey house which, at its closest point, would be 2 metres from the boundary with Cairnlea. The deed of conditions prevented any building within 7 metres. Accordingly, the owners of plot 2 applied to have this condition varied or discharged. The application was opposed by the owners of Cairnlea, who were willing to allow a bungalow on the proposed footprint but not a house of the height which was currently proposed.

The Tribunal indicated that it would refuse the application but, at the request of the parties, delayed the decision in order to give the applicants an opportunity to make alternative proposals.

As often, the Tribunal began with factor (f) in s 100 of the Title Conditions (Scotland) Act 2003. The purpose of the condition was plainly to protect the amenity of Cairnlea, in respect both of light and privacy (para 22). It was true (para 23) that 'the relevance of the purpose of a title condition may be rendered less relevant, or even no longer relevant, by changes of circumstances since the condition had been created' but not in this case. In effect the purpose determined the nature of the condition's benefit (factor (b)). In the Tribunal's view, the proposed building would have a 'substantial effect on the amenity of Cairnlea' (para 13), dominating the view from the front of the house as well as significantly reducing the amount of light in the lounge. Admittedly, the condition caused considerable problems for the applicants (factor (c)), particularly as the location and nature of Whitemills prevented building close to that boundary. Indeed, the Tribunal accepted 'that the effect on Cairnlea might not seem to match the extent of the burden on the applicants' (para 29). But to be set against this was the fact that the condition was relatively new (factor (e)) (para 26):

> It is of course correct that our jurisdiction does allow us to discharge or vary conditions which may have been created very recently, and this factor tends to lose force if there have been relevant changes of circumstances, but we see this as a factor which supports the respondents' position and is of at least some force. Generally, the condition may be said to have been created during the course of a phase of residential development of this locality which is continuing, ie it was created not only recently in time but in general circumstances which remain much the same, as opposed to having been created during some different phase of development.

(15) Gallacher v Wood
2007 GWD 37-647, Lands Tribunal

The applicants, who owned a detached bungalow at 28 Greenbank Grove, Edinburgh, obtained planning permission for a rear extension, including a substantial extension at roof level which went beyond the house's footprint. The extension was contrary to conditions in a feu contract of 1933, which applied to a wide area. The applicants sought to have the conditions varied to the extent of permitting the extension. The owner of No 30 opposed the application insofar as it related to the roof-level element of the extension. It was accepted that he had enforcement rights by virtue of s 53 of the Title Conditions (Scotland) Act 2003.

The application was granted. The Tribunal saw its task as coming down 'substantially, to balancing burden and benefit' (para 37), ie factors (b) and (c) of s 100 of the Title Conditions Act. On factor (b), the Tribunal concluded that the impact of the proposed extension on No 30 would be 'slight' (para 32), adding (para 30) that 'someone not used to the present position would barely notice the extension and we think it reasonable to anticipate that even the respondent and his family will in quite a short space of time become used to it'. On factor (c), the Tribunal thought that the inability of the applicants to proceed with their plans would be 'a considerable impediment' to their enjoyment of the property (para 35). 'The applicants are, as everyone agrees, undertaking what is in modern times a normal and reasonable development of their family home' (para 25). Moving house in order to achieve the extra accommodation would be much more expensive (para 17).

In relation to factor (f) (purpose of condition), the Tribunal expressed its now familiar view that conditions of this kind, in a feudal writ, did not have 'a particular purpose of protecting neighbours although of course neighbours would be among the proprietors who would benefit incidentally from maintenance of the general character' (para 35).

Planning permission had been obtained (factor (g)), and the Tribunal accepted (para 26):

> that as the issue of the effect of the proposals on immediate neighbours' amenity is considered in the planning process as well as under our jurisdiction it is relevant to consider how planning guidance in relation to that applied in this particular case. This is not the same as applying the same standard.

The Local Plan policy was to allow extensions which 'will not result in an unreasonable loss of privacy or natural light to neighbouring properties' (para 29). But the Tribunal accepted 'that the planners' apparent satisfaction on issues of daylighting and privacy does not remove these areas from our consideration'.

Weighing all these factors the Tribunal decided, without apparent difficulty, that the application should be granted. A claim for compensation under s 90(7)(a) ('a sum to compensate for any substantial loss or disadvantage suffered by … the owner, as owner of the benefited property') was refused on the basis that there was no evidence that the value of No 30 would be reduced because of the extension. Solatium was excluded because the loss must be suffered in a person's capacity as owner. The Tribunal, however, added (para 40): 'We would not go so far as to say that there can be no other relevant basis for an award of compensation, although we do not think the respondent either gave notice of one or even identified one in submission.'

(16) Hamilton v Robertson
2008 GWD 8-149, Lands Tribunal

A development of five houses, built in the 1980s, was subject to a deed of conditions which prohibited further building. The applicants wished to build a further house in their garden. At this stage there were no absolutely firm plans, although for the purposes of the site visit by the Tribunal the likely footprint was marked out by garden canes. The application was opposed by the owners of three of the other houses. It was refused. As usual in such cases, the Tribunal had to balance the obvious amenity benefit to the neighbours in being able to prevent further development (factor (b)) against the obvious impediment to the applicants' enjoyment of their property if they were unable to build a second house. Departing from a view which it had expressed in some of the earlier cases, the Tribunal said that (para 24): 'An owner of property is generally entitled to make any legitimate use of it, including for development.' In other cases the Tribunal has tended to regard the impediment as outweighing the benefit, and so to grant the application. But in the present case, unusually, the precise nature of the proposed building was unclear, and the Tribunal was unwilling to give the applicants what would amount virtually to a blank cheque (para 27):

> This site is on a sensitive part of the development. There is a real prospect of substantial detriment to the amenity if another house is built in that position. We cannot on the information available accept that this would not have an adverse effect.... It is not beyond the bounds of possibility that a modest building could be designed sufficiently sympathetically to the site. However, although they have located the likely site, the applicants have given no indication of the type of house or the design.... We are considering the application without any idea what the house would look like. Granting the application would leave the owners of the subjects free to build any type of house which, either now or at some later date, would satisfy the planners, and correspondingly leave the adjoining proprietors with no rights beyond the right to make representations in the planning process.

(17) Lawrie v Mashford
2008 GWD 7-129, Lands Tribunal

In *Ord v Mashford* 2006 SLT (Lands Tr) 15 (*Conveyancing 2005* Case (13)) – which can probably be regarded as the leading case on variation under the Title Conditions (Scotland) Act 2003 – a real burden was varied so as to allow the erection of a house. This case is a sequel. The house having been built, the applicants wanted to add a garage. The owners of the benefited property, opposite, were willing to consent to a garage but wanted (i) compensation of £3000, and (ii) a restriction on the height and roof pitch of the garage, in the same way as the previous Tribunal order had done in respect of the house itself. The Tribunal acceded to (ii) (but in any event the applicants' proposals, for which planning permission had been obtained, complied with the proposed restrictions). Compensation, however, was refused. Although it was true that the garage would be visible from the respondents' house, the visual intrusion was not felt to be serious, particularly as other buildings were already equally visible (para 8):

It is our view that the new garage will 'blend in' to the surroundings: the respondents may very naturally continue for some time to be conscious of it, but, looking at it objectively as we must, we doubt very much whether, for example, any prospective purchaser of No 4 would pay any particular attention to it or be adversely influenced.

Further, the garage would not necessarily leave the respondents worse off, given that the space which it will occupy could otherwise be used for things which were visually intrusive, eg the parking of lorries or for leaving children's toys lying around.

(18) Graham v Parker
2007 GWD 30-524, Lands Tribunal

A mid-terraced house had the benefit of a servitude for access over its end-terraced neighbour, dating from a feu disposition of 1990. The access was used mainly to move the refuse bin from the garden to the street. The owners of the end-terraced house sought to have the route of the servitude varied so that, instead of passing close to the rear of their house, it passed at the foot of their garden. This would allow them to build an extension. The variation was granted, mainly on the basis that factor (b) (extent of benefit) was outweighed by factor (c) (extent to which enjoyment of the burdened property is impeded). The present route of the servitude prevented the applicants from making an ordinary use of their house. The Tribunal continued (para 23):

> Their inability to carry out such plans will diminish the worth of their property. By contrast we do not consider that any re-routing of the access will cause any measurable diminution in the value of the respondent's house.

The diversion was only a modest one. Following a line of argument first used in *Church of Scotland General Trs v McLaren* 2006 SLT (Lands Tr) 27 at para 39, the Tribunal further found that, since the purpose of the servitude (factor (f)) was to provide access (and therefore not to restrict building as such), the fact that the proposed extension would overshadow the respondent's house was of no relevance; for that would be a result of the building and not, directly, of the moving of the servitude.

To a small extent the Tribunal founded on factor (a) (change in circumstances), in respect that many of the houses in the locality (including those owned by the parties) were former council houses now in private ownership, and 'owner-occupiers are much more likely to want to invest in their own properties which is likely to include extending the existing house' (para 19).

(19) MacNab v McDowall
24 October 2007, Lands Tribunal

When the council house was sold at 20 Kincraig Avenue, Maybole, there was reserved in favour of the neighbouring council houses (numbers 16 and 18):

a servitude right of pedestrian access over the footpath tinted blue on the Title Plan and that for the carriage to and from the rear of the said subjects 16 and 18 Kincraig Avenue, of coal, manure, garden refuse and items of a heavy or bulky nature which it would be unreasonable to carry through the dwellinghouse on the said subjects and that for tradesmen calling at the said subjects and for no other purpose.

The route of the servitude followed the side of the house at No 20.

The owners of No 20 obtained planning permission to build a rear extension. Because of its width, this would leave no room for the path. The owners applied to the Lands Tribunal to have the route of the servitude varied so that, when it reached the extension, it would be diverted onto land which was part of No 18. The application was opposed by the owners of No 18, who were in their late 80s and had lived in the house (formerly as tenants) since 1953. They complained that the re-routing would increase the length of the path and add to the cost of maintenance (for which they were partially liable), that the path would encroach onto their land, and that the extension would block out their light.

The Tribunal granted the application. In the Tribunal's view, the advantage to the owners of No 18 from the current route (factor (b)) was modest compared to the disadvantage to the owners of No 20 from insisting on it (factor (c)) – for it would prevent the building of the extension. Other relevant factors were that many other such houses now had rear extensions (factor (a)) and that planning permission had been granted (factor (g)).

As the previous case showed, the Tribunal is quite willing to re-route servitudes. See also *George Wimpey East Scotland Ltd v Fleming* 2006 SLT (Lands Tr) 2. An unusual feature of the present case, however, is that the path was being partially re-routed on to one of the dominant tenements (No 18).

Following the re-routing, the path will not be able to be used by the owners of No 20 to the extent that it now runs on part of No 18; for the owners of the former have never had a servitude over the latter. The effect on No 16 is even less satisfactory. The Tribunal's order was to 'grant variation of the title condition to the extent of substituting the new route of footpath, for the former route' (p 9). That means that the owners of No 16 can no longer use the former route; but it seems that they cannot use the new route either, to the extent that it passes over No 18. This is because, while the Tribunal can relieve No 20 of an existing servitude, it has no power to impose a new servitude on No 18.

(20) Brown v Richardson
2007 GWD 28-490 (merits), 2007 GWD 38-666 (expenses), Lands Tribunal

This is the first case of opposed renewal of a burden following the service of a notice of termination under s 20 of the Title Conditions (Scotland) Act 2003. (In an earlier case, *Hornbuckle Mitchell Trustees Ltd v Sundial Properties (Gilmerton) Ltd* 13 February 2006, Lands Tribunal (*Conveyancing 2006* Case (34)), the application for renewal was dropped and the only remaining issue was one of expenses.) Notices of termination are available only for real burdens which are more than 100 years old (which is why the procedure is sometimes referred to as the 'sunset rule'). Once served, a notice can be resisted by an owner of any benefited property through an application to the Lands Tribunal for the burden to be renewed (s 90(1)(b)(i)). The application proceeds just like an ordinary application for variation or discharge, except that the onus of proof is on the benefited owner and not on the burdened. If the application is successful, the burden survives, but only in relation to the applicant's benefited property.

The present case concerned a group of terraced houses in Duthie Terrace, Aberdeen. The owners of No 14 had obtained planning permission for a large extension to the rear, which would increase the area of the ground floor by more than 40%. The first part of this extension was built hard up on the boundary with No 16.

A substantial area of land, including Duthie Terrace, was affected by a feu charter of 1888. Among its burdens were the following:

> [A]nd any alteration upon or re-erection of said houses or other buildings shall always be made according to a plan and elevation to be approved by me or my foresaids;
>
> Declaring that my said disponees and their foresaids shall not be entitled to erect any other buildings of any kind on the said feu without the express consent in writing of the superior....

With the abolition of the feudal system, all references to superiors fall to be disregarded (Abolition of Feudal Tenure etc (Scotland) Act 2000 s 73(2), (2A)). Although the second burden would then survive as an unqualified prohibition, it is hard to see how any content would be left to the first: see *At.Home Nationwide Ltd v Morris* 2007 GWD 31-535, discussed in *Conveyancing 2006* pp 109–113. But in any event, no doubt prudently, the owners of No 14 served a notice of termination in respect of both burdens. The owner of No 16 responded by making this application for the burdens to be renewed.

As usual, the Tribunal began by considering the purpose of the burden (Title Conditions Act s 100, factor (f)) (pp 18–19):

> Is there a purpose which can still be achieved? Although it can be difficult in some cases to discern the purpose of title conditions, the burdens in this case fall within a very frequently encountered category of feudal burden related to residential development, particularly in deeds pre-dating the system of general planning control introduced in 1947. The superior retained general planning control not only over the original development but also over both alterations or rebuilding and further building. The control over the former – plans and elevations to be approved – is expressed at a lower level than that over the latter – no other buildings without express consent.... The superior had his own interest both in relation to the value of the other building land which he acquired from the estate and in relation to securing the feuduties. We are not persuaded that the purpose was to protect individual proprietors from further building or extending by their neighbours. Not only are neighbours given no right to enforce these burdens (they are expressly given some very limited rights later in the deed) but there is nothing which might indicate a purpose of protecting neighbours from further building which might be regarded as overbearing or interfering with their light or their privacy. There is no indication of any particular restriction of building or extending close to neighbouring properties. Certainly, the burdens are

about preserving amenity, in which all the proprietors would have an interest, but only in a general way.

In some previous cases, the Tribunal has used this kind of argument to discount any benefit which the condition confers on neighbouring properties (ie factor (b)) on the ground that it was unintended. See eg *Daly v Bryce* 2006 GWD 25-565 (*Conveyancing 2006* Case (26)). But, in what seems a preferable approach, the Tribunal in this case explained that factor (f) 'was only one factor' (p 25), and accepted 'that there may be benefit to the benefited proprietor even although that was not the original purpose' (p 23). In the context of the particular building proposal, however, that benefit was thought to be relatively slight, because the impact of the extension on No 16 would be 'quite limited' (p 19). By contrast, the Tribunal gave considerable weight to factor (c) (the extent to which the condition impedes enjoyment of the burdened property) (p 21):

> Looking at the particular situation here, we consider that the respondents are proposing an extension and improvement of their property of an essentially normal and reasonable type, in line with modern living. We can in this day and age readily accept that a possible alternative of buying a larger property of comparable location and attractiveness would be expensive in comparison. In accepting that this is quite a substantial burden and interference with the right of proprietors to develop their property to the extent permitted under public planning control, we do not ignore the applicants' willingness to agree to a smaller extension, of about half the area and rather lower. The proposed extension is large, creating, along with the existing room now to be developed as a kitchen and utility area, a very large living area which might perhaps be reduced to some extent without any serious damage to the concept. That would, however, interfere with the respondents' reasonable wish to develop their own property.

Another consideration (factor (g)) was that planning permission had been granted, and that the planners had insisted on changes in order to protect privacy and daylight at No 16. Finally, the Tribunal noted, but discounted, the fact that the superior had apparently failed to police the burdens for many years, while leaving the question 'open for submission in other cases' (p 22).

Without any real difficulty, the Tribunal concluded that the application for renewal should be refused. The Tribunal then had a choice between (i) outright refusal (in which case the burdens would fall), (ii) qualified refusal, varying the burdens to the extent of permitting the extension proposed by the owners of No 14, and (iii) qualified refusal, varying the burdens to the extent of permitting the lesser extension which the owners of No 16 indicated would be acceptable. Since the Tribunal is in practice reluctant to grant an outright discharge of burdens, the effective choice was between (ii) and (iii). 'Quite narrowly' (p 24), the Tribunal opted for (ii).

Expenses were awarded to the owners of No 14, but restricted to one third. This reflected (a) the divided success on the merits, in respect that the owners of No 14 had sought outright refusal of renewal, and (ii) success by the owners of No 16 on the question (see Case (8) above) of title to enforce.

(21) Sheltered Housing Management Ltd v Jack
11 October 2007, Lands Tribunal

The application concerned a sheltered housing development known as Dunmail Manor, Dunmail Avenue, Cults, Aberdeen. Until the appointed day for feudal abolition (28 November 2004), the development was factored by the superior, Sheltered Housing Management Ltd ('SHML'). After the appointed day, the owners exercised their powers under s 28(1) of the Title Conditions (Scotland) Act 2003 to replace SHML, choosing instead Peverel Ltd. They also drew up a new deed of conditions to replace the original one, which had been couched in feudal terms and had involved the management of the development by the superior.

One of the key changes in the new deed was a provision that certain parts of the development belonging to SHML – which owned the warden's flat, warden's office, guest bedrooms, a garage, a potting shed and certain store rooms – were to be used only for purposes ancillary to the development. Thus the warden's flat, for example, was to be used only for occupation by the warden. In exchange, the other owners were to pay SHML £6000 a year, with a provision for upwards adjustments in line with the RPI.

Naturally, SHML was opposed to the change. But under s 33 of the 2003 Act – read, in the case of sheltered housing, with s 54(5)(b) – existing community burdens can be varied by the owners of two thirds of the units in the community. In the present case, two thirds of the owners had signed the deed. On the other hand, changes made under s 33 can be challenged by means of an application to the Lands Tribunal under s 90(1)(c), and SHML duly applied to have the existing deed of conditions preserved unchanged. The application was refused: see 2007 GWD 32-533 (*Conveyancing 2006* Case (35)).

In the current phase of the application SHML was seeking compensation under s 90(6)(b), (7)(a) in respect of the 'substantial loss' which it claimed to have incurred due to the fact that its property was now subject to real burdens. This raised a novel point. Normally compensation is payable for the *removal* of burdens from a neighbouring property; but in this case it was being claimed, as the Act allowed, for the *imposition* of burdens on the claimant's property.

It was accepted by both sides that the annual payment of £6000 should be capitalised at 7% giving a value to SHML's property of £85,714. SHML argued that, before the imposition of the burdens, its property had been worth significantly more, and claimed for the difference. Various figures were suggested. The Tribunal took the view (i) that only the warden's flat and the garage were sufficiently separate from the development to have an independent value, (ii) that the garage could be valued at full market value, but (iii) that the flat was in practice so tied into the development – and was something for which there was no real market – that only a reduced figure could be accepted. The Tribunal accepted a total figure of £94,892, and so awarded compensation of £9,178. The Tribunal rejected an argument for the owners of the units that the figure did not represent a 'substantial' loss within the legislation and so should not be paid. Further, while the Tribunal accepted that it had an overriding discretion as to whether to award compensation or not, it decided that the award of this level of compensation was fair.

We understand that there is to be an appeal against the Tribunal's decision (including the earlier decision on the merits).

PUBLIC RIGHTS OF WAY AND ACCESS RIGHTS

(22) Hamilton v Dumfries and Galloway Council
[2007] CSOH 96, 2007 GWD 20-347 affd [2007] CSIH 75, 2007 GWD 34-582

A short stretch of public road was stopped up by the local authority in 1989. On 26 May 2005 Dumfries and Galloway Council re-adopted it following an application by some of the frontagers. The owner of the road, wishing to avoid unfettered use by the public, sought judicial review of the Council's decision. His first ground of attack was on the basis that the road was not a 'road' within the Roads (Scotland) Act 1984 s 151(1) in respect that it was not a way over which there was a public right of passage. This failed: see [2006] CSOH 110 (*Conveyancing 2006* Case (37)). The present stage of the litigation was concerned with a new argument.

Under s 16 of the 1984 Act an application for adoption must be made by either a majority of frontagers or such number of frontagers as together own land which includes not less than half of the boundary fronting or abutting the road. In the present case, the application only complied with this definition if the frontagers included the owners of two modern houses which were adjacent to the road. These houses, however, were separated from the road by a pavement built by the original developer of the housing estate. The pavement was not in fact conveyed to the developer, and thus was not thereafter conveyed by the developer to the house buyers. However, the descriptions in all three cases were capable of including the pavement, thus opening the way to the possibility of prescriptive acquisition. The disposition in favour of the developer, dated 13 and 15 May 1995, was recorded in the Register of Sasines on 2 June 1995. Thus on the day on which the road was adopted, the period from the date of recording was fatally short – by one week – from the 10 years required for positive prescription.

It was argued for the Council (i) that a *prima facie* title on the Register of Sasines was all that was needed in order to qualify as a frontager under the 1984 Act, or alternatively (ii) that the pavement was possessed, that the requirements of prescription were met on 2 June 2005, and that prescription operated retrospectively so as to cure any deficiencies in the application process. Both arguments were rejected by the Lord Ordinary (Lord Glennie) and, on appeal, by an Extra Division of the Court of Session. Accordingly, the Council's decision to adopt the road was reduced.

[Other aspects of this case are digested at (56).]

(23) Gloag v Perth & Kinross Council
2007 SCLR 530, Sh Ct

This was an application under s 28(1)(a) of the Land Reform (Scotland) Act 2003 for a declaration that certain land adjacent to the applicant's house was not land in respect of which access rights were exercisable. The applicant argued that the land – some 11 acres in all – fell within the 'privacy exemption' in s 6(1)(b)(iv) of the Act, which applies to 'sufficient adjacent land to enable persons living there to have reasonable measures of privacy in that house and to ensure that their enjoyment of that house is not unreasonably disturbed'. After a proof, the sheriff granted the application. See **Commentary** p 127.

(24) Tuley v Highland Council
2007 SLT (Sh Ct) 97

Highland Council issued a notice under s 14(2) of the Land Reform (Scotland) Act 2003 requiring the owners of Feddonhill Wood to adjust or remove barriers which prevented access to a section of the Wood on horseback. In this action the owners sought recall of the notice, on the basis that taking access by horse would not be a responsible exercise of access rights as required by s 2 of the Act. Recall was refused. See **Commentary** p 135. We understand that the decision has been appealed.

FEUDAL ABOLITION

(25) SQ1 Ltd v Earl of Hopetoun
2 October 2007, Lands Tribunal

Circumstances in which a challenge was made to the validity of a notice served under s 18 of the Abolition of Feudal Tenure etc (Scotland) Act 2000. The challenge failed. See **Commentary** p 147. This decision has been appealed.

EXECUTION OF DEEDS

(26) Dodd v Southern Pacific Personal Loans Ltd
[2007] CSOH 93, 2007 GWD 21-352

A person can execute a deed on behalf of another person. Two such cases are mentioned in the Requirements of Writing (Scotland) Act 1995 – 'notarial' execution on behalf of a person who is blind or unable to write (s 9), and execution under a power of attorney (s 12(2)). In the latter case, how is the mandatary to sign? Normally, of course, he will sign with his own name and, if he does so, there can be no doubt as to the validity of the execution. But can he sign using (only) the name of the person on whose behalf he is signing?

In *Dodd v Southern Pacific Personal Loans Ltd* the pursuer sought reduction of a standard security on the ground that his signature had been forged by his wife. The latter pled, rather curiously: 'Mrs Dodd believes she may have subscribed the loan agreement and standard security in favour of the first defenders on behalf of the pursuer. She does not precisely recall doing so.' After proof, at which expert handwriting evidence was led, it was found that Mrs Dodd had indeed signed using her husband's name. However, it was also found that she had acted with her husband's consent. As a result the Lord Ordinary (Lord Bracadale) held that the security had been validly executed.

The decision seems wrong. Apparently the court was not referred to s 7(2) of the 1995 Act, which provides that 'a document … is signed by an individual natural person as a granter *or on behalf of a granter of it* if it is signed by him' by the various permitted methods of which the normal one is '(b) with his surname, preceded by at least one forename (or an abbreviation or familiar form of a forename)'. In the present case Mrs Dodd had done no such thing. Instead of signing with her own name she had signed with the name of her husband. It is hard to see how such a method of signing can be valid.

Although it was not necessary for the decision, the court also gave brief consideration to whether it would have been possible, under the 1995 Act, for Mr Dodd to adopt the signature by Mrs Dodd if it had been originally made without his authority. Lord Bracadale thought that there was 'some force' in the view that this was not allowed under the Act (para 102). We would go further and say that adoption is not possible under the 1995 Act.

The decision presupposes that a mandate to execute a deed can be given orally. This question is not one that is free from difficulty. The case does not, however, discuss it.

LAND REGISTRATION

(27) Yaxley v Glen
[2007] CSOH 90, 2007 SLT 756, 2007 Hous LR 59

Held: where someone is a 'proprietor in possession', he is so not only as to the right of ownership but also as to a servitude that is a pertinent of the property. *Griffiths v Keeper of the Registers of Scotland* 20 December 2002, Lands Tribunal (*Conveyancing 2003* case (26)) disapproved. See **Commentary** p 121.

TRANSFER OF OWNERSHIP

(28) Nabb v Kirkby
26 October 2007, Stranraer Sheriff Court, A169/01

This case was covered in *Conveyancing 2006* Case (45) when it was at debate stage. Proof before answer was allowed, and that has now taken place. We have unfortunately not found it easy to follow the sheriff's opinion, and what follows is subject to that proviso. We understand that there may be an appeal.

The pursuers were the owners of Knocknassie House Hotel in Wigtownshire. Wishing to retire, they concluded missives to sell to the defenders, who at that time were tenants of a pub in England. Missives were concluded on 15 August

2001 and they provided for settlement on the same day: perhaps not an auspicious beginning. Part of the price (£150,000) was to be paid at settlement, and the balance (£60,000) some weeks later. The buyers were to give the sellers a standard security for the outstanding balance. The missives did not expressly provide that the standard security was to be delivered at settlement. By the date of settlement the standard security had not yet been executed and it seems that its terms had not yet been fully adjusted between the respective agents. At the settlement date the buyers' solicitors sent a cheque for the agreed first stage payment, with a covering letter saying it was to be held as undelivered until dispatch of the executed dispositions. (There were two dispositions because the property was held on two titles.) The sellers' solicitors lodged the cheque with their bank and posted the dispositions, under a covering letter:

> Thank you for your letter of 15 August 2001 and we acknowledge safe receipt of your cheque in respect of the initial instalment of the purchase price. We are presenting this to the bank today on the basis that it was only this morning (16 August 2001) that our clients signed the relative deeds. In that connection we are pleased to enclose herewith the following:
>
> 1. Title deeds following to be delivered.
> 2. Two executed dispositions.... Please acknowledge safe receipt of the enclosures which should be held by you as undelivered pending your confirmation that you hold the executed standard security in favour of our client and pending return to us of the completed Minute of Agreement.

The buyers' agents registered the dispositions without sending the standard security. It appears that the balance of £60,000 has never been paid and the standard security has never been delivered. A few days after the letter (above) was sent, the buyers took possession. They soon had second thoughts, finding the hotel less profitable than they had anticipated. They continued to run it until 2005, when they closed it. In the end they accused the sellers of having induced them to buy the property by means of fraudulent or negligent misrepresentations.

In the present action, which has been in court since 21 December 2001, the sellers sought rectification of the Land Register by the removal of the names of the buyers, on the ground that the dispositions had never been delivered to the buyers, who therefore could not have competently registered them. The sellers also sought violent profits of £80,000 on the ground that the buyers' possession was unlawful. It is unclear to us whether the sellers were seeking rescission of the contract. At one stage at least there was a crave for payment of the balance of £60,000, which would be inconsistent with rescission, but it is not clear if that crave was still in the record when the proof was heard. As for the defenders, they counterclaimed for damages for misrepresentation. The sum sought was £150,000, which is the same as the sum originally paid. It is unclear to us whether the defenders sought rescission or not.

On the underlying dispute, the sheriff held that there had in fact been no misrepresentations and accordingly he rejected the defenders' counterclaim. At the same time he held against the pursuers in respect of both (i) the claim for violent profits and (ii) the claim for the rectification of the Land Register.

On the question of whether the dispositions had been validly delivered to the buyers, the sheriff held that they had been. If we understand the opinion correctly, he held that the dispositions were constructively delivered as soon as the sellers' solicitors cashed the cheque, even though at that stage the dispositions were physically still held by the sellers' solicitors. If that is what was decided, and if it is correct, then it is an interesting and significant decision. It is a familiar fact that legal delivery can happen *later* than physical delivery, as when a deed or cheque is physically delivered, but to be held as undelivered until a condition has been purified. But here the decision seems to be that a document can also be legally delivered *before* it is physically delivered. In theory that may well be possible. A solicitor can act for more than one person, including a person who is not a paying client, and thus the Nabbs' solicitors could act for the Kirkbys. Such acting seems implied by the idea that the solicitors held the deeds for the Kirkbys. But if this conclusion is not inconceivable, it is unclear to us by what precise route it was arrived at.

Arguably the sellers were not entitled to impose a 'held as undelivered' condition on the buyers, because they had cashed a cheque which itself was to be held as undelivered unless the dispositions were delivered. But equally it is not clear that the buyers were entitled to send the cheque to be held as undelivered in the first place. (And yet the fact that someone is not entitled to impose a 'to be held as undelivered' clause perhaps does not alter the fact that it *has* been imposed, however wrongfully; and the fact that something is wrongful does not necessarily mean that it can be disregarded. Wrongful non-delivery is not the same as delivery. This argument, if sound, might be ammunition for *both* sides.) Although the missives did not say expressly that the standard security was to be delivered at settlement, it is difficult to see what other date could be implied. As against that, it may be that the delay in the drafting of the standard security was to be laid at the door of the sellers. If the appeal goes ahead, these various issues may be clarified.

COMPETITION OF TITLE

(29) Hamilton v Ford
[2007] CSOH 15, 2007 GWD 10-177

Mr Hamilton concluded missives to buy a leasehold property at Leitholm, Berwickshire in 1994. He directed the seller to grant the assignation to his wife's nephew (the first defender). This was done. The nephew raised part of the purchase price by means of a loan secured over the property. Mr Hamilton and the nephew agreed that the property would be held in trust for Mr Hamilton, who would free and relieve the latter for all payments due under the secured loan.

In 2002 Mr Hamilton and his wife were divorced. In 2003 the nephew sold the property to third parties (the second defenders). At this stage Mr Hamilton raised an action against the first and second defenders, seeking (i) declarator that the pursuer and his nephew (the first defender) had entered into an oral agreement in 1994 that the nephew would hold the property in trust for the pursuer, (ii) declarator that the assignation to the nephew was in trust for the pursuer, (iii) reduction of the conveyance to the third parties (who, the pursuer averred, knew of the trust), and (iv) decree ordaining the nephew to convey to the pursuer.

The Lord Ordinary (Glennie) noted (at para 9):

> It is a curious feature of this litigation that the first defender admits, or at least does not dispute, a large part of the pursuer's case against him. His defence to the action is, essentially, that the pursuer delayed unreasonably in taking title back into his own name; and that, in some way, this entitled him to sell the property to a third party without giving any prior notification to the pursuer. The legal basis for such a defence was not explained.

The defenders made various attacks on the relevancy and specification of the pursuer's averments, but these were repelled and proof before answer allowed.

(30) Rehman v Secretary of State
[2007] UKSSCSC CSIS_639_2006
23 March 2007, Social Security Commissioner

As in *Hamilton v Ford* (above), the issue here was whether property was or was not held in trust. The curious feature of the present case is that it was the alleged trustee himself who was claiming that he held the property in trust.

Mr Rehman's claim for social security payments was refused on the ground that he owned a property which, not being his own residence, was to be brought into account as a relevant capital asset. He appealed to the Commissioner. His argument was that although he owned the property, he did so in trust for someone else. As evidence, he produced the following affidavit, which we reproduce *verbatim* from the report:

> At Glasgow on the Twenty Ninth day of July Two Thousand and Five, in the presence of Pravin Jain, Notary Public, Glasgow compered Abdul Rehman residing at Flat 2/1, 3 Windsor Street, Glasgow, G20 7NA, whom being solemnly sworn depones as follows:
>
> 1. My full name is … I presently reside at Flat 2/1, 3 Windsor Street, Glasgow, G20 7NA. I was born on the second day of April 1953 and am presently 52 years of age.
> 2. I confirm that I purchased the property at 25 Parkbrae Avenue, Glasgow on around December 2001. This property was purchased for the benefit of my son, due to the fact that he was unable to obtain a mortgage at that time. Whilst no formal agreement was made at the time of purchase, I received and continue to receive no benefits from the property and it has been agreed between me and my son that if the house were to be sold in the future, that I would not receive any monies from the house sale. The monies received would be applied to repay the

mortgage and thereafter would fall to benefit my son. No formal documentation recording this was ever made, however it is an agreement between myself and my son.

3. I can confirm that my son, is in contact with Financial Advisors which will enable the said property to transferred to him.

ALL OF WHICH IS THE TRUTH AS THE DEPONENT SHALL ANSWER TO GOD.

The Commissioner (D J May QC) refused the appeal. There was no satisfactory evidence that a trust had ever been set up. Moreover, there were two further hurdles, apart from lack of evidence, which the claimant's case could not surmount. In the first place, a trust in which the truster and the trustee are the same person has to be in writing: Requirements of Writing (Scotland) Act 1995 s 1(2)(a)(iii). In the second place, in a truster-as-trustee trust there has to be some equivalent of transfer from the truster as an individual to himself as a trustee, and there was no evidence of any such transfer. (Here the Commissioner might have cited *Allan's Trs v Lord Advocate* 1971 SC (HL) 45.) Mr Rehman's argument that the affidavit could itself be regarded as a deed of trust failed.

(31) Marshall v Marshall
[2007] CSOH 16, 2007 GWD 10-188

In this divorce action the pursuer argued that the two farms which he held in joint names with his brother were partnership property and thus not matrimonial property. The defender, his wife, argued that the terms of the titles in the Register of Sasines said nothing about partnership property and that it was not open to the pursuer to lead evidence to contradict the terms of the recorded deeds. **Held**, that the pursuer was free to lead evidence that the farms were partnership property.

(32) Strathclyde Associated Property Holdings Ltd v Kah Ltd
[2007] CSOH 210

A liquidator sought reduction of five leases purportedly granted by the company in favour of the defender. Each lease had an ish of 2024 and an annual rent of £1. The defender could not produce the leases themselves but only photocopies: the last page of each of the five appeared to be identical. Though they bore to be dated in October 2005, the pursuer averred that in fact they had been granted after the company had gone into liquidation in May 2006. The pursuer's position was that the leases were void, and, even if not void, were voidable as gratuitous alienations. The pursuer averred that the shares in the company were held by Ronald Hannah and his former wife Fiona Gibbons, and that Kah Ltd (the defender) was controlled by the latter. The Lord Ordinary (Hodge) noted (para 4) that 'the only explanation of the transactions which the first defenders have proposed in their defences is that the leases were granted in consideration of Fiona Gibbons' claim for financial provision on divorce. That is not a relevant defence'. Decree of reduction was granted.

RIGHT-TO-BUY LEGISLATION

(33) McLaughlin v Thenew Housing Association Ltd
2007 Hous LR 18, Sh Ct

A public-sector tenant exercised her right to buy. The landlord made an offer at a figure of £21,000. Missives were concluded. At that point the landlord realised that it had made a mistake in applying the rules for calculating discount. The property should have been offered at a figure of £49,000. In this action by the tenant to enforce the missives it was held that the error had rendered the missives void.

LEASES

(34) Campbell v Aberdeen City Council
2007 Hous LR 26, Sh Ct

Under a residential tenancy agreement the landlord was to keep the property 'wind and water-tight'. When the landlord was carrying out certain repairs, high-pressure water jetting was required. This was done by an independent contractor. Some of the water penetrated the interior, causing loss to the pursuer. The pursuer claimed damages from the landlord not on the basis of the law of delict but on the basis of breach of contract. She was successful and damages of £2,900 were awarded.

(35) Warren James Jewellers Ltd v Overgate GP Ltd
[2007] CSIH 14, 2007 GWD 6-94

A unit in Dundee's Overgate Shopping Centre was held on a 15-year lease beginning in September 2000. The tenant, Warren James (Jewellers) Ltd, ran a jewellery business. The lease contained an exclusivity clause, whereby the landlord bound itself:

> 4.3 [F]or so long as the said Warren James (Jewellers) Ltd is the Tenant under this Lease, not in respect of any first letting (which means the first time the Landlord lets the Lettable Unit in question and not in respect of any subsequent lettings) of any Lettable Unit to lease any such Lettable Unit (other than the Premises and two other Lettable Units only) with its Permitted Use having specified as its principal trade or business the retail sale of jewellery.

At the time (September 2000) there were already two other jewellery businesses in the centre. The landlord then granted two further leases to jewellery businesses, thus bringing the total to five. Warren James (Jewellers) Ltd claimed that this constituted a breach of contract, and sued for £400,000 which it said was its trading losses as a result of the landlord's breach. The quoted clause is hard to make sense of, and whilst judges are sometimes too quick to criticise contract drafting, here their criticisms were surely justified. In the Outer House it was held that the clause should be construed in the way contended for by the tenant: [2005] CSOH

142, 2006 GWD 12-235 (*Conveyancing 2005* Case (26)). The landlord reclaimed and the Inner House has now affirmed the Lord Ordinary's decision.

(36) Comhairle Nan Eilean Siar v Collins
2007 SLT (Sh Ct) 122, 2007 SCLR 567

Comhairle Nan Eilean Siar owned an industrial estate in Lewis. In 2002 it leased two units to Mr Collins. In 2003 Mr Collins assigned the lease to the Xaverian Missionaries. He continued working there as an employee of the Missionaries. It appears that his work was to repair African road vehicles. In 2006 the pursuer 'became aware that the subjects were being kept in poor condition, that vehicle shells were being dumped around the estate, restricting access and creating a nuisance to other tenants and that complaints were received from various parties' (para 2). The pursuer complained to the Xaverian Missionaries and as a result the lease was terminated by mutual agreement.

When it appeared that Mr Collins was continuing to occupy the units, the pursuer raised the present action, craving (1) (a) declarator that the defender had no right to occupy the subjects, (b) decree ordaining him to remove, and (2) interdict from occupying the subjects or storing property on any part of the industrial estate. Decree in absence was granted. Mr Collins then sought to be reponed, arguing that the writ had not been validly served.

Mr Collins offered as his substantive defence that the Xaverian Missionaries had assigned the lease back to him orally in 2005. The Xaverian Missionaries said that this was not true. Mr Collins added that the pursuer had consented to this by a telephone conversation: the pursuer denied any such consent. Though the defender claimed to be the tenant he conceded that he paid no rent.

The sheriff principal **held** that this defence was unstateable in relation to the first crave (para 28): 'It seems to me that, if this matter were ever to get to the stage of a proof, the chances of the sheriff believing the defender's account of the supposed re-assignation of the lease having taken effect on 31 March 2005 must be regarded as more or less nil.' Nevertheless with some reluctance the reponing motion was granted because a possible defence was available to the second crave.

(37) Douglas Shelf Seven Ltd v Co-operative Wholesale Society Ltd
[2007] CSOH 53, 2007 GWD 9-167

The pursuer was the landlord of a shopping centre in Dundee's Whitfield area. The defender was tenant of the supermarket unit. The lease contained a 'keep open' clause of a type that is standard in shopping centre leases. Most litigation about such clauses is about their specific implement (see eg *Highland and Universal Properties Ltd v Safeway Properties Ltd* 2000 SC 297). This was about damages for breach.

The supermarket was shut in 1995 and had remained shut since. The present action has been in court since 1999. The defender argued that the property had been sub-leased, so that the defender was the mid-landlord, and that since this sub-lease had been consented to by the head landlord (ie the pursuer), the keep-open obligation no longer bound the defender, in as much as the obligation was one that had to be performed by the sub-tenant. This argument was rejected. The granting of a sub-lease does not free a tenant from the obligations of the lease. Apart from that argument, the rest of the case was concerned with damages. On this aspect, see M Hogg, 'Damages for breach of a keep-open clause' (2007) 11 *Edinburgh Law Review* 416.

(38) Maris v Banchory Squash Racquets Club Ltd
[2007] CSIH 30, 2007 SC 501, 2007 SLT 447, 2007 Hous LR 54

This case is about the possibility of purging an irritancy, and raises issues about the nature of irritancy. See **Commentary** p 104.

(39) Clydeport Properties Ltd v Shell UK Ltd
[2007] CSOH 92, 2007 SLT 547, 2007 Hous LR 49

The landlord sought payment of the sum of £6,815,000 in respect of dilapidations. One of the defences was negative prescription. Were the tenant's obligations 'obligations relating to land' and therefore subject to the 20-year prescriptive period rather than the 5-year one? (See sch 1 para 2(e) of the Prescription and Limitation (Scotland) Act 1973.) **Held** that they were indeed obligations relating to land. But held further that 'an obligation arising out of a breach of an obligation relating to land is not the same thing as an obligation relating to land' (para 17, adopting Lord Coulsfield's analysis in *Lord Advocate v Shipbreaking Industries Ltd* 1991 SLT 838), so that obligations to pay damages for breach of the primary obligations would be subject to the 5-year prescription.

(40) Allen v McTaggart
[2007] CSIH 24, 2007 SC 482, 2007 SLT 387, 2007 Hous LR 29

The 'tenancy-at-will' is a mysterious type of right which would probably be of little interest except that s 20 of the Land Registration (Scotland) Act 1979 says that tenants-at-will have the right to buy their property at a discount of 96% below market value. Given that incentive one may doubt whether any such tenancies can still exist. The present case supports such a conjecture, for the pursuers were **held** by the Inner House not to be tenants-at-will.

The pursuers were tenants of huts at Rascarrel Bay, Kirkcudbrightshire. That in itself was not a promising start, for tenancies-at-will can exist only where there exists a local custom to that effect and it does not appear that any such tenancy has ever been recognised in Kirkcudbrightshire. (So far as we know the only counties where such tenancies have hitherto been recognised are Aberdeenshire, Banffshire, Lanarkshire, Ross-shire and Sutherland.)

Nobody has ever been quite sure what amounts to a tenancy-at-will. Section 20 of the 1979 Act has a definition but it does not take one very far. (And while saying that the holder is *not* a tenant (s 20(8)(a)(i)) it nevertheless calls him a 'tenant' and recognises that he pays 'rent' (s 20(8)(b).) In *Allen* the Inner House held that whatever a tenancy-at-will may be, the pursuers' pleadings failed to aver sufficient facts to support the existence of such tenancies (para 21 *per* Lord Nimmo Smith, giving the opinion of the court):

> It is clear from the statute that, at the date at which a tenancy-at-will is claimed by an applicant to exist, it must be possible to prove that the necessary custom and usage have become established in the locality. The averments for the appellants pay no more than lip-service to the concept of custom and usage. They make no attempt to define the locality in which, the inhabitants among whom or the terms and conditions on which the custom and usage are alleged to operate. The averments go no further than to establish that there has been an arrangement under which the respondents and their predecessors in title have permitted the occupiers of the eight huts to occupy them in exchange for payment of a ground rent which has varied from time to time. There is no averment which would serve to establish who was responsible for the erection of any of the huts in the first place. The facts, so far as averred, would indicate the existence of informal leases from year to year, not tenancies-at-will without ish. The absence of any averments sufficient to establish the necessary custom and usage, and the admissions about rent increases, therefore appear to us, as the latter did to the Tribunal, to render the applicants' pleadings fundamentally irrelevant.

This affirms the decision of the Lands Tribunal, reported as *Harbinson v McTaggart* 2006 SLT (Lands Tr) 42 (*Conveyancing 2006* Case (69)). See further David Cabrelli, 'Tenancies-at-will: *Allen v McTaggart*' (2007) 11 *Edinburgh Law Review* 436.

(41) Stephen v Innes Ker
[2007] CSIH 42, 2007 SC 501, 2007 SLT 625

This concerns the succession to a share in an agricultural tenancy. It affirms the decision of the Lord Ordinary: [2006] CSOH 66, 2006 SLT 1105 (*Conveyancing 2006* Case (67)). See **Commentary** p 102.

(42) Little Cumbrae Estate Ltd v Island of Little Cumbrae Ltd
[2007] CSIH 35, 2007 SC 525, 2007 SLT 631, 2007 Hous LR 40

There was a 5-year lease of (and here we quote the sheriff principal, James Taylor) 'the island of Little Cumbrae, the motor vessel named Bean Mhadh and the dumb barge'. The lease provided that the landlord would insure, and that any proceeds from an insurance claim would be spent on making good the loss. The tenant was to reimburse the insurance premiums, and also 'to repair and maintain or renew the Premises except where the damage necessitating such repair, maintenance or renewal is caused by any of the Insured Risks'.

In January 2005 a storm caused extensive damage. The landlord claimed on the insurance policy and the insurance company paid. But the amount paid did not meet the full cost of repairs. The tenant argued that the shortfall was the landlord's responsibility, while the landlord argued that it was the tenant's.

When it was held by the sheriff that the shortfall was the landlord's responsibility, the landlord appealed to the sheriff principal, but without success: see *Conveyancing 2006* Case (73). The tenant's obligation was only in relation to uninsured types of loss, and this loss was insured. Hence the tenant was not responsible. It is true that the lease did not impose responsibility on the landlord either. But, said the sheriff principal, 'if the obligation to repair is not the tenant's obligation then it must be the landlord's obligation. At common law the obligation to repair would fall upon the landlord'. So the landlord was responsible for the shortfall.

The landlord appealed once again and the Inner House has now reversed the decision. It agreed that, since the lease was silent about it, the shortfall was subject to the common law (para 19): 'In so far as the express terms of a lease do not cover, or replace, the provisions implied at common law in such contracts, those provisions will apply.' But the Inner House did not agree that the common law rules allocated responsibility to the landlord. Had these been ordinary repairs that would have been the case. But it held that storm damage of this type is to be classified as a *damnum fatale*. 'In so far as the insurance arranged against *damnum fatale* should prove lacking, the common law rule will apply to the uninsured *damnum fatale*.' At common law, it held, such damage is the responsibility of *neither* party (para 16):

> The common law position in both urban and rural tenancies has been that in the event of damage or destruction constituting *damnum fatale* neither party is under any obligation, owed to the other, to repair or re-build. Each may have an interest to do so; the tenant to resume enjoyment; the landlord to recover his rental income, since otherwise the rent is subject to whole or partial abatement.

(43) City Wall Properties (Scotland) Ltd v Pearl Assurance plc
[2007] CSIH 79, 2008 GWD 5-93

This prolonged litigation concerned a property at East Green Vaults under Aberdeen's Market Street. The property was a car park. The rent review clause provided that:

> The rent so payable shall be subject to review at the instance of the Landlords at the relevant review date by addition per space of the product of 96 multiplied by 'the car park factor' (as hereinafter defined) applying at the relevant review date. For the purposes of the Lease 'the car park factor' shall mean the average of increased daily rates (ie the 9 hour rate from 0830 to 1730 hours charged to the public) at the Trinity Centre, Bon Accord Centre and the multi-storey College Street public car parks in Aberdeen....

Did 'the car park factor' mean (i) the average *increase* at the comparator car parks, or (ii) the *total* new average rent at the comparator car parks? Thus, suppose that the average comparator rate increased over the review period from £10 to £11. Would the 'car park factor' then be (i) £1, or (ii) £11? On the actual figures in the case, the first interpretation would have produced a new rental of £37,774, whereas the second would have produced a new rental of £64,083 – about 70% higher.

The Lord Ordinary held that the meaning of the clause was not self-evident and fell to be interpreted against the factual matrix. After proof, he decided that the interpretation more favourable to the tenant was the one to be preferred: see [2005] CSOH 139, 2005 GWD 35-666 (*Conveyancing 2005* Case (32)). The landlord reclaimed, and the Inner House has now affirmed the Lord Ordinary's decision.

(44) Scottish Ministers v Pairc Crofters Ltd
17 August 2007, Scottish Land Court

Although in this series we do not cover crofting tenure, this case is worth noting. Pairc Crofters Ltd owned an estate in Lewis. (Despite its name, it did not represent crofters.) It leased the estate to an associated company, Pairc Renewables Ltd, which then sub-leased an area to SEE Generation Ltd for a windfarm. Since this area was part of the common grazings, a question arose as to its effect in relation to crofting rights. The Scottish Ministers made a reference to the Land Court under s 81 of the Land Reform (Scotland) Act 2003. The Land Court **held** that the arrangement was not inconsistent with crofting legislation and did not require the consent of the Crofters Commission. It remains to add that the question of the interaction of such leases with the crofting community right to buy has now been addressed by s 31 of the Crofting Reform etc Act 2007, inserting a new s 69A into the Land Reform (Scotland) Act 2003.

(45) O'Donnell v McDonald
[2007] CSIH 74

Property was let as a riding school. The tenant had the right to graze horses. When the landlord served a notice to quit, the question arose as to whether the tenancy was an agricultural holding. The sheriff held that it was. The sheriff principal disagreed: see 2006 GWD 28-615 (*Conveyancing 2006* Case (60)). The Inner House has now taken the same view as the sheriff principal.

The case also touches on a more general point. The landlord had required the tenant to remove as at 31 March. This was a mistake since the anniversary date was 7 February. It was held that this mistake did not invalidate the notice. The Lord Justice Clerk (Gill) commented at para 33: 'It was not suggested by the counsel for the defender that the period of notice was insufficient; and since the notice specified a date of removal that was later than the true anniversary date, the defender was not prejudiced in any way by the error.' That leaves open the converse case, where the notice period is sufficient but the stated removal date was too early. For instance, suppose the date specified had been 6 February. Would that have been valid, as from 7 February, or invalid?

(46) Credential Bath Street Ltd v Venture Investment Placement Ltd
[2007] CSOH 208

Credential was landlord of property in Glasgow for 25 years from 2001. The tenant, Callpoint Europe Ltd, had gone into liquidation. Venture, which belonged to the same group as Callpoint, was the guarantor of the tenant's obligations. The guarantee had a time limit: 'The guarantor shall be deemed to be released from its obligations under these presents on 1 January 2005 save in respect of any antecedent breach of the guarantee occurring prior to 1 January 2005.'

During 2004 the landlord had served on both tenant and guarantor a schedule of dilapidations, but no actual demand was made on the guarantor to pay for the repairs prior to 1 January 2005. By the time that such a demand was made, the time limit had passed. The guarantor argued that the demand came too late. The landlord argued (a) that the phrase 'breach of the guarantee' really meant 'breach of the terms of the lease', and (b) that even if that were not the correct reading, the service of the schedule of dilapidations could be deemed to be a demand against the guarantor.

The Lord Ordinary (Reed) held against the pursuer on both arguments. As to the first, he gave a long and possibly controversial exposition of modern developments in the law of interpretation of documents, in doing so siding with the new contextualist school of interpretation. (We believe that this is the first Scottish case to refer to Wittgenstein.) Despite this outlook, the Lord Ordinary did not think that contextualist construction could help the pursuer on the first argument. The provision as written was a commercially possible one. To quote the Lord Ordinary (para 36):

> It appears to me that the commercial considerations on which the pursuers rely come nowhere near the standard set by the authorities. This is not a case in which it can be said, in the language used by Lord Hoffmann ... that 'something must have gone wrong with the language', or that the natural reading of clause 3.4 would 'attribute to the parties an intention which they plainly could not have had'. If the pursuers are not protected against disrepair which was latent when the guarantee expired, that is not, in Lord Diplock's words ... 'a conclusion that flouts business common sense'.

As to the second argument, the Lord Ordinary held (para 47) that 'the question is whether the reasonable recipient of the letter would have said to himself, "I am being called on to do the work specified in the schedule"'. The answer to that test was, he considered, clearly a negative one.

As well as covering the tenant's obligations, the guarantee contained a step-in obligation under which the winding-up of the tenant would trigger an obligation on the guarantor to take over the lease. The pursuer's attempts to have the tenant wound up did not succeed until after the guarantee had expired. The pursuer argued that the guarantee contained an implied term not to delay a winding-up, and that the defender had breached that term. Perhaps unsurprisingly, this argument failed. (We note that the petition for winding up was presented on 12 July 2004. Section 129(2) of the Insolvency Act 1986 says that 'the winding up of a company by the court is deemed to commence at the time of the presentation of the petition for winding up'. This line of argument seems not have been advanced.)

(47) Ben Cleuch Estates Ltd v Scottish Enterprise
[2008] CSIH 1, 2008 GWD 7-135

This case was about whether a break option had been validly exercised. Scottish Enterprise held a lease of premises at 45 North Lindsay Street, Dundee at an annual rent (at the time of the litigation) of £210,700. The lease was from 1991 to 2016, except that it had a break option. The break would take effect at Candlemas 2006, provided that notice exercising the option was served on the landlord by Candlemas 2005.

Notice was timeously served on Bonnytoun Estates Ltd. But that company was not the landlord: the landlord was Ben Cleuch Estates Ltd. The reason that notice was served on Bonnytoun was that the letting agents issued rent invoices on behalf of Bonnytoun, not on behalf of Ben Cleuch. The agents acted as agents for more than one company in the Bonnytoun group. The companies in the group were closely related and all had the same registered office. A Mr Cairns was a director of both Bonnytoun and Ben Cleuch and seems also to have been, directly or indirectly, the main shareholder. Mr Cairns saw the letter exercising the break option, but noticing that it was addressed to the wrong company said nothing until the deadline had passed. Ben Cleuch then sought declarator that the break option had not been validly exercised. In the Outer House the pursuer was successful: [2006] CSOH 35, 2006 GWD 8-154 (*Conveyancing 2005* Case (61)). The defender reclaimed.

The defender's first argument was that the notice had been sent to the right address – Bonnytoun and Ben Cleuch had the same address – and that that was sufficient. That argument was rejected. The second was that the pursuer was personally barred from denying the validity of the break notice, on the ground that the rent invoices, being issued on behalf of Bonnytoun, would naturally lead the tenant to believe that Bonnytoun was the landlord. It is true that the tenant was informed of transfers of the landlord's interest, and there had been several such transfers over the years, most recently to a company called Pacific Shelf 1145. Although it turned out that that had been the name by which Ben Cleuch had previously been known, it was reasonable, argued the defender, for it to assume that it was the previous name of Bonnytoun. This personal bar argument had been put to the Lord Ordinary, but without success. The Inner House accepted it, and accordingly held that the break option had been validly exercised.

One provision in the lease that came under particular scrutiny was clause 17:

> Any notice or document required or permitted to be given or served under this Lease may be given or served personally or by leaving the same or sending the same by first class recorded delivery post at or to the registered office of the party (where it is a company) for the time being, or (in the case of a firm or an individual) to its or his address as shown in the Preamble to this Lease, or at or to such other address as shall have been last notified to the other party for that purpose. Any notice or document given or received by post shall be deemed to have been duly given or served on the second business day after the letter containing the same was posted and in proving

that any notice or document was so given or served it shall be necessary only to prove that the same was properly addressed and posted.

The court called this clause 'ill-drafted' and commented (para 70) that:

> the reference (in the case of a firm or individual) to the address shown in the preamble to the Lease is inept, since neither of the original parties was a firm or an individual. Moreover, the defenders, and their predecessors as tenant, were not a limited company, nor a firm, nor an individual. Neither of the primary provisions of Clause 17 could therefore apply to them.

Another difficulty concerned the phrase 'or at or to such other address as shall have been last notified ...'. Did this apply only to 'a firm or an individual' or did it also apply to 'a company'? The court adopted the latter, broader, interpretation, though at the end of the day the point was not crucial to the decision reached. The court's criticisms of the drafting seem justified. Long sentences devoid of punctuation may be traditional, but the traditional path is not always the best path. Lawyers have often refused to use the word 'it', preferring 'the same'. We know of no justification for this, or even explanation. In itself it does no more than slow down comprehension and make a text look like legalese (plain English campaigners might say 'gobbledegook'). But like other symptoms that are in themselves harmless, it is nevertheless a symptom, and what it is symptom of is an overvaluation of style as against sense.

STANDARD SECURITIES

(48) Bank of Scotland v Forman
[2007] CSIH 46

The pursuer held a standard security over the defender's property. In 1998 it served a calling-up notice and later raised the present action seeking declarator of a power of sale and also decree of removing. The action was dismissed on various grounds, one of which was time bar, for s 19(11) of the Conveyancing and Feudal Reform (Scotland) Act 1970 provides that 'a calling-up notice shall cease to have effect for the purpose of a sale in the exercise of any power conferred by the security on the expiration of a period of five years'. The text of this statutory provision is obscure, but the basic idea is clear enough. Since more than 5 years had passed since the service of the notice, the sheriff held that it had lapsed: see *Conveyancing 2005* Case (36) (discussed further at pp 116–118 of that volume).

The pursuer appealed. The argument about the calling-up notice was that it ceased to be valid only 'for the purpose of a sale' and so the pursuer could still found on it to support its crave for the removal of the defender. The Inner House has now refused the appeal on the ground that the crave for removing was merely ancillary to the crave seeking declarator of the power of sale. Since the first crave had fallen because of s 19(11), the ancillary crave must fall too. On the other matters in issue between the parties the court reserved its opinion. It appears that the pursuer may now raise a fresh action. The case is another example of how long property litigation often seems to take: this dispute has been in court since 1999 and seems nowhere near an end.

SOLICITORS, ESTATE AGENTS, SURVEYORS

(49) Countrywide North Ltd v GWM Developments Ltd
[2007] CSOH 60

An estate agent sued for payment of commission. The contract provided that conclusion of unconditional missives would trigger liability for commission, whether or not the purchaser had been introduced by the estate agent. Later, there was a supplementary agreement to cover the case of missives which might be concluded subject to a condition suspensive on the obtaining of planning permission. This supplementary agreement did not repeat the previous provisions about the estate agent being entitled to commission whether or not the purchaser had been introduced by the estate agent. Relations between the parties seem to have broken down after this. Eventually missives were concluded, subject to planning permission, the buyer not having been introduced by the estate agent. The seller declined to pay commission, arguing that commission would only have been due in these circumstances if the missives had been unconditional. **Held**, that the original agreement and the supplementary agreement had to be read together, so that commission was payable. In addition, averments by the seller that the estate agents had been in breach of contract in the manner they had marketed the property were rejected as not having been adequately pled.

(50) Murray v J & E Shepherd
2007 GWD 7-108, Sh Ct

A proprietor sued a firm of surveyors for loss that, he averred, had been caused by their failure, in a survey done many years earlier, to report the presence of asbestos in the property. It was **held** that the pursuer's written pleadings did not relevantly set forth the alleged link between the defenders' fault and any loss the pursuer may have suffered.

(51) Watts v Bell & Scott WS
[2007] CSOH 108, 2007 SLT 665

This was an action for damages against a law firm for having failed to send an offer in before the closing date. See **Commentary** p 143.

(52) Khosrowpour v Murray Beith & Murray WS
[2007] CSOH 132, 2007 GWD 24-419

Mehdi Khosrowpour ('MK') was the tenant of a fast-food restaurant. He granted a 10-year sub-lease or licence to Hamid Khosrowpour ('HK') in return for a grassum of £50,000 plus a rental of £500 per week. The agreement provided: 'in event that [MK] is unable to hold his tenancy of the aforementioned premises, within the period of the Agreement with [HK], therefore in consequence [MK] or his estate will repay the whole of the License Fee back to [HK]'. It seems, rather strangely, that this sum would be repayable regardless of whether the trigger event happened after just a few months or near the end of the 10-year period.

Later, HK bought the property, thus becoming MK's landlord. When MK fell into rent arrears, HK instructed the defenders to irritate the tenancy. After the irritancy notice was served, MK raised an action of declarator that the tenancy remained in effect, and he was successful. HK then raised the present action against the defenders, arguing that the failure to irritate the tenancy validly was attributable to their negligence. His claim for damages rested on the quoted clause, which would have enabled him to obtain repayment of the grassum. His claim was thus based on what he allegedly lost as sub-tenant or licensee rather than as head landlord.

This stage of the case turned on whether the pursuer's averments about loss had been stated with sufficient relevancy and specification. The core of the difficulty concerned the meaning to be ascribed to the curious expression 'unable to hold his tenancy'. Proof before answer was allowed.

(53) Christie Owen & Davies plc v Campbell
2007 GWD 24-397 affd December 2007, Glasgow Sheriff Court

A firm of estate agents sued the seller's law firm for having failed to remit to them the estate agency commission. See **Commentary** p 145.

(54) Henderson v Sayer
[2007] CSOH 183, 2007 GWD 37-655

This was an action against a solicitor for allegedly having failed to inform the purchasers of an onerous and unusual title condition. See **Commentary** p 144.

BOUNDARY DISPUTES/PRESCRIPTION

(55) Mackenzie v Grant
2007 GWD 16-298, Sh Ct

'This lamentable litigation', says the sheriff, 'concerns a distance of 380 millimetres, although even on that measurement there were a few minutes of debate between the parties' solicitors, before a consensus was reached, as to whether it might be 375mm or 400mm. The proof lasted 12 days and took over a year to complete.'

In December 2003 Mrs Mackenzie disponed part of her garden to Mr and Mrs Grant as a building plot. The disposition contained both a plan and also a detailed verbal description of the boundaries. The disposition was registered in the Land Register on 5 February 2004 but a land certificate was not issued until more than a year later, in March 2005. During the period between registration of the disposition and the issuing of the land certificate, a dispute arose between the parties as to the precise boundaries between the properties. Matters came to a head in August 2004 when, on two separate occasions, Mrs Mackenzie stood in front of a digger to stop it digging on ground which, she claimed, was owned by her. On both occasions she suffered minor injuries, on the first occasion from Mr Grant's dog and on the second from Mr Grant himself. Both were unintentional. Thereafter Mrs Mackenzie obtained interim interdict.

The current phase of the litigation concerned expenses. Now that the land certificate had been issued, it was accepted that the Grants had indeed been encroaching on Mrs Mackenzie's land. But the encroachment was innocent because, the sheriff found – after a proof – it was impossible to tell from the disposition and the plan where the boundary lay. With some qualifications, expenses were awarded to Mrs Mackenzie. The expenses incurred in litigating about the expenses exceeded the expenses being litigated about. In the sheriff's words: 'The purpose of the proof is for the court to decide upon whom the expense of the action should fall, notwithstanding that, on any view, the expense of the proof must have been far more than the expense of the action to that point.'

The facts of this case illustrate some of the difficulties which can arise if there is a long wait for a land certificate. No doubt it is for the parties to make clear provision as to boundaries in a disposition. But if they fail to do so, the boundary will be settled by the land certificate (subject to the possibility, remote in practice, that the title plan is challenged as inaccurate). As registration takes effect from the day on which the application is received and not from the day on which the land certificate is issued (Land Registration (Scotland) Act 1979 s 4(3)), it follows that the parties are immediately subject to a ruling as to the boundary without being able to discover its details for many months. It was the parties' misfortune in the present case that it was precisely during this blind period that the dispute arose.

(56) Hamilton v Dumfries and Galloway Council
[2007] CSOH 96, 2007 GWD 20-347

(1) A 1920 disposition conveyed lands 'as delineated and coloured pink on the sketch or plan annexed and subscribed as relative hereto'. The disposition further provided that 'the accuracy [of the plan] is not warranted'. The roads running through the lands in question were not coloured pink. **Held:** that they were not carried by the disposition. On the provision as to warranty, Lord Glennie said (para 14):

> I do not think that anything turns on the wording in the disposition to the effect that the accuracy of the plan is not warranted. Such a disclaimer is intended to cover errors in the plan and also to make it clear, for example, that field boundaries may not be precisely drawn. But it does not remove altogether the relevance of the plan. The plan is important, for example, to identify which fields are disponed. By the same token, it is relevant for the purpose of identifying that there is no intended disposition of any interest in the public roads running through the land.

(2) A 1926 disposition of the same area conveyed land 'delineated and coloured pink on the Plan thereunto annexed and subscribed by me'. This time the roads *were* coloured pink. It was **held** that the roads were nonetheless excluded. One (but not the only) reason for this was that the plan was said by the disposition to be 'descriptive merely and not taxative'. Lord Glennie's view – rather surprisingly in view of the indulgence shown to the plan in the previous disposition – was that 'with such wording, any inference that might be drawn from the colouring of the plan is very weak' (para 17).

(3) A developer laid a pavement and a road bell-mouth on land to which it had only an *a non domino* title. Thereafter, it was averred, the owners of two houses in the housing estate, which the pavement adjoined, and whose title derived from the developer, weeded and swept the pavement and kept it clear of snow, as well as driving over the bell-mouth. In the event, the question of whether there was sufficient possession for prescription did not have to be answered. But Lord Glennie said this (para 34):

> The difficulty is in finding some act of 'possession' which can be said to be 'un-equivocally referable' to their claimed titles of ownership. Driving out through Townhead Park does not fall within this category. Such an act is in no way referable to the claim to ownership. There were no doubt many others living within the development doing the same without pretending to any title.... For similar reasons, I was not persuaded that the routine acts of sweeping the pavements, weeding them and clearing them of snow were unequivocally referable to the claim to ownership. However, the developers constructed the pavement at some time after 1992, and it seems to me that the act of constructing the pavement and keeping it there could be said to be an act of possession which was unequivocally referable to a claim to ownership. In those circumstances, had it been necessary for me to decide this point, I would, on balance, have held that by 2 June 2005 the title enjoyed by Mr Hyslop and Mr and Mrs Marshall was exempt from challenge.

Would such prescription operate retrospectively? Surely correctly, Lord Glennie said no (para 33):

> The effect of their having done so [ie having the requisite possession) would be to make their titles exempt from challenge from that point on. But it would not have the effect of retrospectively validating actions which took place before the expiry of 10 years. Insofar as it is necessary to examine what occurred before the expiry of 10 years, that examination must proceed upon the basis of what the position was then. Otherwise one would have the absurd situation that the validity of a decision by the roads authority to adopt a road [valid only if the authority were the owner at the time] would alter merely by the passage of time. In the present case, the decision taken on 26 May 2005 would have been invalid at the time it was taken but, on Mr Olson's argument, would have become valid about a week later without anyone doing anything to achieve that. ... The system would be unworkable if the effect of the exemption from challenge in s 1 of the 1973 Act had the effect of retrospectively validating prior acts.

Lord Glennie's decision in this case was affirmed on a different point at [2007] CSIH 75, 2007 GWD 34-582. [Another aspect of this decision is digested at (22).]

BARONY TITLES

(57) Lindberg Ptr
2 April 2007, Lyon Court

This petition for arms by Dr Lars Lindberg was refused by the Lord Lyon on the grounds of absence of jurisdiction. Dr Lindberg was a Norwegian who had never visited Scotland and whose only connection with Scotland was a barony title. One result of the abolition of the feudal system was to separate barony titles from the land: see Abolition of Feudal Tenure etc (Scotland) Act 2000 s 63(2). The Lord Lyon gave his views on their new status as follows:

> I do not accept that a barony remains a noble fief to the extent that the holder has a special heraldic privilege or right. A fief is a landholding and the dignity of baron after the commencement of the 2000 Act ceases to be an incident of landholding. No hereditary office is involved in a barony. In my view a barony is no longer a heritable office held of the Crown.
>
> What has arisen after the 2000 Act is in effect a new species of property, 'the dignity of baron' as it is styled in the Act. The dignity is a social 'advantage', or benefit, but it is shorn of a connection to land albeit that it has historically related to a Crown grant of land. The 2000 Act has altered the character of the dignity. Prior to the Act it was a dignity associated with landholding; the 2000 Act has done away with that association. There remains, however, a historic relationship with the Crown in so far as the dignity was, at some point in the past, a benefit conferred by the Crown.
>
> The dignity of baron, after the coming into force of the 2000 Act, has a heritable character. That determines the manner in which it is to transfer on the death of the holder, but that is not synonymous with a feudal relationship. It is merely a pragmatic way of dealing with the right. It has a noble character in that it is a right which historically originated in a Crown grant.

Previously the Lyon Court had jurisdiction to confer arms on barons – even those with no other connection to Scotland – because, in holding a barony title, they also owned corporeal heritable property (ie land) in Scotland. But a post-feudal barony title has no connection with the land. It is only incorporeal heritable property. In the Lord Lyon's view, that was not enough by itself to confer jurisdiction.

MISCELLANEOUS

(58) De Lathouwer v Anderson
[2007] CSOH 54, 2007 SLT 437

In the late 1970s Mr and Mrs Ross, who were then living in Belgium, wanted to buy a house in Crieff. Lacking the necessary funds, they entered into an arrangement with Mr and Mrs de Lathouwer of Houston, Texas, whereby Mr and Mrs de Lathouwer would buy the property and Mr and Mrs Ross would pay them back over a period of years. In the meantime, title was to remain with Mr and

Mrs de Lathouwer. On the basis of this arrangement, Mr and Mrs de Lathouwer acquired the property. In 1981 Mr de Lathouwer disponed his half share to Mrs de Lathouwer. In 1982 the arrangement was varied, and Mrs de Lathouwer disponed the property to Mr and Mrs Ross and the survivor of them even though the full amount due had not yet been paid. At the same time a probative agreement was entered into between Mrs de Lathouwer (or Moberg, the name she used in the agreement) on the one hand and Mr and Mrs Ross on the other hand, spelling out the terms of the agreement, and containing this provision:

> We [Mr and Mrs Ross] and the survivor of us undertake to leave and bequeath the said house to the said Dolores Althea Moberg; And we further declare that such bequest shall be irrevocable.

Eventually all the instalments were paid. In 1990 Mr Ross died, and his half share passed to Mrs Ross. In 2000 Mrs Ross died. Her will left her estate mainly to a Mrs Wilson. In 2001 Mrs de Lathouwer raised an action to require the executor (Mr Anderson) either to convey the property to her or to pay damages for breach of the 1982 agreement. In 2003 Mrs Wilson raised an action under s 8 of the Law Reform (Miscellaneous Provisions) (Scotland) Act 1985 to have the 1982 agreement rectified so that the quoted provision would be subject to the proviso that the obligation to bequeath would lapse when the last instalment was paid off. This action was unsuccessful. Meanwhile the present action has continued and reached the stage of debate in 2007. The pursuer's argument that the 1982 agreement was itself an irrevocable legacy was rejected. But the Lord Ordinary (Emslie) allowed proof before answer on the second branch of the pursuer's case. The outcome of that proof is not known to us.

One can only speculate about the real intentions of the parties. If the de Lathouwers were providing a loan, one wonders why a standard security was not used. If the intention was that the Rosses would have the property for their joint lives, after which it would go to the de Lathouwers, one wonders why a liferent – either a proper liferent or a trust liferent – was not used.

(59) Stewart v Henderson
[2007] CSOH 14

In October 1983 George Henderson died, leaving his house in liferent to his daughter, and the fee equally to the daughter, to her son, and to her two brothers. In August 1985 the family signed a deed of variation whereby the daughter was to have the property absolutely, and would pay her brothers the value of their share in the fee (which she did). In this action the daughter sought to compel one of her brothers to grant her a disposition of his share. Her difficulty was that the deed of variation could not be found. The defender did not deny signing it, nor did he deny being paid. But he did not admit that he was bound to do anything further. He also pled prescription. Counsel for the defender admitted that her client's position was an 'unattractive' one.

Proof was allowed, but it appears that the case has been sisted to allow the pursuer to raise an action of proving the tenor of the lost deed of variation. On the prescription point, the action had been raised in August 2005 and it was unclear whether by then 20 years had passed or not. The Lord Ordinary's opinion does not discuss the current state of the title, but one assumes that a one-quarter share had been conveyed to the defender prior to the deed of variation, for otherwise the present action would be difficult to understand.

(60) Young v Campbell
[2007] CSOH 194

Mr and Mrs Campbell had a property in Ross-shire. Part of it was co-owned and the remainder was owned by Mrs Campbell alone. The house, which was their home, stood on the co-owned area, except for the kitchen, which stood on the area owned by Mrs Campbell alone. The Bank of Scotland held a standard security over the co-owned area. It seems that it did not cover the area owned by Mrs Campbell alone, and so did not cover the kitchen. We do not know the reason why the security was limited in this way. Although it seems that the kitchen was a later extension to the original building, there is some evidence in the case that the extension was already there when the standard security was granted. The title to both areas was in the Register of Sasines.

The Campbells got into financial difficulties. In June 2004 Mr Campbell was sequestrated. In the same year Mrs Campbell sold the area of which she was the sole owner to her daughter for £250: title was completed on 30 November 2004. (The pleadings say that this was in the GRS but in fact it was the Land Register – as the date would itself indicate.) By that time Mrs Campbell had been inhibited, but it does not appear that any attempt was made to reduce the disposition. In February 2005 Mrs Campbell granted a trust deed. In September 2005 the daughter, Miss Campbell, granted a standard security over her area in favour of a Mr Redpath for a debt of £6,000. After sundry abortive negotiations, the trustee under the trust deed petitioned for Mrs Campbell's sequestration. One of his reasons was that he wished to reduce the sale to the daughter as a gratuitous alienation. (It may be remarked that a trustee under a trust deed normally has this power anyway – see eg W W McBryde, *Bankruptcy* (2nd edn 1995) para 12–50 – and so we do not wholly follow the logic of this argument.)

The Lord Ordinary (Lady Paton) **held** that the statutory grounds for sequestration had been satisfied. Accordingly the trustee's petition was successful. The next round in this case will presumably be an action of reduction at the instance of the trustee in sequestration.

While the action was proceeding, Miss Campbell disponed the area to Mr Campbell, the date of entry being 13 June 2007 and registration being 5 July 2007. We do not know the date of his sequestration in 2004, but we assume that matters were so arranged as to ensure that he acquired no rights in relation to the property before the third anniversary of his sequestration, the third anniversary being the normal date of a discharge. (The standard discharge period will in future be shorter: see the Bankruptcy and Diligence etc (Scotland) Act 2007 s 1.) The consideration was stated as being £6,000.

(61) AB v CD and Bank of Scotland Trust Company (International) Ltd [2006] CSOH 200, 2007 Fam LR 53

This was a divorce case. The husband had put most of his assets into a discretionary trust established in Jersey. He argued that these assets should not be classified as matrimonial property, since the trust was discretionary, and he was merely one of various potential beneficiaries. The wife argued that in reality he controlled the assets. The Lord Ordinary (Brodie) agreed and awarded her £1,000,000. The case shows that the off-shore discretionary trust is not necessarily bomb-proof.

PART II

STATUTORY DEVELOPMENTS

STATUTORY DEVELOPMENTS

Bankruptcy and Diligence etc (Scotland) Act 2007 (asp 3)

This Act was passed by the Scottish Parliament at the end of 2006 and received the Royal Assent in January 2007. It replaces adjudication with a new diligence called land attachment, and also makes major changes to the law of bankruptcy, inhibitions, and floating charges. For a summary of its provisions as they affect conveyancers, see *Conveyancing 2006* pp 131–138.

The **Bankruptcy and Diligence etc (Scotland) Act 2007 (Commencement No 1) Order 2007, SSI 2007/82** brought into force in March 2007 various amendments to the Debt Arrangement and Attachment (Scotland) Act 2002, which provides for the debt arrangement scheme and for the diligence of attachment of corporeal moveable property. A provisional timetable for future commencement can be found at www.aib.gov.uk/Policy/AiB%20Policy%20 Page.htm.

Legal Profession and Legal Aid (Scotland) Act 2007 (asp 5)

Although this Act has no specific connection to conveyancing, its potential impact on the legal profession in general means it should be noted here.

Crofting Reform etc Act 2007 (asp 7)

This Act makes important changes to crofting law. Although crofting is not a subject covered in this series, we mention some highlights of the new legislation. The changes are effected mainly by amendments to the Crofting (Scotland) Act 1993. Provision is made for the creation of new crofts, including the extension of crofting tenure beyond the crofting counties (Argyll, Inverness, Ross and Cromarty, Sutherland, Caithness, Orkney and Shetland). There are changes to the rules about assignation of crofts, succession to a deceased crofter, termination of crofting tenancies, reorganisation schemes, development schemes, common grazings, decrofting, sub-letting, the crofting community right to buy, the jurisdiction of the Land Court and the function of the Crofters Commission. The commencement date for much of the Act was 25 June 2007 (**Crofting Reform etc Act 2007 (Commencement No 1) Order 2007, SSI 2007/269**), and for the balance 28 January 2008 (**Crofting Reform etc Act 2007 (Commencement No 2) Order 2007, SSI 2007/568**).

Adult Support and Protection (Scotland) Act 2007 (asp 10)

Part 2 of this Act amends the Adults with Incapacity (Scotland) Act 2000 in relation to continuing powers of attorney and welfare powers of attorney.

Planning-gain Supplement (Preparations) Act 2007 (c 2)

This is a 'paving the way' statute. What it paves the way for is neatly summarised by its long title: 'An Act to permit expenditure in preparation for the imposition of a tax on the increase in the value of land resulting from the grant of permission for development.'

Finance Act 2007 (c 11)

For changes to stamp duty land tax, see **Commentary** p 153.

Consumers, Estate Agents and Redress Act 2007 (c 17)

In recent years there has been pressure to toughen up the provisions of the Estate Agents Act 1979. This new Act does so, though it does not go as far as to require all estate agents to be licensed, which is what many had been calling for. Its provisions affect only non-solicitor estate agents.

The Act deals with a wide range of issues. As to estate agency, the main provisions are: (a) estate agents must belong to a redress scheme in relation to the marketing of residential property; (b) there are new requirements for estate agents to make and keep records; (c) the Office of Fair Trading is given power to require production of records; (d) there are extended powers for the OFT to take regulatory action against estate agents who have acted improperly.

Money Laundering Regulations 2007, SI 2007/2157

The Money Laundering Regulations 2007 came into force on 15 December 2007, replacing the Money Laundering Regulations 2003, SI 2003/3075. They transpose the Third Money Laundering Directive (2005/60/EC). Some minor amendments were made by the **Money Laundering (Amendment) Regulations 2007, SI 2007/3299**.

The Solicitors (Scotland) Accounts etc Rules 2001 have been altered to bring them into line with the 2007 Regulations. There is a useful article by Morag Newton and James Ness at p 26 of the May issue of the *Journal of the Law Society of Scotland* and a further article by Morag Newton in the July issue at p 30. The Law Society of Scotland's website (www.lawscot.org.uk/Members_Information/moneylaundering) also has helpful coverage. The Society gives official guidance, divided into two parts. Part 1 is identical with part 1 of the Joint Money Laundering Steering Group Guidance. (The JMLSG is a government-sponsored body. The Law Society of Scotland is a member.) The JMLSG guidance can be found at www.jmlsg.org.uk/content/1/c6/01/14/56/Part_I_-_HMT_approved.pdf, and at 159 pages it is not a quick read. Part 2 of the Society's guidance is specific to Scottish solicitors, and is given in full – and is happily brief.

The 2007 Regulations are far from being a mere revised version of the 2003 Regulations, even if at the end of the day the results are likely to be fairly similar. But major legislative overhauls are seldom problem-free. Our crystal ball suggests that there may be problems with the concept of 'beneficial owner'. Regulation 5 says:

'Customer due diligence measures' means –

(a) identifying the customer and verifying the customer's identity on the basis of documents, data or information obtained from a reliable and independent source;

(b) identifying, where there is a beneficial owner who is not the customer, the beneficial owner and taking adequate measures, on a risk-sensitive basis, to verify his identity so that the relevant person is satisfied that he knows who the beneficial owner is, including, in the case of a legal person, trust or similar legal arrangement, measures to understand the ownership and control structure of the person, trust or arrangement....

Paragraph (a) is fairly straightforward, but para (b) is not. What is a 'beneficial owner'? That is dealt with by reg 6 which, like much of the 2007 Regulations, is closely based on the Directive. The length of the definition is so great that the text cannot be reproduced here. That in itself is an ominous sign. We think that this mammoth definition – which every solicitor is supposed to know and understand – is likely to prove problematic.

Tenements (Scotland) Act 2004

With the **Tenements (Scotland) Act 2004 (Commencement No 2) Order 2007, SSI 2007/17**, which brought s 18 into force on 24 January 2007, the Tenements (Scotland) Act 2004 is now fully in force. Section 18 provides for compulsory insurance against fire and the other risks set out in the **Tenements (Scotland) Act 2004 (Prescribed Risks) Order 2007, SSI 2007/16**. See **Commentary** p 141.

Housing (Scotland) Act 2006

Home reports/single survey

In February 2007 the Scottish Executive issued a consultation document about the regulations for what were then still called 'purchaser's information packs' to be made under ss 98–119 of the 2006 Act. (On those provisions see *Conveyancing 2005* pp 124–130.) The Law Society of Scotland's response, assisted by the results of an online questionnaire, can be found at www.lawscot.org.uk/Members_ Information/convey_essens/PIP/Response.aspx. (And see an article by Peter Nicholson at p 50 of the March issue of the *Journal of the Law Society of Scotland*.) A Scottish Executive report on the views of consultees was published in August 2007 under a title of studied neutrality, *The Single Survey: Fairer for Everyone* (www. communitiesscotland.gov.uk/stellent/groups/public/documents/webpages/cs 019860.pdf). On 30 January 2008 the Scottish Government announced that the new system would come into operation on 1 December 2008, and that purchaser's information packs would be renamed 'home reports': see www.scotland.gov.uk/News/Releases/2008/01/30105839.

In England and Wales 'home information packs' have already arrived (see *Conveyancing 2006* pp 63–64) but not without some changes of mind. The original Home Information Pack Regulations 2006, SI 2006/1503 were amended by the Home Information Pack Regulations 2007, SI 2007/992, and both were revoked before they could come into force by the Home Information Pack (Revocation) Regulations 2007, SI 2007/1525. Their replacement, the Home Information Pack (No 2) Regulations 2007, SI 2007/1667, were promptly amended by the Home Information Pack (Amendment) Regulations 2007, SI 2007/3301. These Regulations came fully into force on 14 December 2007, having previously been brought into force first for houses with four or more bedrooms (1 August 2007) and then for houses with three bedrooms (10 September 2007).

So far as Scotland is concerned, the necessary statutory instruments are now being put into place for commencement. The **Housing (Scotland) Act 2006 (Penalty Charge) Regulations 2007, SSI 2007/575** is the first, and comes into force on 1 October 2008. The background is that, once the relevant provisions are in force, a person who is responsible for marketing a house must have and make available home reports. Breach of this duty attracts a 'penalty charge notice' by a trading standards officer from the local authority. Under the Regulations, the amount of a penalty charge will be £500, which is the maximum allowable in terms of the powers in para 2 of sch 3 to the 2006 Act. By contrast, in England the corresponding figure is a paltry £200 – too low, perhaps, to compel compliance with the statutory requirements.

A draft of main regulations – the Housing (Scotland) Act 2006 (Prescribed Documents) Regulations 2008 – was published on 8 January 2008. As expected, the home report is to comprise two documents: (a) a survey report (including a report on energy efficiency) and (b) a property questionnaire. These must follow the forms in, respectively, schedules 1 and 2 of the Regulations. The property questionnaire covers a number of topics which, at present, are covered in missives, including alterations, water supply and other services, shared maintenance, dry rot and other infestations, and statutory notices. As a result it will be necessary to consider whether some of the missives clauses currently in use need to be modified, or can be deleted altogether. It should be borne in mind, however, that the property questionnaire is a call for information rather than a legal warranty. Further, the draft Regulations allow the information – and the survey as well – to be up to 12 weeks out of date at the time when the property is first put on the market, with the result that more recent developments (eg new statutory notices) do not need to be owned up to.

The Scottish Regulations are mercifully shorter and easier to understand than their English equivalents. The English Regulations are prolix and fussy: for instance they actually have rules about the *order* in which the documents must be inserted into the HIP, and they are followed up by a dessert course of no fewer than twelve schedules. Nevertheless there is some copy-and-paste in the draft Scottish Regulations, just as much of the Housing (Scotland) Act 2006 was copied from the Housing Act 2004.

One important point of difference between England and Scotland concerns registration. Section 104 of the 2006 Act authorised the setting up of this new register, in which all home reports would have to be registered. That was based, needless to say, on the English proposals. But whereas the English have actually gone ahead with this idea, the draft Scottish Regulations quietly drop it. Another difference worth noting is about providers: in Scotland RICS surveyors are to be authorised to provide home reports and nobody else.

Form of repayment charge

Section 30 of the 2006 Act introduces a new type of repairs notice known as a works notice. If a works notice is not complied with, the local authority can carry out the work and recover the cost (ss 35, 59). As part of the recovery process, s 172 allows the local authority to make a 'repayment charge' in its own favour. On registration this constitutes 'a charge' – whatever that is – which has priority over existing heritable securities (s 173(2)). The form of a repayment charge, and its discharge, has now been prescribed by the **Housing (Scotland) Act 2006 (Repayment Charge and Discharge) Order 2007, SSI 2007/419**, as follows:

Form of Repayment Charge

We [ ] (i),in exercise of the power conferred on us by section 172 of the Housing (Scotland) Act 2006, CHARGE the subjects described in the schedule with a repayable amount of [ ] (ii) sterling, payable in thirty equal annual instalments of [ ] (iii), the first instalment being payable on [ ] (iv) in 20[ ] and subsequent instalments on the same date in every succeeding calendar year. IN WITNESS WHEREOF (v)

SCHEDULE

DESCRIPTION OF SUBJECTS (vi)

    (i) Insert the name and address of the local authority.
    (ii) Insert in words the repayment amount.
    (iii) Insert the amount of the annual instalment.
    (iv) Insert a date after the making of the charge for the first instalment to be paid.
    (v) The deed should be executed here and at the end of the Schedule.
    (vi) Insert a full description of the subjects by reference to the postal address and, as appropriate, either (a) a competent conveyancing description to enable recording in the General Register of Sasines, or (b) the registered title number to enable registration in the Land Register.

Form of Discharge of Repayment Charge

We [ ] (i), DISCHARGE the Repayment Charge made by us on [ ] (ii) over the subjects [ ] (iii) and [either] (iv) registered in the Land Register under Title Number [ ] (v) on [ ] (vi) [or] recorded in the Division of the General Register of Sasines for the County of [ ] (vii) on [ ] (viii) IN WITNESS WHEREOF

(i) Insert the name and address of the local authority.
(ii) Insert the date of execution of the original Repayment Charge.
(iii) Insert postal address of subjects.
(iv) Delete as appropriate.
(v) Insert Title Number in Land Register.
(vi) Insert date of registration of Repayment Charge.
(vii) Insert name of County in the General Register of Sasines.
(viii) Insert date of recording of Repayment Charge in the General Register of Sasines.

Commencement

A substantial number of provisions are brought into force by the **Housing (Scotland) Act 2006 (Commencement No 5, Savings and Transitional Provisions) Order 2007, SSI 2007/270**. (For previous commencement orders, see *Conveyancing 2006* p 65.) These include ss 12 ff (in force from 3 September 2007) which impose enhanced obligations on private landlords to keep houses in repair, as well as providing for a right of application by tenants to the Private Rented Housing Panel, when the landlord is alleged to be in breach of these obligations, and a right for local authorities to carry out works determined by a Private Rented Housing Committee and which a landlord cannot or will not do. See *Conveyancing 2005* pp 26–28. Further provision for applications to the Private Rented Housing Panel is made by the **Private Rented Housing Panel (Applications and Determinations) (Scotland) Regulations 2007, SSI 2007/173**.

Form of path order

Under s 22 of the Land Reform (Scotland) Act 2003, local authorities and National Park Authorities have compulsory powers to delineate a path over land in respect of which access rights are exercisable. The **Land Reform (Scotland) Act 2003 (Path Orders) Regulations 2007, SSI 2007/163** is an enabling provision setting out the form which path orders must take. No path order has yet been made.

New conservation bodies

Conservation bodies are bodies which are able to create and hold conservation burdens under s 38 of the Title Conditions (Scotland) Act 2003. A conservation burden is a personal real burden which preserves or protects the natural or built environment for the benefit of the public. The first list of conservation bodies, prescribed by the Title Conditions (Scotland) Act 2003 (Conservation Bodies) Order 2003, SSI 2003/453, was amended by the Title Conditions (Scotland) Act 2003 (Conservation Bodies) Amendment Order 2004, SSI 2004/400, the Title Conditions (Scotland) Act 2003 (Conservation Bodies) Amendment Order 2006, SSI 2006/110, and the Title Conditions (Scotland) Act 2003 (Conservation Bodies) Amendment (No 2) Order 2006, SSI 2006/130. The **Title Conditions (Scotland) Act 2003 (Conservation Bodies) Amendment Order 2007, SSI 2007/533** adds two further bodies: Glasgow City Heritage Trust and Stirling City Heritage Trust.

The complete list of conservation bodies is now:

All local authorities
Castles of Scotland Preservation Trust
Aberdeen City Heritage Trust
Alba Conservation Trust
Edinburgh World Heritage Trust
Glasgow Building Preservation Trust
Glasgow City Heritage Trust
Highlands Buildings Preservation Trust
Plantlife – The Wild-Plant Conservation Charity
Scottish Natural Heritage
Solway Heritage
St Vincent Crescent Preservation Trust
Stirling City Heritage Trust
Strathclyde Building Preservation Trust
Tayside Building Preservation Trust
The John Muir Trust
The National Trust for Scotland for Places of Historic Interest or Natural Beauty
The Royal Society for the Protection of Birds
The Scottish Wildlife Trust
The Trustees of the Landmark Trust
The Trustees of the New Lanark Conservation Trust
The Woodland Trust
United Kingdom Historic Building Preservation Trust

New rural housing bodies

Rural housing bodies are bodies which are able to create and hold rural housing burdens under s 43 of the Title Conditions (Scotland) Act 2003. A rural housing burden is a personal right of pre-emption. This may only be used over rural land, ie land other than 'excluded land'. 'Excluded land' has the same meaning as in the Land Reform (Scotland) Act 2003, namely settlements of over 10,000 people.

The first list of rural housing bodies was prescribed by the Title Conditions (Scotland) Act 2003 (Rural Housing Bodies) Order 2004, SSI 2004/477. The Title Conditions (Scotland) Act 2003 (Rural Housing Bodies) Amendment Order 2006, SSI 2006/108, added more names, and a further nine are now added by the **Title Conditions (Scotland) Act 2003 (Rural Housing Bodies) Amendment Order 2007, SSI 2007/58** and the **Title Conditions (Scotland) Act 2003 (Rural Housing Bodies) Amendment (No 2) Order 2007, SSI 2007/535**. These are:

Argyll Community Housing Association
Colonsay Community Development Company
Commmunity Self-Build Scotland Limited
Down to Earth Scottish Sustainable Self Build Housing Association Limited
Dumfries and Galloway Small Communities Housing Trust
Fyne Initiatives Limited
HIFAR Limited

North West Mull Community Woodland Company Limited
West Highland Rural Solutions Limited.

The complete list of rural housing bodies is now:

Albyn Housing Society Limited
Argyll Community Housing Association
Barra and Vatersay Housing Association Limited
Berneray Housing Association Limited
Buidheann Taigheadais na Meadhanan Limited
Buidheann Tigheadas Loch Aillse Agus An Eilein Sgitheanaich Limited
Cairn Housing Association Limited
Colonsay Community Development Company
Comhairle nan Eilean Siar
Community Self-Build Scotland Limited
Down to Earth Scottish Sustainable Self Build Housing Association Limited
Dumfries and Galloway Small Communities Housing Trust
Dunbritton Housing Association Limited
Ekopia Resource Exchange Limited
Fyne Homes Limited
Fyne Initiatives Limited
HIFAR Limited
Isle of Jura Development Trust
Lochaber Housing Association Limited
Muirneag Housing Association Limited
North West Mull Community Woodland Company Limited
Orkney Islands Council
Pentland Housing Association Limited
Rural Stirling Housing Association Limited
Taighean Ceann a Tuath na'Hearadh Limited
The Highlands Small Communities' Housing Trust
The Isle of Eigg Heritage Trust
The Isle of Gigha Heritage Trust
The North Harris Trust
Tighean Innse Gall Limited
West Highland Housing Association Limited
West Highland Rural Solutions Limited.

Building regulations

Amendments to building regulations

The Building (Scotland) Regulations 2004, SSI 2004/406, were amended with effect from 1 May 2007 by the Building (Scotland) Amendment Regulations 2006, SSI 2006/534. The **Building (Scotland) Amendment Regulations 2007, SSI 2007/166** add some provisions omitted by mistake from the 2006 Regulations.

Amendments to procedural requirements

The Building (Procedure) (Scotland) Regulations 2004, SSI 2004/428, set out the procedures for obtaining a warrant, presenting a completion certificate, using

Approved Certifiers and handling dangerous and defective buildings. The 2004 Regulations are now amended by the **Building (Procedure) (Scotland) Amendment Regulations 2007, SSI 2007/167** in order to implement in part the EC Directive on the Energy Performance of Buildings (2002/91/EC), to simplify the submission of completion certificates, and to clarify access to Building Standards Registers.

Forms

The **Building (Forms) (Scotland) Amendment Regulations 2007, SSI 2007/168** make minor amendments to the Building (Forms) (Scotland) Regulations 2005, SSI 2005/172, in order to implement the EC Directive on the Energy Performance of Buildings (2002/91/EC). This follows the significant amendments previously made by the Building (Forms) (Scotland) Amendment Regulations 2006, SSI 2006/163.

Fees

The **Building (Fees) (Scotland) Amendment Regulations 2007, SSI 2007/169** make a minor change to the fees laid down in the Building (Fees) (Scotland) Regulations 2004, SSI 2004/508.

Name and designation of charities in conveyancing documents

Important new rules are introduced by the **Charities References in Documents (Scotland) Regulations 2007, SSI 2007/203**. In terms of reg 2, any body entered in the Scottish Charity Register:

> must state, in legible characters –
>
> (a) the registered number allocated to it by OSCR as part of the registration process;
> (b) its name as entered in the Scottish Charity Register;
> (c) any other name by which it is commonly known; and
> (d) where the name entered in the Scottish Charity Register does not include 'charity' or 'charitable', that it is a charity by using one of the terms referred to in section 13(1) or (2) of the Charities and Trustee Investment (Scotland) Act 2005,
>
> on all documents listed in regulation 4 and which are issued or signed on behalf of the charity after 31st March 2008.

The terms referred to in s 13(1) or (2), mentioned in para (d) above, are:

> charity
> charitable body
> registered charity
> charity registered in Scotland
> Scottish charity
> registered Scottish charity.

The last two may only be used if the body is established under Scots law or is managed or controlled wholly or mainly in Scotland.

The list of documents, in reg 4, in which these names and designations must be used is extensive:

(a) business letters and e-mails;
(b) advertisements, notices and official publications;
(c) any document which solicits money or other property for the benefit of the charity;
(d) bills of exchange, promissory notes, endorsements and orders for money or goods;
(e) bills rendered;
(f) invoices, receipts and letters of credit;
(g) statements of account prepared in accordance with either regulation 8, 9 or 14 of the Charities Accounts (Scotland) Regulations 2006;
(h) educational or campaign documentation;
(i) conveyances which provide for the creation, transfer, variation or extinction of an interest in land;
(j) contractual documentation.

The last two should be particularly noted.

What is the sanction for failure to comply? On this matter, both the Regulations and the enabling provision (Charities and Trustee Investment (Scotland) Act 2005 s 15) are silent. Compare the possible criminal and civil sanctions which apply in the case of the equivalent provisions for companies (ss 83 and 84 of the Companies Act 2006). It seems that a disposition which does not comply with the Regulations will be perfectly valid – provided of course that the body in question is named and designed in a way which allows it to be identified. But presumably persistent breach of the Regulations may attract the unwelcome attentions of OSCR (see eg ss 28–33 of the 2005 Act). Finally, the new provisions run in tandem with s 112(6) of the Companies Act 1989, which has comparable provisions for Scottish charities that are incorporated under the Companies Acts.

PART III
OTHER MATERIAL

OTHER MATERIAL

Sharp v Thomson

The Scottish Law Commission published its Report on *Sharp v Thomson* in December 2007 (Scot Law Com No 204, available on www.scotlawcom.gov.uk). The Commission was asked to look into the issues raised by that case by the Justice Department. Since then, a number of developments have taken place, including:

(i)   the Enterprise Act 2002, which is gradually phasing out receivership, at least for most types of floating charge;

(ii) the introduction of ARTL, which cuts down a buyer's exposure to the risk of the seller's insolvency;

(iii) s 17 of the Bankruptcy and Diligence etc (Scotland) Act 2007, which implements most of proposal 4 in the Commission's earlier Discussion Paper on *Sharp v Thomson* (Scot Law Com DP No 114 (2001)); and

(iv) the case of *Burnett's Tr v Grainger* 2004 SC (HL) 19, which gave a narrow interpretation to *Sharp v Thomson* (see *Conveyancing 2004* pp 78–85).

In the light of these developments, the package of reforms recommended by the Law Commission is limited in its scope. The recommendations aim mainly at enhancing the transactional security of a buyer (or other grantee) where the seller (or other granter) is a company. The recommendations are:

(1) Voluntary liquidations should be registered forthwith, thus eliminating the current 15-day blind period.

(2) Petitions for winding up should be registered forthwith. At present they are not registered at all.

(3) The rule that a floating charge cannot attach without registration, which at present applies in some cases but not others, should apply in all cases.

(4) Section 25 of the Titles to Land Consolidation (Scotland) Act 1868, which allows a liquidator to complete title instantly, should be repealed.

The Register of Insolvencies goes online

The Register of Insolvencies (which is kept not by the Keeper but by the Accountant in Bankruptcy) has now gone online: www.aib.gov.uk/ROI/. The value of this register is perhaps under-appreciated by conveyancers. Although to some extent it duplicates information that can be located in the Register of Inhibitions or the Register of Companies, it also contains information that cannot readily be obtained elsewhere.

Letters of obligation

The Law Society of Scotland's website (www.lawscot.org.uk) now has a valuable section on letters of obligation. It covers such topical matters as ARTL, notices of potential liability for costs, and the changes to the forms brought about by the Land Registration (Scotland) Rules 2006, SSI 2006/485.

Housing policy

In October 2007 the Scottish Government issued a *Discussion Paper on the Future Direction of Housing Policy in Scotland* (ISBN 9780755955381). Of the many issues raised in this paper, the one that caught the attention of the media was the possibility of exempting new-build properties from the ambit of the right-to-buy legislation.

Crown Estate Review Working Group Report

The subject of Crown Estate is a controversial one, especially in certain parts of the country. The Crown Estate Review Working Group (CERWG) was set up by six local authorities in the Highlands and Islands, together with Highlands & Islands Enterprise and the Convention of Scottish Local Authorities. The Group's report, though dated December 2006, was published in February 2007: www. highland.gov.uk/yourenvironment/landandwater/crownestatereviewwg.htm. The Crown Estate Commission lost no time in issuing a negative response: www. thecrownestate.co.uk/newscontent/92_cerwg_report_response.htm.

Registers of Scotland

ARTL

A little later than expected, ARTL began to be used in the autumn of 2007, but only for a small number of firms and lending institutions and only for standard securities and discharges. According to the *Journal of the Law Society of Scotland* for January 2008 (p 17), the system should begin to be available for transfers of title by the end of March 2008. The first step will be to sign firms up with digital signatures. The order of sign-up will generally follow the order in which counties became operational on the Land Register:

- Renfrew, Dumbarton, Lanark, Glasgow, Argyll, Bute;
- East Lothian, West Lothian, Midlothian;
- Angus, Fife, Stirling, Kinross, Clackmannan, Perth, Kincardine;
- Aberdeen, Banff, Caithness, Moray, Orkney & Shetland, Ross & Cromarty, Sutherland, Inverness, Nairn;

- Ayr, Dumfries, Kirkcudbright, Wigtown, Berwick, Peebles, Roxburgh, Selkirk.

James Ness gives an account of a typical ARTL transaction at p 52 of the July 2007 issue of the *Journal of the Law Society of Scotland*. His final heading – not, we hope, a hostage to fortune – is 'nothing to fear'.

The Automated Registration of Title to Land (Electronic Communications) (Scotland) Order 2006, SSI 2006/491, empowers the Keeper to issue 'directions' and in 2007 two were issued: Keeper's Direction No 1 of 2007 and Keeper's Direction No 2 of 2007. For information about ARTL, including the texts of these two directions, see the ROS website. This says of the first Direction:

> Direction No 1 sets the standard of electronic signature within the ARTL system which will be accorded the same legal presumptions of authenticity as are accorded a hand-written signature on a paper deed. The Direction will exclude from ARTL technologically insecure digital certificates and legally insufficient checks on identity.

Direction No 1 is a technofest. Those who do not know what is meant by cryptography standard ITU-T X509 (08/05) should probably take the Direction on trust. By comparison, the second Direction is plain sailing, providing that in the initial phase ARTL will be available for standard securities and discharges of standard securities. As already mentioned, that initial phase began in the autumn of 2007.

Reorganisation of HBOS

On 17 September 2007 The Governor and Company of the Bank of Scotland was registered as a public company under the Companies Act 1985 and its name changed to Bank of Scotland plc. In addition, the business, property and liabilities of Halifax plc, Capital Bank plc and HBOS Treasury Services plc transferred to and vested in Bank of Scotland plc. See further the HBOS Group Reorganisation Act 2006. The implications for standard securities and discharges are set out in Registers of Scotland, *Update 22* (available at www.ros.gov.uk/pdfs/update22.pdf). On the basis that Bank of Scotland plc is the same legal person as the Governor and Company of the Bank of Scotland, there are no implications for discharges of securities granted in favour of the latter, except of course that the granter should be the former. But where a security was granted in favour of Halifax plc, Capital Bank plc or HBOS Treasury Services plc, a discharge will need to deduce title (Sasine deeds) or list the midcouples in form 4. The midcouples are the HBOS Group Reorganisation Act 2006 and the Notice in the *Edinburgh Gazette* on 17 August 2007. That Notice reads:

HBOS GROUP REORGANISATION ACT 2006

NOTICE IS HEREBY GIVEN, under section 9 of the above Act, that the Board of the Governor and Company of the Bank of Scotland ('the Bank') has appointed 17

September 2007 as the 'appointed day' for the undertakings of Halifax plc, Capital Bank plc and HBOS Treasury Services plc ('the transferor companies') for the purposes of Part 3 of the above Act.

On the appointed day, the entire undertakings of the transferor companies will be transferred to the Bank in accordance with the above Act.

Harry Baines, Company Secretary
The Governor and Company of the Bank of Scotland

17 August 2007.

Update 22 gives guidance on the transitional case where a deed is executed before 17 September 2007 but presented for registration on or after that date.

Turnaround times

As at September 2007 the annual turnaround times were 13.7 working days for Sasine writs, 25.3 working days for dealings with whole, and 79.3 working days for domestic first registrations. In all cases these were comfortably within ministerial targets.

Decisions by the Scottish Information Commissioner

Decisions of the Scottish Information Commissioner in respect of applications under the Freedom of Information (Scotland) Act 2002 can be found at: www. itspublicknowledge.info/ApplicationsandDecisions/Decisions/Decisions.php. A number are of interest to conveyancers.

Decision 37/2007

MacRoberts, acting on behalf of an undisclosed client, requested data from the Application Record in the Land Register. The Keeper declined the request on the ground that the data were available as part of the Land Register, and so were not subject to an FoI request: s 25 of the Freedom of Information (Scotland) Act 2002. MacRoberts took the case to the Scottish Information Commissioner, who upheld the Keeper's position.

Decision 112/2007

MacRoberts requested copies of all extant statutory notices from Glasgow City Council. They pointed out that the information sought was currently provided to a client of theirs under the 2002 Act at no charge by 15 of the 26 local authorities from whom the information had been requested, while a further two local authorities supplied the information under the Act while charging a fee. An additional five local authorities provided the information by means outwith the 2002 Act, such as through direct e-mail correspondence, or by access through Council offices or websites. MacRoberts therefore asserted that only four local authorities out of the 26 approached refused to supply their client with equivalent information, one of which was Glasgow City Council. Nonetheless the Council refused to supply the information arguing both that it was already publicly available (2002 Act s 25(1)), and also that disclosure of the information would or would be likely to prejudice substantially the commercial interests of the Council (s 33(1)(b)) because it could be used by competitors to provide property enquiry certificates.

Both defences were rejected by the Information Commissioner and disclosure was ordered. In relation to the first defence, the information could be obtained only by buying individual PECs. As there were approximately 300,000 properties within the Council's geographic boundaries, and the charge for an individual PEC was approximately £62, the total cost of accessing information through the methodology proposed by the Council would be in the region of £18.6 million. In relation to the second defence, an investigation by the Commissioner of the position in certain other local authorities which supplied information of this kind suggested that their commercial position had not been affected. Further, the Commissioner took

> into account the fact that most, if not all, of the core information sought by MacRoberts' client is currently obtainable through access to publicly accessible registers and minutes of relevant Council meetings. Indeed, it is my understanding that it is this information which principally informs the PEC's which are currently produced by the Council's commercial competitors.

It is understood that this decision has been appealed to the Court of Session.

Decision 139/2007

This was a request by MacRoberts to Dundee Council for details of statutory notices. The result and the reasoning were much the same as for Decision 112/2007.

Decision 123/2007

Millar & Bryce requested Renfrewshire Council to supply a list of all properties in its area which had outstanding debts in respect of statutory notices. The Council refused, founding on s 25 of the 2002 Act (information otherwise available). The Information Commissioner rejected this defence and ordered disclosure. The Commissioner found that the only way in which this information was otherwise available would be by buying property enquiry certificates for each of the individual houses in Renfrewshire – of which there were more than 75,000 – at a cost of over £5.5 million.

Decision 160/2007

Mr Patterson had been involved in a boundary dispute. This dispute had been determined by the Lands Tribunal: *Patterson v The Keeper of the Registers of Scotland,*

LTS/LR/1992/2, decided on 27 July 1993 (available at www.lands-tribunal-scotland.org.uk/register.html). In 2006 Mr Patterson made a FoI request to the Keeper for all documents that might bear on that dispute. The Keeper copied to him some documents but not others, the latter being withheld on the basis of s 36 of the 2002 Act (confidentiality). These documents were letters between the Keeper and his legal advisers. The Information Commissioner upheld the Keeper's position.

Scottish Barony Register

One response to the severance of barony titles from the land, effected by s 63(2) of the Abolition of Feudal Tenure etc (Scotland) Act 2000, was the setting up of an unofficial Scottish Barony Register in order to keep a record of transfers. In the December 2007 issue of the *Journal of the Law Society of Scotland* (p 53), Alistair Rennie, the 'Custodian' of the Register, gave the following report:

> The Scottish Barony Register opened for business on 28 November 2004, the famous 'appointed day' when the feudal system was abolished in Scotland. While, in the ensuing three years, business has not been as brisk as we might have hoped, there is evidence that the register is fulfilling the purpose for which it was designed, that is to provide a source of information about the transfer of baronial dignities now that such transactions cannot be registered in either the Sasine Register or the Land Register of Scotland.
>
> So far there have been 20 registrations, but this appears to be a reflection of slow market activity rather than any lack of faith in the register. Our information suggests that the vast majority, if not all, transfers of dignities in the three year period have been registered. Perhaps more importantly, it is becoming common practice to search the register before a transaction settles. We also know of cases where the payment of the price for a dignity, or a significant part thereof, has been made contingent on the application to register being accepted. In such cases the selling solicitors require a letter of confirmation from the Custodian, a service we have been happy to introduce.
>
> Not all applications have been made as the result of sales. In one case the proprietor was selling the land to which the dignity was formerly attached, but retaining the dignity, and wished to have his entitlement registered as the fact of the retention was not going to be patent from the public registers. Having such information in a readily accessible source can undoubtedly help prevent fraud.

A difficulty is that a barony title can now be transferred by assignation alone, and there is no need, in a legal sense, to register in what is only an unofficial register – although plainly it would be prudent to do so. It is presumably that consideration which lies behind the Lord Lyon's statement, in *Hamilton Ptr* 15 May 2006 (*Conveyancing 2006* Case (87)) that:

> I do not consider that a private Register, managed by a person appointed by a private company with no public scrutiny, and operated under terms which allow complete discretion as to what evidence is to be provided, is an acceptable source of evidence in an application before the Court of the Lord Lyon.

Standard missives

Residential missives

The Borders are the latest region to have produced standard missives (based on a draft commissioned from Professor Reid). Meanwhile, the Faculty of Solicitors of the Highlands has produced an updated version of its well-established missives. Both are available on www.lawscot.org.uk/Members_information/convey_essens/stdmissives. The time cannot be long away to try to prepare a Scotland-wide style.

Commercial missives

Following the success of regional missives for residential sales (see above), the Property Standardisation Group (www.psglegal.co.uk) has now produced a national equivalent for commercial missives. This is an offer to sell rather than an offer to buy, and is based on vacant possession. A further style will follow for an investment offer to sell. Meanwhile, Ian Macniven has argued cogently that standard clauses should now be produced for commercial leases: see pp 46–47 of the October 2007 issue of the *Journal of the Law Society of Scotland*. His starting point is with the depressing observation that: 'Many property lawyers spend a large part of their working day wasting their time and that of their clients.'

Interest clauses

In *Conveyancing 2006* we explained that the form of interest clause then in use required to be changed in the light of a number of court decisions. Interest clauses make provision for two different situations. One is where the buyer pays late. The other is where the buyer never pays at all. In relation to the first situation, the traditional wording, which requires payment of interest at, typically, 4% above base, is straightforward and effective. But there are real difficulties in deciding how to respond to the second situation. Plainly, the seller should be allowed to rescind the contract after a certain period (such as two weeks). But what then? The approach in recent years has been to require the buyer to pay liquidated damages. But quite apart from the technical difficulties with such a provision – exposed by the new case law – this is potentially unfair to the buyer and can lead to liability which is unreasonable or even absurd.

In *Conveyancing 2006* we offered three possible styles for a new clause, our preferred style (Option A on p 94) being one which abandoned liquidated damages in favour of the ordinary common law. Such a clause allows the seller to recover what he has actually lost, no more and no less, rather than the uncontrolled amounts which might be due under a liquidated damages provision. This, we suggested, struck a fair balance between the parties, in the spirit of standard missives.

We are glad to report that the new PSG clause for commercial missives (above) follows this approach. In the light of that clause, and of helpful discussions with a number of practising solicitors, we now offer a revised version of Option A, as follows:

(1) If the price is paid after the due date, in whole or in part, the Seller is entitled to –

    (i) interest on the amount outstanding at the rate of 4% *per annum* above the Royal Bank of Scotland plc base rate from the due date until the date when payment is made; and

    (ii) to the extent that loss caused by the Buyer's breach is not sufficiently compensated by (i), damages in respect of that loss.

(2) If the price remains unpaid in whole or in part at any time more than two weeks after the due date, the Seller is entitled to rescind the contract, and to damages for loss caused by the Buyer's breach.

(3) The loss for which damages are due may include (but is not limited to) –

    (i) any shortfall in the price on resale of the property;

    (ii) the expenses of such a resale;

    (iii) the cost of a bridging or other loan to enable the Seller to complete a purchase of another property;

    (iv) the amount of any liability which the Seller may incur to a third party owing to the Seller's inability to pay that third party money which is or becomes due.

(4) In this clause the 'due date' means whichever is the later of –

    (i) the date of entry;

    (ii) the date on which payment of the price was due, having regard to the circumstances of the case including any entitlement to withhold payment owing to non-performance by the Seller.

There are two main changes as compared to the previous version. First, subclause (1) makes explicit what was merely implicit before, namely that not only interest but also common law damages are potentially due in the case of late payment. Secondly, subclause (3) provides a fuller (though still non-exhaustive) list of possible heads of damages.

Residential conveyancing: the biggest headaches

In an online survey carried out by the Law Society in March 2007 (and reported on p 51 of the May *Journal*), almost 300 respondents identified what they regarded as the two most common causes of problems for clients. In order of severity these were (the figures in brackets are for the percentage of solicitors who identified the cause in question as one of the two most common):

late or incomplete loan instructions (64%)
unauthorised alterations (60%)
appliances/heating warranties (23%)
deliberate underpricing of the property (16%)
lack of information about the property (11%)
offers subject to survey (10%)
anti-money laundering compliance (8%)
multiple surveys (8%).

In relation to alterations, some of the main figures to emerge in the results are that:

- 31% report that alteration enquiries are necessary in at least 60% of transactions, though 26% put the proportion in the 20–40% band;
- only a minority of cases are resolved by the seller providing additional documentary evidence, or seller and buyer agreeing a compromise; local authority re-inspection and consent are the more common outcome;
- 42% consider the volume of enquiries to be stable, 43% say it is increasing and only 15% report a declining trend;
- 33% estimate the average delay to the conveyancing process at 5 to 10 days, 24% at 10 to 15 days and 18% put it at over 15 days;
- costs to the client (including legal fees) from seeking retrospective consent amount to over £250 in 35% of cases and between £150 and £250 in a further 47%;
- only 18% consider the retrospective consent process to be consistently applied in all cases (58% some of the time; 24% not at all); similar figures apply to the good/average/poor rating of the information provided.

Treasure trove

The Queen's and Lord Treasurer's Remembrancer is now issuing annual reports on 'treasure trove': www.treasuretrovescotland.co.uk/downloads/ANNUAL%20 TT%20REPORT%202004–06.pdf.

Property factors

In August 2007 the Scottish Consumer Council published a case study of consumer experiences of property management services in the private sector in Dennistoun in Glasgow. See www.scotconsumer.org.uk/publications/reports/ reports.htm. This recorded a high level of dissatisfaction with communication, costs and timescales for repairs. Over half of the survey respondents indicated that they had complained about the service they received, and most (86%) were dissatisfied with the response. The Scottish Consumer Council supports the suggestion, made originally by the Housing Improvement Task Force, that there should be a national accreditation scheme for property managers.

Meanwhile, on 26 March 2007 Gordon Jackson MSP lodged a proposal for a Property Factors (Scotland) Bill. This fell with the dissolution of the Parliament. On 19 October 2007 Patricia Ferguson lodged a similar proposal, which was out for consultation until 20 January 2008. The proposal says that:

The system of property management in Scotland offers little opportunity for people who are unhappy with the service their manager or 'factor' provides to question their activity. Constituents complain that it is sometimes impossible to query the need for repairs or improvements and some raise issues about the invoices which are often unclear, excessive and subject to high rates of interest and penalty charges. In Scotland, property managers are largely unregulated; they do however operate from a position of some power, trust and influence. Often the owners of flats in tenement properties are required by their title deeds to appoint a factor and many have no choice as to who is appointed. This bill proposal has two main aims. Firstly, to create a registration scheme where persons appointed to manage properties would be required to meet a 'fit and proper person' test. This would help eliminate unreasonable practices. Secondly, the Bill would provide a form of straight-forward dispute resolution where homeowners and factors can resolve contractual disputes without having to incur prohibitive legal expenses or costs.

Books

James Barrowman, *Residential Evictions* (Legal Services Agency 2006)

William W McBryde, *The Law of Contract in Scotland*, 3rd edn (W Green 2007; ISBN 9780414016064)

Kenneth G C Reid and George L Gretton, *Conveyancing 2006* (Avizandum Publishing Ltd 2007; ISBN 9781904968177)

Adrian Stalker, *Evictions in Scotland* (Avizandum Publishing Ltd 2007; ISBN 9781904968184)

Articles

Craig Anderson, 'Survivorship destinations and s 142 of the Inheritance Tax Act 1984' 2007 SLT (News) 241

Craig Anderson, 'Servitudes, the Land Register and the proprietor in possession' 2007 SLT (News) 275

Ross Gilbert Anderson, 'Fraud on transfer and on insolvency: ta ... ta ... *tantum et tale*?' (2007) 11 *Edinburgh Law Review* 187

David Bartos, 'Advance to free parking? – *Moncrieff v Jamieson*' (2007) 75 *Scottish Law Gazette* 203

Hazel Bett, 'Another update on transfers of title in matrimonial disputes' (2007) 88 *Greens Property Law Bulletin* 3

Stewart Brymer, 'Protecting the purchaser in insolvency situations' (2007) 86 *Greens Property Law Bulletin* 6

Stewart Brymer, 'The long and winding road to better information' (2007) 89 *Greens Property Law Bulletin* 4

David Cabrelli, 'Tenancies-at-will: *Allen v McTaggart*' (2007) 11 *Edinburgh Law Review* 436

David Cabrelli, 'Conditional break options' (2007) 86 *Greens Property Law Bulletin* 1

David L Carey Miller, 'Right to annual crops' (2007) 11 *Edinburgh Law Review* 274 (considering *Boskabelle Ltd v Laird* 2006 SLT 1079)

Colin Christie, 'Access or excess?' (2007) 52 *Journal of the Law Society of Scotland* May/48 (considering the law of trespass in the light of the Land Reform (Scotland) Act 2003)

George B Clark, 'Get it sorted' (2007) 88 *Greens Property Law Bulletin* 4 (discussing problems in settlements)

Malcolm Combe, 'Good neighbour agreements – bad law?' (2007) 52 *Journal of the Law Society of Scotland* Aug/50

Lorne D Crerar, 'The single survey – the view of the Edinburgh Conveyancers Forum: a reply' (2007) 89 *Greens Property Law Bulletin* 1

Candice Donnelly, 'From possession to ownership: an analytical study of the declining role of possession in Scottish Property Law' 2006 *Juridical Review* 267

Andrew Duncan, 'Serving development – the powers and duties of utilities' (2007) 88 *Greens Property Law Bulletin* 5 and (2007) 89 *Greens Property Law Bulletin* 6

Alasdair G Fox, 'Breaking down a brick wall?' (2007) 52 *Journal of the Law Society of Scotland* March/42 (discussing whether it is possible to create agricultural tenancies of a duration of between 5 and 15 years)

Alasdair G Fox, 'Lessons in improvements' (2007) 52 *Journal of the Law Society of Scotland* June/42 (considering *Telfer's Exrs v The Buccleuch Estates Ltd*, 15 December 2006, Scottish Land Court)

Alasdair G Fox, 'Activity in the courts' (2007) 52 *Journal of the Law Society of Scotland* Sept/41 (considering recent decisions on agricultural law)

Alasdair G Fox, 'Camels and common sense' (2007) 52 *Journal of the Law Society of Scotland* Dec/41 (considering recent cases on agricultural tenancies)

Richard Hamer, 'Letting in the disabled' (2007) 52 *Journal of the Law Society of Scotland* Jan/48 (discussing new duties for landlords in relation to disabled tenants)

Chris Hardie, 'The single survey – the view of the Edinburgh Conveyancers Forum' (2007) 86 *Greens Property Law Bulletin* 4

Martin Hogg, 'Damages for breach of a keep-open clause' (2007) 11 *Edinburgh Law Review* 416

Sinead Lynch, 'Not the best option' (2007) 52 *Journal of the Law Society of Scotland* Jan/46 (advocating promotion agreements rather than options in the acquisition of land for development)

Ian Macniven, 'Leases: the war is over?' (2007) 52 *Journal of the Law Society of Scotland* Oct/46

William W McBryde, 'A question of interest' (2007) 11 *Edinburgh Law Review* 242 (considering interest clauses on the unpaid price)

Frankie McCarthy, 'Positive prescription in the human rights era' 2008 SLT (News) 15

James Ness, 'ARTL – now and then?' (2007) 52 *Journal of the Law Society of Scotland* July/52 (giving an account of a typical ARTL transaction)

Morag Newton, 'CDD is the new ID' (2007) 52 *Journal of the Law Society of Scotland* July/30 (considering customer due diligence under the Money Laundering Regulations 2007)

Morag Newton and James Ness, 'Money laundering to change again' (2007) 52 *Journal of the Law Society of Scotland* May/26

Peter Nicholson, 'PIPs' hour approaches' (2007) 52 *Journal of the Law Society of Scotland* March/50

Peter Nicholson, 'Possession undisturbed' (2007) 52 *Journal of the Law Society of Scotland* June/51 (considering *Yaxley v Glen* [2007] CSOH 90)

Roddy Paisley, 'Clear view' (2007) 52 *Journal of the Law Society of Scotland* Dec/50 (considering *Moncrieff v Jamieson* [2007] UKHL 42, 2007 SC 790, 2007 SLT 989)

Ian Quigley, 'On the wrong track?' (2007) 52 *Journal of the Law Society of Scotland* Feb/48 (discussing the tension between case law and practice in commercial leases)

Kenneth G C Reid, 'Interest to enforce real burdens: how material is "material"?' (2007) 11 *Edinburgh Law Review* 440 (considering *Barker v Lewis* 2007 SLT (Sh Ct) 48)

Robert Rennie, 'Real burdens – a question of interest' 2007 SLT (News) 89 (considering *Barker v Lewis* 2007 SLT (Sh Ct) 48)

Robert Rennie, 'Noting title in a non feudal era' 2007 SLT (News) 157

Lynn Richmond, 'Private rights and public interest' 2007 SLT (News) 233 (discussing *Gloag v Perth & Kinross Council* 2007 SCLR 530)

Kenneth Ross, 'Contaminated land – where are we now?' (2007) 52 *Journal of the Law Society of Scotland* Sept/52

Peter Smith, 'Energy performance of buildings' (2007) 87 *Greens Property Law Bulletin* 4

Ken Swinton, 'Missives, PIPS and warranties' (2007) 75 *Scottish Law Gazette* 12

Ken Swinton, 'When do you suspect it is reasonable to disclose?' (2007) 75 *Scottish Law Gazette* 52 (discussing disclosure of activities which may constitute money laundering)

Ken Swinton, 'The "good" old days' (2007) 75 *Scottish Law Gazette* 92 (discussing good and marketable title)

Ken Swinton, 'What comes after?' (2007) 75 *Scottish Law Gazette* 128

Ken Swinton, 'Future access rights: *Peart v Legge*' (2007) 75 *Scottish Law Gazette* 169

Ken Swinton, 'A roaming I shan't go' (2007) 75 *Scottish Law Gazette* 154

Andrew Todd, 'Light work: servitude right of light created by prescription or implication' (2007) 87 *Greens Property Law Bulletin* 3

Robin M White, 'Parking's fine: the enforceability of "private" parking schemes' 2007 *Juridical Review* 1

Adam Wilkie, 'Illegal parking – to clamp or not to clamp' (2007) 88 *Greens Property Law Bulletin* 4

PART IV
COMMENTARY

COMMENTARY

REAL BURDENS

Interest to enforce[1]

Introduction

To enforce a real burden it has always been necessary to have interest as well as title. But under the former law the issue was seldom a live one, because burdens were typically enforced by feudal superiors, whose interest was presumed and virtually impossible to rebut.[2] That has now changed. Section 8 of the Title Conditions (Scotland) Act 2003 provides that: 'A real burden is enforceable by any person who has both title and interest to enforce it'; and a person has such interest, in the normal case, if and only if

> in the circumstances of any case, failure to comply with the real burden is resulting in, or will result in, material detriment to the value or enjoyment of the person's ownership of, or right in, the benefited property.

This provision allows for two possibilities: there must be material detriment either to the value of the benefited property, or to its enjoyment. And in both cases the guardian against inappropriate enforcement is the word 'material'. Only detriment which is 'material' will justify enforcement. Anything less must be endured with the fortitude which is to be expected of a good neighbour.

But how material is 'material'? The word itself does not carry a single and precise meaning. The *Oxford English Dictionary* offers 'of serious or substantial import' but also, more weakly, 'significant' and 'of consequence'.[3] On one view, 'material' is simply the opposite of 'immaterial',[4] but this does little to advance matters, merely shifting the uncertainty of meaning from one word to another. An alternative, but perhaps no more helpful, approach is to say that there is an undistributed middle between 'material' and 'immaterial' leading to a tripartite classification of (i) material, (ii) immaterial, and (iii) neither material nor

---

1 An earlier version of this note was published by Professor Reid as 'Interest to enforce real burdens: how material is "material"?' (2007) 11 *Edinburgh Law Review* 440.
2 K G C Reid, *The Law of Property in Scotland* (1996) para 408.
3 The online version of the *Oxford English Dictionary* was consulted. This is a revised and updated version of the second edition of 1989.
4 As was argued, unsuccessfully, by the pursuers in *Barker v Lewis* 2007 SLT (Sh Ct) 48.

immaterial. In the absence of precise meaning, context is naturally of particular importance, so that the question is not what 'material' means in the abstract but rather what it means in the context in which it appears in the Title Conditions Act.

Barker v Lewis

The meaning of 'material detriment' in section 8 has now been the subject of judicial decision. *Barker v Lewis*[1] concerned a recent development of five houses at Cauldside Farm Steadings, about two miles from St Andrews. Access was by a private road. The development was regulated by a deed of conditions which, among other restrictions, limited the use of each house to 'a domestic dwellinghouse with relative offices only and for use by one family only and for no other purpose whatsoever'. The 'tranquil location' promised by the developer's brochure appeared under threat when one of the owners began to use her house for a bed-and-breakfast business.[2] Eventually, the owners of three of the other houses sought interdict. The sheriff[3] accepted that the business was in breach of the burden in the deed of conditions, and that there was title to enforce.[4] The question of interest, however, was seen as more difficult. It was true that life for the pursuers had been made less pleasant. The defender's business attracted around 250 visitors a year, leading to more traffic, increased noise from late arrivals and early departures, some inappropriate parking, and a general loss of privacy and peace. The disturbance was increased by the otherwise secluded nature of the development, and the fact that the houses were close together. Nevertheless, the sheriff concluded that the pursuers had failed to show interest to enforce, and interdict was refused.

On the evidence as summarised in the judgment, this is a rather unexpected result, although it was evidently a close one, with the sheriff indicating that if the number of guests were to increase in the future, 'there is a real risk' of material detriment to the pursuers' enjoyment of their properties.[5] More important, however, is the general approach which the sheriff chose to adopt. His decision may be said to have rested on three main propositions. First, 'material' detriment means 'substantial' detriment. Secondly, in interpreting 'material' it is helpful to have regard to the law of nuisance. Thirdly, in assessing detriment arising out of non-compliance with a burden it is relevant to consider what detriment might have arisen even if there had been full compliance. While the sheriff deserves sympathy for having to grapple with these issues for the first time, there are real difficulties with the approach he chose to adopt. Taken singly, each of the propositions seems open to question, while, taken together, they present a model

---

1 2007 SLT (Sh Ct) 48.
2 See www.millhouse-standrews.com.
3 Sheriff G J Evans.
4 On this point the sheriff's judgment contains an interesting discussion (at 54–55) of the extent to which *Low v Scottish Amicable Building Society* 1940 SLT 295 is consistent with the decision of the First Division in *Colquhoun's Curator Bonis v Glen's Tr* 1920 SC 737.
5 At 51F (finding in fact and in law 9).

of interest to enforce which is unconvincing as well as damaging to the future usefulness of real burdens.

The three propositions

The first proposition was that 'material' means 'substantial'. That, said the sheriff, was the 'plain meaning' of the word.[1] But the truth is that there is no 'plain meaning' of 'material' – as already seen – so that it is always necessary to consider the context in which it is used. In fact, the Title Conditions Act uses both 'material' and 'substantial', and is careful to do so in different ways. 'Material' detriment is the test for interest to enforce, but when it comes to compensation for variation or discharge by the Lands Tribunal the test is 'substantial' loss or disadvantage.[2] The hierarchy which these words imply is obvious. Where detriment or disadvantage reaches the point of being 'material', there is interest to enforce; but it is only when it is raised to the level of 'substantial' that compensation is due, in the event of variation or discharge by the Tribunal. And because disadvantage is rarely 'substantial', the experience of the last 30 years is that compensation is rarely awarded.[3] In this connection it seems worth observing that, as originally enacted, section 20 of the Abolition of Feudal Tenure etc (Scotland) Act 2000 (which allowed the Lands Tribunal to reallot feudal burdens in certain cases) imposed a criterion of 'substantial' disadvantage, but that this was changed to 'material' detriment by the Title Conditions Act.[4] The distinction can also be found in other provisions of the Title Conditions Act. For example, while section 16(1) requires 'material expenditure' whose benefit has been 'substantially' lost, as a condition of acquiescence, section 54(3) defines a 'sheltered or retirement housing development' as one containing houses with facilities 'substantially' different from those of ordinary houses.

The second proposition linked interest to enforce to nuisance. The result, according to the sheriff,[5] would be that

> in order to find that the disputed activity of the burdened proprietor has resulted, or will result, in material detriment to the enjoyment of the benefited property, the court must be satisfied that the result has been, or will be, more than just sentimental, speculative, trivial discomfort or personal annoyance and that it amounts to substantial inconvenience or annoyance, as judged by the objective standard of what would affect a proprietor of ordinary sensibility and susceptibility and taking into account both the existing character of the locality affected and the extent to which the benefited and the burdened properties are geographically interconnected.

These words are drawn from the law of nuisance and, in part, are a direct quotation from the speech of the Earl of Selborne in one of the leading Victorian

---

1 At 55E.
2 Title Conditions (Scotland) Act 2003 s 90(7)(a).
3 Sir Crispin Agnew of Lochnaw, *Variation and Discharge of Land Obligations* (1999) ch 7. The experience so far under the Title Conditions Act has been the same: see p 98 below.
4 Title Conditions (Scotland) Act 2003 sch 13 para 4, amending s 20(7)(a) of the 2000 Act.
5 At 55H.

cases.[1] The linkage, however, is problematic. For on the one hand, if the test for interest to enforce is the same as the test for nuisance, real burdens would be superfluous in respect of matters which would in any event be governed by the law of nuisance. Conveyancers would have been wasting their time in putting real burdens into deeds. But on the other hand, if the test is different, as appears to be the case, then the linkage is unhelpful and misleading. The leading modern account of nuisance lists materiality as only one of the six factors which may be relevant in order to determine whether a nuisance has occurred.[2]

There are other objections as well. There is nothing in the Act, or in the report which lies behind it,[3] to warrant recourse to the law of nuisance. Nor is it evident why a doctrine of the common law should be thought of as being of assistance in a matter of statutory interpretation. Finally, the suggested linkage tells us nothing about the meaning of 'material' in the many cases where the content of the burden has no parallel in the law of nuisance – for example, in the standard case of a prohibition on building.

The sheriff's third proposition has a certain intuitive attractiveness. Evidently, the disturbance caused by the prohibited use (as a B & B) was no worse than might be caused by other use which would be freely permitted under the titles (eg use by a large family). 'On a change of ownership', the sheriff pointed out, the pursuers 'might end up with a nosey, intrusive neighbour with a large family who all possess peculiar noisy habits and hobbies'.[4] The reasoning, however, is flawed. The risk of a noisy family is one which, under the titles, the pursuers are bound to take. But they are not bound to take the risk of noisy guests in a B & B. Having made special provision in respect of that particular risk, there can be no reason why they do not have interest to enforce it.[5]

Implications for practice

Each proposition in *Barker v Lewis* raises the bar for interest to enforce; cumulatively, they raise the bar too high. Although authority under the former law was meagre and not always easily reconciled, there was little doubt that, for immediate neighbours at least, there was interest to enforce most burdens most of the time.[6] That is as it should be, for otherwise real burdens would be largely pointless. Admittedly, section 8 provides a more exacting test than the former law,[7] especially

---

1 *Fleming v Hislop* (1886) 13 R (HL) 43 at 45.

2 N R Whitty, 'Nuisance', in *The Laws of Scotland: Stair Memorial Encyclopaedia*, Reissue (2001) para 43. Surprisingly, this work is not referred to by the sheriff in *Barker v Lewis*.

3 Scottish Law Commission, Report on *Real Burdens* (Scot Law Com No 181 (2000); available on www.scotlawcom.gov.uk) paras 4.16–4.24.

4 At 57A.

5 The relative ineffectiveness of a burden might well be a relevant factor for the Lands Tribunal in exercising its discretion as to whether the burden ought to be varied or discharged and, if so, whether compensation should then be paid. See *Smith v Elrick* 2007 GWD 29-515; *Lawrie v Mashford* 2008 GWD 7-129, Lands Tribunal. But for as long as the burden remains undischarged, the fact of its alleged weakness is no reason for denying its enforcement.

6 K G C Reid, *Law of Property in Scotland* para 407.

7 R Rennie, 'Real burdens – a question of interest' 2007 SLT (News) 89 at 93.

for those whose property lies at a distance;[1] but it is not as exacting as the sheriff suggests. Those who wish to be relieved of real burdens can ask for a minute of waiver or apply to the Lands Tribunal. But for as long as the burdens remain alive, the question of interest should not normally stand in the way of enforcement by close neighbours.[2]

The sheriff's decision in *Barker* was upheld by the sheriff principal on 5 March 2008. The appellate decision will be analysed in next year's volume, but in brief the appeal succeeded on the law but failed on the facts. The implications for practice are significant. In the first place, clients wishing to enforce burdens against neighbours should hesitate long and hard. In many cases they may fail to surmount the barrier of interest to enforce. Secondly, clients considering breaching a burden of their own can be met with words of encouragement. Sometimes it will be possible to advise that there is no interest to enforce. On other occasions, the line to take might be that only the closest of neighbours have such interest, meaning that a minute of waiver need be taken from those neighbours alone – and not from the owners of the 197 other houses on the estate. Finally, conveyancers may need to re-consider their practice in drafting deeds of conditions. On the basis of *Barker*, some of the relatively trivial burdens found in such deeds are, quite simply, unenforceable.

Title to enforce: section 53

Sections 52, 53 and 56 of the Title Conditions (Scotland) Act 2003 replace and extend the old common law rules of implied *jus quaesitum tertio*. It need hardly be added that, with one transitional exception,[3] they apply only to real burdens created before 28 November 2004, for post-2004 burdens must nominate and identify the benefited property or properties.[4] Of the three provisions, the most important, and certainly the most inscrutable, is section 53. The two Lands Tribunal decisions which considered this provision in 2007 – the first consideration by any court – are therefore particularly welcome.

In *Brown v Richardson*[5] a substantial area of land in Aberdeen had been feued in six lots by a single deed recorded in 1888. The feu charter contained an

---

1 In the Scottish Law Commission's first version of what is now s 8, 'the distance between the benefited and burdened properties' was singled out as a factor of particular importance: see Report on *Real Burdens* para 4.18.
2 Unless, of course, there is no detriment to the benefited property or the detriment is trivial. As the Scottish Law Commission has pointed out (Report on *Real Burdens* para 4.17): 'An obligation not to build prevents rabbit hutches as well as five-storey blocks of flats. But it seems doubtful whether there is interest to prevent the building of rabbit hutches, even on the part of an immediate neighbour.'
3 Where at least one property in a group of properties was conveyed by the burden-imposer before the appointed day, s 53 is capable of applying to post-appointed day conveyances of other properties in the same group. The requirement of dual registration is then dispensed with. See Title Conditions (Scotland) Act 2003 s 53(1), (3A).
4 TC(S)A 2003 s 4(2)(c)(ii), (3).
5 2007 GWD 28-490. The full judgment is available at www.lands-tribunal-scotland.org.uk/decisions/LTS.TC.2006.41.rub.html. The decision should be read subject to the caveat at the opening of the opinion: 'We have considered this case on its own facts and on the submissions made to us. There are issues here which have not previously arisen before the Tribunal, and it may be that

obligation to build 'good and substantial cottages or dwellinghouses' subject to the superior's approval and to certain other conditions. All alterations and new buildings required the superior's consent, and there were further provisions as to use. Different types of building came to be erected on different parts of the feu at different times, and the overall picture was far from uniform. Among the buildings erected on the first lot was a group of terraced houses, 10 to 34 Duthie Terrace. When the owners of No 14 sought to remove certain burdens, under the so-called 'sunset rule', by serving a notice of termination,[1] the notice was opposed by their immediate neighbours at No 16. This involved an application to the Lands Tribunal for renewal of the burdens. Under the Act such an application can only be brought by 'an owner of a benefited property'.[2] A question to be determined, therefore, was whether No 16 Duthie Terrace was a benefited property in respect of No 14.

The feu charter was silent as to rights to enforce. Section 56 of the Title Conditions Act, being confined to facility and service burdens, was plainly inapplicable, whilst section 52 was excluded because the burdens in question made provision for superior's consent (ie contained a 'reservation of a right to vary or waive the real burdens' within section 52(2)). That meant that if the owners of No 16 had enforcement rights, such rights must rest on section 53.

Section 53 imposes two requirements for enforcement rights to arise. In the first place, both properties (ie in this case Nos 14 and 16) must be subject to burdens which were imposed under a 'common scheme'. And secondly, the properties must be 'related' to one another. As usual in such cases, there was no difficulty as to the first requirement, for uniform burdens were imposed on both – as well as on many other – properties.[3] But matters were far less certain in respect of the second requirement. When are properties 'related'? Some help is provided by section 53(2), which lists the following factors as 'giving rise to such an inference':

    (a) the convenience of managing the properties together because they share –
        (i) some common feature; or
        (ii) an obligation for common maintenance of some facility;
    (b) there being shared ownership of common property;
    (c) their being subject to the common scheme by virtue of the same deed of conditions; or
    (d) the properties each being a flat in the same tenement.

But these factors are not exhaustive, and others may also come into play.

---

fuller submissions than we received in this case will point to the need for fuller consideration of the general approach to s 53 and to the application of the new jurisdiction in "sunset rule" cases.' In this connection it should be noted that the owners of No 16 were not legally represented.
1 TC(S)A 2003 s 20.
2 TC(S)A 2003 s 90(1)(b).
3 Although reaching this conclusion, the Lands Tribunal was perhaps more hesitant on the point than seems necessary: see pp 14–15 of the transcript.

In the particular circumstances of *Brown v Richardson*, the Lands Tribunal concluded that none of the statutory factors applied as such, but that the use of a single deed – the feu charter – to impose burdens on a group of different properties was analogous to the use of a deed of conditions mentioned in factor (c):[1]

> It seems to us that a feu charter conveying the ground to the builder and establishing a scheme of conditions to be applied to the housing units to be erected may be of the same character. It may be that all the detail of many modern deeds of conditions is not to be found in this feu charter, and if it had merely regulated the initial development, with no ongoing burdens, we do not think that would have advanced the argument much. However, it seems to us that it did provide an analogous scheme of continuing burdens, in particular regulating further building and requiring maintenance, insurance and (if necessary) rebuilding of the individual houses. These seem to us to make this provision comparable in this context with a deed of conditions. The feu charter may be said to have provided an element of communal protection of amenity.

The argument is certainly persuasive. It is hard to see why a deed of conditions is singled out other than as indicating that its granter saw the affected properties as constituting a single development. Exactly the same may be true of a conveyance which burdens what soon turn out to be separately owned properties. There is also a link to section 52, in respect that the use of a single deed for a group of properties is sufficient to provide notice of the common scheme, and so will usually trigger enforcement rights under that provision as well.

The Tribunal concluded that the properties were 'related', with the result that the owners of No 16 had title to enforce the burdens against the owners of No 14. Another (non-statutory) factor which was thought to support this conclusion was the degree of uniformity in the terrace of which the two properties formed part. Whether the Tribunal would have reached the same decision without this rather slight additional point is unclear, but one suspects that the answer is yes. If that is correct, it would follow that, in the Tribunal's view, a single significant factor (in this case, the use of a single deed for both properties) can be sufficient to make properties 'related'.

The potential importance of burdens being imposed by a single deed rather than in a series of separate grants in feu is brought out by the other case, *Smith v Prior*.[2] This concerned a 1930s development in the Murrayfield area of Edinburgh. The applicants wished to build a modest rear extension to their bungalow in Campbell Road but this was contrary to a no-building provision in the original feu charter of 1934. This was one of a series of feu charters, in similar terms, granted by the same superior in respect of a group of feus. The houses were built by the feuars and varied in style. Although the position was unclear, the applicants took the cautious view that, despite the abolition of the feudal system, their neighbours might have enforcement rights by virtue of sections 52 and 53 of

1 At pp 16–17 of the transcript.
2 2007 GWD 30-523.

the Title Conditions (Scotland) Act 2003. Accordingly, they applied to the Lands Tribunal for the burdens to be varied.

In *obiter* remarks, the Tribunal doubted whether these provisions applied:[1]

> We were told that in the (very common) type of situation with which this case is concerned, where a landowner originally feued out building plots in accordance with a feuing plan, and there is some necessary element of mutuality between immediate neighbours in relation to the position at the boundaries, proprietors of the properties which had been subject to the feudal burdens are being advised that, while there is a degree of uncertainty, their co-proprietors are likely to be held benefited under one or other of these statutory provisions. The applicants in this, as in other, cases, have accordingly (and entirely understandably) proceeded on the basis that their immediate neighbours are benefited. They have not chosen to invoke the jurisdiction which the Tribunal now has, and which can be invoked in the same application as an application to discharge or vary, to test the matter.
>
> The application of these new provisions was therefore not at issue in this case. There remains unfortunately a degree of uncertainty. It was not entirely self-evident to us that the situation in which a landowner historically simply feued out (perhaps over a period of several years) individual building plots on his estate, where despite the reference to a feuing plan and repetition of similar or identical obligations the only actual element of regulation among the feuars was in relation to boundary walls or fences, necessarily involves a 'common scheme' under the 2003 Act. Houses within the area of the former Murrayfield Estate do not seem to fit any of the examples of 'related properties' in section 53(2), although that is not a definitive list. Whether either of those provisions applies will of course depend on the particular circumstances, but without having heard full argument in an appropriate case we wish to reserve our view on that.

In fact there seems no reason to doubt the existence of a common scheme in circumstances where the same superior has imposed the same burdens on a number of feus. But there is certainly an argument to be made that the properties are not 'related' within section 53. Of course, it can be objected to such an argument that, for 'relatedness' to turn on the question of whether one deed was used or many, is to attach too much importance to the conveyancing, or development, preferences of its granter. But if that is so, it is a weighting which can also be found in section 53(2)(c) of the Act.

Developments and deeds of conditions

Section 53 is concerned with old real burdens. But what of new? Typically, new burdens are created in two types of case (though of course other possibilities exist).[2] One is where land is being divided, one part being sold and one retained. So plot A is sold and plot B retained, the idea being that burdens should be imposed on plot A for the benefit of plot B. Burdens of this kind are sometimes

---

1 At pp 15–16 of the transcript.
2 For example, where plot A is sold and plot B retained, with reciprocal burdens ('community burdens') imposed on each.

known as 'neighbour burdens':[1] their characteristic is that one plot is burdened and the other plot is not. The second case is quite different. Here all the plots are being sold, all are to be burdened, and all are to have reciprocal rights of enforcement. In this case the burdens are 'community burdens' – burdens in which each plot is both a burdened property and also a benefited property.[2]

From a conveyancing point of view, the first case is straightforward. Burdens are imposed in the split-off disposition of plot A, and the disposition must then be registered against both plot A (the burdened property) and plot B (the benefited property).[3]

The second case is potentially straightforward as well; but if more than two plots are involved it is straightforward, subject to one transitional case,[4] *only if a deed of conditions is used.* This way of proceeding was, of course, perfectly familiar from the former law. It works like this. Before any other conveyancing is done, a deed of conditions is registered, imposing uniform (or at least equivalent) burdens on each plot, and providing for mutual enforceability. The latter can be spelled out in the deed but is achieved more simply, under the Title Conditions (Scotland) Act 2003, by a declaration that the burdens are to be community burdens. This is because of section 27, which provides that:

> Where, in relation to any real burdens, the constitutive deed states that the burdens are to be community burdens, each unit shall, in relation to those burdens, be both a benefited and a burdened property.

So far as the burdens are concerned, there is nothing more to be done. Split-off dispositions can now be granted for individual plots in the normal way. Importantly, there is no requirement of dual registration because the burdens have *already* been created.[5]

In the case of small developments there is a natural temptation to do without a deed of conditions, and instead to impose the burdens in the individual split-off writs. Under the former law, that was usually satisfactory enough. Under the new law, however – as experience is now beginning to show – the result is likely to be unfortunate or even disastrous.[6]

Take the following example. A development comprises 12 plots. The developer holds on a single title registered in the Land Register. There is no deed of conditions. In the disposition of the first plot to be sold – plot 1 – real burdens are imposed for the benefit of the parent title, less the plot being sold (or in other

---

1 Although the term does not appear in the Title Conditions (Scotland) Act 2003.
2 TC(S)A 2003 s 25(1).
3 TC(S)A 2003 s 4(5).
4 The transitional case arises where at least one of the plots was disponed, and burdened, before the appointed day. Provided that the plots are 'related', mutual enforcement rights arise automatically under TCA(S)A 2003 s 53, and there is no need for dual registration (s 53A(3A)) or indeed for a deed of conditions.
5 At least in the normal case: see TC(S)A 2003 s 4(1). But it is possible to postpone the creation of the burdens until the registration of the split-off dispositions.
6 We are grateful to John Glover of Registers of Scotland for drawing these difficulties to our attention.

words, for the benefit of plots 2–12). Well and good. The disposition must then be registered against both plot 1 (for which a new title sheet will be opened) and the parent title. Now it is the turn of plot 2 to be sold. With the disposition of plot 1 already on the computer, there is nothing more natural than to use the same style for plot 2. So in the disposition of plot 2, burdens are likewise imposed for the benefit of the parent title, less the plot that is being sold, and once again there is dual registration. At first all seems to be well. It is not. The benefited property, ie the parent title, is not the same in both cases. In the case of plot 1, the parent title comprised plots 2–12 (ie 11 plots); by the time that plot 2 comes to be sold, the parent title is reduced to plots 3–12 (ie 10 plots). Nor is this all. As part of the original parent title, plot 2 was a benefited property in respect of plot 1. But once plot 2 is disponed separately from the parent title, the effect of section 12 of the Title Conditions Act is that plot 2 ceases to be a benefited property – unless the disposition provides otherwise. It may be added that section 12 seems not to be as well known as its importance deserves. The end result is this: plot 1 was never a benefited property in respect of plot 2, while plot 2 is no longer a benefited property in respect of plot 1. The previous law would have produced the first of these outcomes but not the second, which is caused by section 12.

The same problem recurs each time that a new plot is disponed, with the result that the benefited property continues to shrink. By the end it has shrunk almost to nothing: the burdens on each of plots 1–11 are enforceable only by the developer and its successors as owners of the one plot remaining in the parent title, plot 12. It is unlikely that this was the outcome that the parties intended.

Of course, with care this result can be avoided. One possibility is the following.[1] The first disposition, of plot 1, is the same as before, but the second is crucially different. In the first place, it declares the benefited property to be the plot already sold (plot 1) as well as the plots still retained in the parent title (plots 3–12). In the second place, the effect of section 12 is eliminated – as the section itself permits – by an express statement that the plot being sold and the parent title being retained are *both* to continue as benefited properties in relation to plot 1. So plot 1 can enforce against plot 2, and vice versa. And provided the rest of the conveyancing is done in the same way, the final result is a set of community burdens, with the owner of each plot able to enforce uniform burdens against the owner of any other plot.

But this is a clumsy way of achieving a simple result. Each disposition (other than the first and last) must contain a statement excluding section 12. Each plot, though burdened by only one deed (the disposition of that plot), is benefited by no fewer than 11 (the dispositions of the other 11 plots), which makes for a crowded and unlovely title sheet. And the registration dues become increasingly expensive as the sales proceed. Compare the first and the last dispositions. The first disposition will require to be registered only twice – against the property being sold (plot 1) and against the parent title being retained (the benefited

---

1 There are others, each with their own difficulties. For example, the dispositions could impose burdens *both* on the plot being disponed *and* on the plots still held on the parent title.

property) which at that stage contains all of plots 2–12. But the last disposition will require to be registered 12 separate times, for by now each of plots 1–11 (the benefited properties) has a title sheet of its own. Every extra title sheet means an extra £30 in registration dues. For the purchaser of plot 1, the costs of dual registration are a mere £30, but for the person unlucky enough to buy plot 12 the costs have risen to £330 – in addition, of course, to the normal fee for registration against plot 12 itself.

There is no need to put up with any of this. If a deed of conditions is used the difficulties disappear. The message could hardly be plainer.

VARIATION AND DISCHARGE BY THE LANDS TRIBUNAL

The decline of the minute of waiver

A superior's minute of waiver was, under the old law, a currency accepted by everyone. Of course, waivers were not always obtainable. The superior might be impossible to trace. He might charge too much. He might say no – though that was rare, superiors being more interested in money than in the integrity of some Victorian feuing plan. Inopportunely, there might be no superior at all, because the burdens were imposed in a disposition – or in a deed of conditions granted in association with dispositions – rather than in a grant in feu. But even here there was often an attempt to find a superior-substitute – the original developers perhaps – a gambit which turned a convenient blind eye to the fact that, if the developers had disposed of all the units in the estate, they ceased to have any title to enforce the burdens, and therefore to grant a minute of waiver.

It is true that law did not always support practice. To get a waiver from the superior was of little value if the neighbours – the co-feuars – were also invested with enforcement rights. In such a case the neighbours must sign too or the burdens lived on. If one was being properly cautious, therefore, each minute of waiver must be accompanied by an anxious inquiry into co-feuars' rights. But this was often overlooked. The law of co-feuars' rights was notoriously difficult. It rested on a whole host of, often contradictory, cases whose very names – *Hislop v MacRitchie's Trs*[1] for example – were a distant and unwelcome memory. For many years before, sensible question-spotters had left out that part of the conveyancing course when preparing for their exam. And so it was that minutes of waiver were usually granted by the superior alone even in cases where there were co-feuars' rights.

In the brave new world of post-feudalism, minutes of waiver remain, of course.[2] But who is now to grant them? The answer is: those who have title to enforce the burdens in question. But immediately there are difficulties.

The *first* difficulty lies in identifying which burdens might require attention. Feudal abolition dispensed with superiors while – quite often – leaving the

---

1 (1881) 8 R (HL) 95.
2 Title Conditions (Scotland) Act 2003 s 15.

burdens in place. But by no means always. A real difficulty is to know whether the burden which blocks a client's intended development is alive or dead.[1]

If the burden is thought to be alive, there is then a *second* difficulty. Who has title to enforce it? The effect of sections 52–56 of the Title Conditions (Scotland) Act 2003 is often to replace the superior with neighbours. But the provisions are no more attractive than the rules about co-feuars' rights which they replace, and in important respects their scope remains uncertain.[2] In all too many cases, therefore, the advice to clients is that the burden in question *might* still be alive and, if it is, that it *might* be enforceable by certain neighbours.[3]

This assessment leads to the *third* difficulty. Often there are too many enforcers or possible enforcers to make a minute of waiver practicable. In a modern housing development, there may be 40 neighbours with enforcement rights, or 400. Admittedly, the Title Conditions Act contains special provisions allowing waivers in respect of 'community burdens' to be granted by smaller numbers – by all neighbours within four metres or, less promisingly, by a majority of all neighbours.[4] But even if the necessary signatures can be obtained, the procedure is slow, cumbersome, and subject to challenge in the Lands Tribunal.[5] Another possibility is to take a view on interest to enforce, and to dispense with the signatures of those whose houses are sufficiently distant to remove any real possibility of enforcement.[6] All this is worth considering, of course; but quite often the conclusion will be that a minute of waiver simply cannot be done.

Why the Lands Tribunal?

In the absence of a minute of waiver, what options are available to a client faced with an awkward burden? If the burden is more than 100 years old, it is possible to use the new 'sunset rule' by which the client executes, intimates and – after waiting some weeks for possible objections – registers a notice of termination.[7] The available figures suggest that this has been used in only about 40 cases so far, a surprisingly low figure for what is a rather useful mechanism.

For more youthful burdens, the choice is stark. One possibility is to breach the burden and hope that some trigger-happy neighbour does not rush for an interdict. If the building work is completed without objection, the burden will be

1 For a discussion, see A Steven and S Wortley, 'Is that burden dead yet?' (2006) 51 *Journal of the Law Society of Scotland* June/46 and July/50.
2 For an analysis of the rules under the Title Conditions (Scotland) Act 2003, see K G C Reid and G L Gretton, *Conveyancing* (3rd edn 2004) paras 13-14–13-17.
3 See p 80 above.
4 Title Conditions (Scotland) Act 2003 ss 35, 36.
5 Since the appointed day (28 November 2004) there have been 10 such challenges in the Lands Tribunal, although only one has so far resulted in a decision: see *Sheltered Housing Management Ltd v Jack* 2007 GWD 32-533, *Conveyancing 2006* Case (35). The challenge was unsuccessful. We are extremely grateful to the Clerk to the Lands Tribunal, Neil Tainsh, for providing us with these and other figures which appear in this section.
6 See p 77 above.
7 Title Conditions (Scotland) Act 2003 ss 20–24. Any benefited proprietor can oppose the notice by applying to the Lands Tribunal for renewal of the burden. The only example so far is *Brown v Richardson* 2007 GWD 28-490, 2007 GWD 38-666.

extinguished, first by the new statutory acquiescence, after 12 weeks, and later – to be on the safe side – by the 5-year negative prescription.[1]

The other possibility is to go to the Lands Tribunal. But it is wrong to present this negatively – as a last resort when all other options have run out. Conveyancers, naturally enough, are suspicious of litigation; but a Lands Tribunal application is often an essentially administrative process. And it has a number of advantages which correspond to the difficulties mentioned earlier. A variation or discharge by the Lands Tribunal has universal effect. On registration it clears the title.[2] Thus the problems of large numbers of enforcers, or their identification, cease to matter. And, in a change from the previous law, it does not even matter if, on a proper view of the law, the burden had already ceased to exist. The Lands Tribunal will discharge it anyway – will kill the already dead.[3] Alternatively, the Tribunal can be asked to pronounce on the validity of the burden – a new jurisdiction – although experience so far shows that this option is rarely chosen.[4]

An obvious benefit of the Lands Tribunal is certainty. A person who proceeds in any other way does so with an element of risk. If he ignores the burden, he runs the risk that it is still alive and that neighbours will reach for interdict. If he seeks a minute of waiver, he runs the risk that he has failed to identify the correct enforcers and so get the correct signatures. But with the Lands Tribunal there is only the risk of failure in the application – and that risk, as we shall see, is a small one. Assuming that the application is successful, the burden is varied or discharged for all time.

The procedure in brief

The Lands Tribunal jurisdiction in respect of real burdens dates from the Conveyancing and Feudal Reform (Scotland) Act 1970. The 1970 Act provisions are repealed and replaced by part 9 of the Title Conditions (Scotland) Act 2003, introducing important changes and – as a general rule – making applications swifter and, as it seems at the moment, more likely to be attended with success.

Under the 2003 Act, any person who is subject to a real burden is entitled to apply for its variation or discharge.[5] For negative burdens, this means not only the burdened owner but also any tenant or person having use of the property.[6] In the case of community burdens, there is a new rule that the owners of at least one quarter of the units are entitled to make an application for global discharge, ie discharge as regards the whole community.[7] Applications are made on form TC90(1)(a).[2]

---

1 TC(S)A 2003 ss 16, 18.
2 TC(S)A 2003 s 104(2).
3 TC(S)A 2003 s 90(1)(a) allows the Lands Tribunal to discharge 'a title condition (or purported title condition)'.
4 TC(S)A 2003 s 90(1)(a)(ii). For an example, which was undefended, see *Halladale (Shaftesbury) Ltd* 20 June 2005, Lands Tribunal, *Conveyancing 2006* Case (23).
5 TC(S)A 2003 s 90(1).
6 This is because such a person is subject to the burden: see TC(S)A 2003 s 9(2). A 'negative burden' is one which consists of an obligation to refrain from doing something (s 2(1)(b), (2)(b)).
7 TC(S)A 2003 s 91.
8 Lands Tribunal for Scotland Rules 2003, SSI 2003/452, sch 2.

On receipt of an application, the Tribunal must intimate it to various parties, notably the benefited owner(s) (or the holder of the burden, in the case of a personal real burden).[1] Intimation must also be made to the burdened owner if he or she is not the applicant. The Tribunal may intimate to other parties, for example tenants, if it thinks fit.[2] The parties to whom intimation is made must be given at least 21 days to make representations.[3] Any party wishing to do so must give a written statement of the facts and contentions upon which it is intended to rely.[4] A fee of £25 is payable.[5]

What happens next depends on whether the application is opposed (ie representations are made) or unopposed. If the application is unopposed, the Tribunal must (with minor exceptions) grant it without further inquiry.[6] If it is opposed, the Tribunal makes a site visit and there is then usually a hearing – although the case can also be disposed of on the basis of written submissions if the parties agree.[7]

Will the application be opposed?

If the application is unopposed, the process will be swift – about two months from start to finish – and the result sure. It will also be quite cheap: a fee of £238[8] plus advertising and other expenses (and of course legal fees). So at the outset it is important to consider whether an application is likely to meet with opposition. Much of course will depend on the circumstances of individual cases, and the client may have a good idea as to the likely attitudes of neighbours. But the statistics are highly encouraging. A survey carried out for the Scottish Law Commission of 40 applications, mainly from 1997, showed that 50% were unopposed.[9] The figures so far under the new law are more favourable still: of the 35 cases disposed of by the Tribunal in 2006,[10] as many as 26 were either unopposed or the initial opposition was withdrawn – some 74% of cases in all. Of course it is early days and it is possible that these figures will prove to be untypical. Yet, given the new rules on expenses (discussed below), it is not hard to understand why opposition has become less attractive than formerly.

---

1 TC(S)A 2003 s 93(1).

2 TC(S)A 2003 s 93(3).

3 TC(S)A 2003 s 94(a)(ii).

4 TC(S)A 2003 s 96(1).

5 Item 23 in sch 2 of the Lands Tribunal for Scotland Rules 1971, SI 1971/218, as inserted by the Lands Tribunal for Scotland Amendment (Fees) Rules 2004, SSI 2004/480.

6 TC(S)A 2003 s 97. The exceptions are for facility burdens, service burdens, and burdens in sheltered or retirement housing developments.

7 As happened for example in *Graham v Parker* 2007 GWD 30-524.

8 This comprises an application fee of £150 and a further fee of £88 for making the order. See items 17 and 21 in sch 2 of the Lands Tribunal for Scotland Rules 1971, as amended in particular by the Lands Tribunal for Scotland Amendment (Fees) Rules 2003, SSI 2003/521, and the Lands Tribunal for Scotland Amendment (Fees) Rules 2004, SSI 2004/480.

9 Scottish Law Commission, Report on *Real Burdens* (Scot Law Com No 181 (2000); available on www.scotlaw.gov.uk) para 6.3.

10 Excluding six which were withdrawn by the applicant and one which was ruled incompetent.

If the application is opposed, will it succeed?

In only one quarter of cases – on the figures given above – will an application be opposed. And of those one quarter, the prospects of ultimate success seem very high indeed.

In the 1997 survey already mentioned, applications in opposed cases achieved a 70% success rate. Under the Title Conditions (Scotland) Act 2003 the success rate has, so far, been even higher. The tables below detail every opposed application for variation or discharge of real burdens which the Tribunal has decided under the Act. Of the 15 cases which proceeded to final judgment,[1] the application was granted in 12 – a success rate of 80%.[2] Furthermore, failure first time round does not necessarily mean failure for ever: indeed in two out of the three cases of refusal, the Tribunal gave some hope that a reformulated application might meet with success.[3] A feature of many of these cases is how easily the Tribunal came to its decision: usually, it seems, the arguments in favour of discharge are seen to be overwhelmingly strong.

Restriction on building

Name of case	Burden	Applicant's project in breach of burden	Application granted or refused
Ord v Mashford 2006 SLT (Lands Tr) 15; Lawrie v Mashford 2008 GWD 7-129	1938 deed of servitude. No building.	Erection of single-storey house and garage.	Granted. Claim for compensation refused.
Daly v Bryce 2006 GWD 25-565	1961 feu charter. No further building.	Replace existing house with two houses.	Granted.
J & L Leisure Ltd v Shaw 2007 GWD 28-489	1958 disposition. No new buildings higher than 15 feet 6 inches.	Replace derelict building with two-storey housing.	Granted subject to compensation of £5,600.
Faeley v Clark 2006 GWD 28-626	1967 disposition. No further building.	Erection of second house.	Refused.
West Coast Property Developments Ltd v Clarke 2007 GWD 29-511	1875 feu contract. Terraced houses. No further building.	Erection of second, two-storey house.	Granted. Claim for compensation refused.
Smith v Prior 2007 GWD 30-523	1934 feu charter. No building.	Erection of modest rear extension.	Granted.

---

1 Two cases are omitted: *McPherson v Mackie* 2007 SCLR 351 (which was settled after the decision of the Inner House), and *At.Home Nationwide Ltd v Morris* 2007 GWD 31-535 (where the burden in question was found to be void, making it unnecessary to discharge it).

2 If servitudes are included (for which see below), the success rate is 12 cases out of 15, or 83%.

3 The exception was *Faeley v Clark* 2006 GWD 28-626, *Conveyancing 2006* Case (29).

Name of case	Burden	Applicant's project in breach of burden	Application granted or refused
Anderson v McKinnon 2007 GWD 29-513	1993 deed of conditions in modern housing estate.	Erection of rear extension.	Granted.
Smith v Elrick 2007 GWD 29-515	1996 feu disposition. No new house. The feu had been subdivided.	Conversion of barn into a house.	Granted.
Brown v Richardson 2007 GWD 28-490	1888 feu charter. No alterations/new buildings.	Erection of rear extension.	Granted. This was an application for renewal, following service of a notice of termination.
Gallacher v Wood 2007 GWD 37-647	1933 feu contract. No alterations/new buildings.	Erection of rear extension, including extension at roof level which went beyond bungalow's footprint.	Granted. Claim for compensation refused.
Cattanach v Vine-Hall 3 Oct 2007	1996 deed of conditions in favour of neighbouring property. No building within 7 metres of that property.	Erection of substantial house within 2 metres.	Refused, subject to the possibility of the applicants bringing a revised proposal.
Hamilton v Robertson 2008 GWD 8-149	1984 deed of conditions affecting 5-house development. No further building.	Erection of second house on site, but no firm plans.	Refused, although possibility of later success once plans firmed up was not excluded.

Other restriction on use

Name of case	Burden	Applicant's project in breach of burden	Application granted or refused
Church of Scotland General Trs v McLaren 2006 SLT (Lands Tr) 27	Use as a church.	Possible development for flats.	Granted.
Wilson v McNamee 16 Sept 2007	Use for religious purposes.	Use for a children's nursery.	Granted.

Flatted property

Name of case	Burden	Applicant's project in breach of burden	Application granted or refused
Regan v Mullen 2006 GWD 25-564	1989. No subdivision of flat.	Subdivision of flat.	Granted.

Sheltered and retirement housing

Name of case	Burden	Applicant's project in breach of burden	Application granted or refused
At.Home Nationwide Ltd v Morris 2007 GWD 31-535	1993 deed of conditions. On sale, must satisfy superior that flat will continue to be used for the elderly.	No project: just removal of an inconvenient restriction.	Burden held to be void. Otherwise application would have been refused.

Miscellaneous

Name of case	Burden	Applicant's project in breach of burden	Application granted or refused
McPherson v Mackie 2006 GWD 27-606 rev [2007] CSIH 7, 2007 SCLR 351	1990 deed of conditions. Housing estate: maintenance of house.	Demolition of house to allow the building of a road for access to proposed new development.	Discharged by agreement on 25 April 2007.

What arguments should be used?

For success it is necessary to advance the right kinds of argument. And it should be borne in mind that the statutory criteria under the Title Conditions (Scotland) Act 2003 are different from those under the previous legislation.[1] In formulating arguments the first cases decided under the Act are – and are intended to be – of considerable assistance.

Admittedly, in the most important of those cases, *Ord v Mashford*,[2] the Lands Tribunal warned that:

> Even under the 1970 Act our experience had been that while a grasp of case law helped parties to understand the approach taken by the Tribunal to the inter-related provisions of section 1(3), the detail of previous decisions was seldom of assistance in the direct assessment of reasonableness.
>
> One reason why reference to apparently similar previous cases tended to provide little real assistance is that it has been the experience of the Tribunal that a site inspection plays a significant part in many decisions. Even with the benefit of hearing oral evidence and studying maps, plans and photographs, the Tribunal has often been influenced by the impression derived on site. That element cannot readily be assessed from the text of reported decisions. Litigants seeking to make comparisons

---

1 The previous legislation was the Conveyancing and Feudal Reform (Scotland) Act 1970 s 1(3), now repealed. The Lands Tribunal has doubted whether the new criteria will make any difference 'in substance': see *George Wimpey East Scotland Ltd v Fleming* 2006 SLT (Lands Tr) 2 at 10F; *Ord v Mashford* 2006 SLT (Lands Tr) 15 at 19L.

2 2006 SLT (Lands Tr) 15 at 20D–F.

with previous cases usually do so without the benefit of plans and photographs. While broad guidance to our approach under the new Act will, we hope, be derived from our decisions as they emerge, we think it likely that attempts to rely on apparently close factual comparison will seldom be worthwhile.

The 'broad guidance' given by the first decisions is certainly of help;[1] and it may be that the Tribunal over-states the extent to which previous cases cannot be used on their facts. Unfortunately, most of the decisions are unreported, although some are available on the Tribunal's website: www.lands-tribunal-scotland.org.uk.

The statutory factors

In reaching a decision in an opposed application, the Tribunal is required to decide whether it is reasonable to grant the application, having regard to the factors set out in s 100.[2] These factors are:

(a) any change in circumstances since the title condition was created (including, without prejudice to that generality, any change in the character of the benefited property, of the burdened property or of the neighbourhood of the properties);
(b) the extent to which the condition –
  (i) confers benefit on the benefited property; or
  (ii) where there is no benefited property, confers benefit on the public;
(c) the extent to which the condition impedes enjoyment of the burdened property;
(d) if the condition is an obligation to do something, how –
  (i) practicable; or
  (ii) costly,
  it is to comply with the condition;
(e) the length of time which has elapsed since the condition was created;
(f) the purpose of the title condition;
(g) whether in relation to the burdened property there is the consent, or deemed consent, of a planning authority, or the consent of some other regulatory authority, for a use which the condition prevents;
(h) whether the owner of the burdened property is willing to pay compensation;
(i) if the application is under section 90(1)(b)(ii) of this Act [application for renewal of a burden which would otherwise be extinguished by compulsory purchase], the purpose for which the land is being acquired by the person proposing to register the conveyance; and
(j) any other factor which the Lands Tribunal consider to be material.

Obviously, all factors are not of equal importance. Factor (i), for example, is confined to cases of compulsory purchase. The rather puzzling factor (h) seems to be disregarded in practice. Factor (d) is confined to affirmative burdens, which are rarely the subject of Lands Tribunal applications. Factor (j) has not so far proved to be of importance.

---

1 For a detailed discussion, see K G C Reid and G L Gretton, *Conveyancing 2005* pp 102–114. Naturally, this does not take account of the most recent decisions.
2 Title Conditions (Scotland) Act 2003 s 98.

Nor is the order in the statute of significance. In fact the Tribunal usually begins its consideration with factor (f).

Factor (f): purpose of condition

The reason for having factor (f) at all is not entirely clear.[1] All the other factors contain an implied question, the answer to which points either in favour of discharge or against it. So for example, if the condition which is the subject of the application impedes development (factor (c)), or if planning permission has been granted (factor (g)), these answers support the granting of the application. But if the condition confers significant benefit (factor (b)), that is an answer which favours refusal. Factor (f) is of a different kind. Uniquely, it cannot stand alone, for no particular conclusion can be drawn from identifying the purpose of the condition. As a result, factor (f) can only be used *in conjunction* with some other factor. So far the Tribunal's approach has been to use it in conjunction with factor (a) – and sometimes, and more controversially, in conjunction with factor (b).

In fact, the 'purpose' of most burdens is usually found to be rather general and anodyne – typically to preserve the amenity of the group of properties which it burdens.[2] With one exception, which we will come to, not much can be learned from that.

Factor (a): change in circumstances

After factor (f) the Tribunal tends to consider whether any change of circumstances has occurred which might disturb the initial purpose of the condition and, perhaps, even defeat it entirely (factor (a)). In *West Coast Property Developments Ltd v Clarke*,[3] for example, changes of circumstances (the flatting of all the houses in the terrace in question and the building of mews houses) were found to be decisive in favour of granting the application. But this is untypical. The experience so far is that factor (a) is usually of secondary importance.

Factor (b): extent of benefit to benefited property

Instead the crucial factors will be factors (b) and (c). They are intended to be used together. Most conditions will *both* confer benefit on the benefited property and *also* impede use of the burdened, so that the question becomes whether the benefit is of greater value than the impediment.[4]

Benefit is rarely considered in the abstract, for in practice the applicant usually has a particular project in mind. Indeed in the only case so far in which no precise project was put forward, the application was rejected, partly on that ground.[5]

---

1 It was absent from the original list produced by the Scottish Law Commission.
2 See eg *Smith v Elrick* 2007 GWD 29-515.
3 2007 GWD 29-511, *Conveyancing 2006* Case (30).
4 Eg in *Gallagher v Wood* 2007 GWD 37-647, the Tribunal described its task as coming down 'substantially, to balancing burden and benefit' (para 37).
5 *Hamilton v Robertson*, 2008 GWD 8-149, Case (16) above. This is because the Tribunal is reluctant to grant the applicant a blank cheque to build whatever the planning authorities will allow.

Typically the project involves extending an existing building or erecting a new one. That project is prevented by the burden – hence the application. And as the benefit to the proprietor of the benefited property is the chance to stop the project, the Tribunal's task is to evaluate that benefit by considering the project's likely impact. Often one or both sides will lead expert evidence, but the Tribunal will make up its own mind, particularly in the light of a site visit. Indeed in *Faeley v Clark*[1] – one of only three cases so far in which an application was refused – the result of the site visit was for the Tribunal to reject the evidence of the applicants' expert to the effect that the proposed development would have only a limited impact.

All new building, of course, involves the initial inconvenience of the construction phase, but it has been said by the Inner House that 'if the long-term user is acceptable it will usually be difficult to deny its allowance on the basis of short-term construction disturbance'.[2]

In some early cases, the Tribunal chose to read the burden narrowly, in the light of its purpose (ie factor (f)). Benefit consistent with that purpose was accepted and evaluated, but benefit of a different kind was rejected as irrelevant for factor (b). So for example where a burden was imposed to preserve only *general* amenity and over-development, it was of little consequence, on this approach, that the new building proposed by the applicant would have the highly particular effect of restricting the light in the objecting neighbour's sitting room. The burden's purpose was not to protect a neighbour's light.[3] This approach, however, caused difficulties for burdens of feudal origin, for where burdens were originally imposed by a superior – and in particular by an absentee superior – it was easy to conclude that their purpose was general and public and not specific and private. At any rate they were not for the benefit of immediate neighbours. The Title Conditions Act then seemed to pull in two different directions. On the one hand, it took care to ensure the survival of the burdens by transferring enforcement rights from superiors to neighbours;[4] but on the other hand – at least on the approach under discussion – it made such burdens easy to remove because, in an application to the Tribunal, the neighbours were unable to show any relevant benefit. Perhaps because of this, the Tribunal seems now to accept that a burden may confer relevant benefit even if that benefit was not within the purpose for which the burden was originally imposed. So in *Brown v Richardson*,[5] for example, the Tribunal agreed 'that there may be benefit to the benefited proprietor even although that was not the original purpose'.[6]

Finally, the Tribunal may try to assess the effectiveness of the burden as a whole. A burden which, while preventing the applicants' particular development,

1 2006 GWD 28-626.
2 *McPherson v Mackie* [2007] CSIH 7, 2007 SCLR 351 at para 16 per Lord Eassie. For a discussion, see J J Robbie, 'Short-term benefit and the Lands Tribunal' (2008) 12 *Edinburgh Law Review* 114.
3 *Daly v Bryce* 2006 GWD 25-565, *Conveyancing 2006* Case (26). See also *Church of Scotland General Trs v McLaren* 2006 SLT (Lands Tr) 27, *Conveyancing 2005* Case (14).
4 Title Conditions (Scotland) Act 2003 ss 52–56.
5 2007 GWD 28-490 at p 23 of the transcript.
6 See also *Smith v Prior* 2007 GWD 30-523.

would not prevent other developments which would be more harmful still, is likely to be varied or discharged as being of little real benefit.[1]

Factor (c): extent to which enjoyment of burdened property impeded

Against factor (b) there must be balanced factor (c).[2] If, as typically, the burden restricts alterations and building, the Tribunal tends to view such restrictions as a serious impediment which can be justified only if, under factor (b), the proposed alterations or building would have a major impact on the benefited property. The following comments are typical:

> The applicants' motives for extending are not of importance. They are exercising a normal wish to enjoy their property by extending their house. It would be a considerable hardship to them if they were unable to do so.[3]

> Looking at the particular situation here, we consider that the respondents are proposing an extension and improvement of their property of an essentially normal and reasonable type, in line with modern living. We can in this day and age readily accept that a possible alternative of buying a larger property of comparable location and attractiveness would be expensive in comparison.[4]

Although further arguments are not usually necessary, it is possible to identify two which are likely to strengthen factor (c). The first is the degree of need for the project proposed by the applicant, or at least for *some* building project. In *J & L Leisure Ltd v Shaw*[5] the applicant's properties were derelict and urgently in need of replacement. In *Daly v Bryce*[6] – less dramatically but still helpfully – the applicant's house, a 1960s bungalow, was outmoded and said to be in need of major refurbishment or replacement.

The second is the absence of alternative uses for the property, at least for as long as the condition stands unmodified. In *J & L Leisure Ltd v Shaw*, where the property was in a conservation area, the Tribunal accepted that the 'single storey housing [allowed under the condition] firstly might not be approved by the planners and secondly would be uneconomic'.[7] Furthermore:[8]

> the proposed housing development [which would breach the condition] seems not only eminently reasonable but also the only type of development which can be seriously considered. Accordingly, the burden on the applicants of the title condition restraining development to this height is very considerable.

---

1 *Ord v Mashford* 2006 SLT (Lands Tr) 15 at 25B; *Smith v Elrick* 2007 GWD 29-515.
2 Initially, the Tribunal had been inclined not to give factor (c) much weight, on the basis that the burden was voluntarily assumed by the applicant and was reflected in the price paid. See *Ord v Mashford* 2006 SLT (Lands Tr) 15 at 25L. But that rather unrealistic analysis has not prevailed.
3 *Anderson v McKinnon* 2007 GWD 29-513 at p 10 of the transcript.
4 *Brown v Richardson* 2007 GWD 28-490 at p 21 of the transcript.
5 2007 GWD 28-489, *Conveyancing 2006* Case (27).
6 2006 GWD 25-565, *Conveyancing 2006* Case (26).
7 At p 9 of the transcript.
8 At p 14.

In *Wilson v McNamee*[1] it was not easy to find a tenant for a hall which could only be used 'for religious purposes'. By contrast, one of the reasons for refusing the application in *Faeley v Clark*[2] was that the benefited proprietors (neighbours) had given consent in the past to new buildings which were, from their point of view, less objectionable, and might be expected to do so again in the future.

A third factor was initially treated by the Tribunal as pointing the other way. This was where the proposed development was being pursued only for commercial gain. In *West Coast Property Developments Ltd v Clarke*, for example, the Tribunal accepted, as a factor unhelpful to the applicant, that 'this may simply be a speculative development with a view to realising profit'.[3] However, in *McPherson v Mackie*,[4] the Inner House took issue with the Tribunal's refusal, at first instance, to place weight on the 'potential windfall development value' which would accrue to the applicants if the condition was discharged and as a result they were able to demolish their house and sell the site as an access road to a proposed new development. '[I]n its characterisation of the development as "windfall", with the possible moral judgment implied in the selection of that adjective, the Tribunal may have fallen into error.'[5] Whether in response to this view or not, the Tribunal has emphasised in a recent case that 'the applicants' motives for extending are not of importance'.[6]

As already mentioned, the Tribunal reaches its decision largely by weighing factor (b) against factor (c). If factor (b) is very strong – if, in other words, the applicant's building project will be seriously detrimental to the objector's property – the application will be refused. That was the situation in *Faeley v Clark*. But, at least on the basis of the cases decided so far, a lesser degree of prejudice is unlikely to block the application. Indeed, as was pointed out in *J & L Leisure Ltd v Shaw*, the very fact that the Act provides for compensation in respect of 'substantial loss and disadvantage' (s 90(7)(a)) shows that it was contemplated that applications could be granted even where to do so would have a material impact on the benefited owner.[7] Given the way in which factors (b) and (c) are currently interpreted, it seems likely that the vast majority of applications will continue to succeed.

Factor (e): age of the condition

The only other factor which need be discussed is factor (e). As already mentioned, if a burden is more than 100 years old, it is possible for the burdened proprietor to secure its discharge by the execution, intimation and registration of a notice of termination.[8] This is the so-called 'sunset rule'. But if a burden is elderly but

---

1 6 Sept 2007, Lands Tribunal, Case (13) above.
2 2006 GWD 28-626, *Conveyancing 2006* Case (29).
3 2007 GWD 29-511, *Conveyancing 2006* Case (30), at p 25 of the transcript. See also *Daly v Bryce* 2006 GWD 25-565 at p 21 of the transcript: 'this is not a case in which … the proposal to demolish and replace with two houses was motivated only by financial profit'.
4 2007 SCLR 351, *Conveyancing 2006* Case (28).
5 At para 23.
6 *Anderson v McKinnon* 2007 GWD 29–513 at p 10 of the transcript.
7 2007 GWD 28-489 at pp 16–17 of the transcript.
8 Title Conditions (Scotland) Act 2003 ss 20–24.

less than 100 years old, this is a factor which argues for its discharge in a normal application to the Lands Tribunal. In *Smith v Prior*, the Tribunal had this to say about a restriction on building which had been imposed in 1934:[1]

> [T]o the extent that rights of control may produce sterility, there must come a time when, however attractive to its immediate neighbours, that should be at last relaxed. Holding the applicants to a prohibition on extension more than 70 years after it was imposed would seem to us to require quite strong justification.

The converse would also be true: the Tribunal would be reluctant to discharge a burden which was imposed only last year.[2] Most burdens, of course, are neither very new nor very old, and in such cases factor (e) is likely to be of little importance.[3]

Timing and cost

An opposed application is likely to take from four to six months. For all applications, there is a fee of £238 plus advertising costs plus legal costs. If the application is opposed there is in addition a fee of £155 for each day that the Tribunal sits.[4] But, assuming that the application is successful, it should be possible to get some of this back by way of an order for expenses against the unsuccessful objector. On the other hand – if much more rarely – the applicant may face a requirement to pay compensation to the objectors. To both of these subjects we now turn.

Expenses

Section 103(1) of the Title Conditions (Scotland) Act 2003 provides that:

> The Lands Tribunal may, in determining an application made under this Part of this Act, make such an order as to expenses as they think fit but shall have regard, in particular, to the extent to which the application, or any opposition to it, is successful.

That is an important change in law and practice. Until the Title Conditions Act came into force, the Tribunal's practice in relation to opposed applications was as follows.[5] Where an application was unsuccessful, the applicant met the expenses of both sides. But where it was successful – where, in other words, the opposition

---

1 2007 GWD 30-523 at p 22 of the transcript.
2 *Cattanach v Vine-Hall* 3 Oct 2007, Lands Tribunal.
3 It is in this sense that one should read the *dictum* in *Ord v Mashford* 2006 SLT (Lands Tr) 15 at 25L that '[M]ere duration tells us little as to whether it [the condition] can be regarded as out of date, obsolete or otherwise inappropriate. At first blush, therefore, there might be little weight to attach to this factor.'
4 See item 20 in sch 2 of the Lands Tribunal for Scotland Rules 1971, as amended by the Lands Tribunal for Scotland Amendment (Fees) Rules 2003 and the Lands Tribunal for Scotland Amendment (Fees) Rules 2004.
5 *West Coast Property Developments v Clarke* 2007 GWD 29-511, *Conveyancing 2006* Case (30), at p 12 of the transcript.

failed – the applicant nonetheless had to meet his own expenses. This was because the possibility of being relieved of burdens – an innovation in 1970 – was felt to be a privilege for which the applicant might reasonably be expected to pay, while at the same time those opposing the application should not be penalised simply for seeking to uphold their rights. From time to time the Tribunal did in fact award expenses against unsuccessful objectors, but only where they had acted unreasonably.

Section 103 proceeds on a different view of title conditions. On this view, title conditions need not – perhaps should not – last for ever. Indeed if they are more than 100 years old they are presumptively obsolete, and can be discharged under the sunset rule. Even within the 100-year period, however, variation or discharge is a normal, even an expected, outcome. From the point of view of the owner of the burdened property, the opportunity to be relieved of title conditions is a right and not merely a privilege, reluctantly conceded. A contested application before the Lands Tribunal is thus a competition between two different kinds of right – between the right of the objectors to maintain the title condition and the right of the applicant to be free of it. And in deciding which right is the stronger, the Tribunal will, like any other court, award expenses against the party who is unsuccessful.

The Tribunal has set out its approach to expenses in *Donnelly and Regan v Mullen*.[1] No expenses are normally due for the period before the objector makes representations, including for the costs of legal research and drawing up the application. But thereafter expenses should follow success, subject to two qualifications.

The first qualification arises from the language of section 103 itself, which directs the Tribunal to have regard to '*the extent* to which the application, or any opposition to the application, is successful'. This is consistent with the usual rule on expenses in a case of divided success. The Tribunal views the qualification in this way:[2]

> We think that this is a reference to the extent of success of the *application* (or the opposition to it) rather than of individual arguments. For example, we do not think it justifies any approach of counting up success in relation to the individual factors listed in section 100, unless some particular chapter or area of evidence and submission (on which the applicant has not been successful) can be identified as having taken up a substantial amount of time. It does, however, clearly seem to permit consideration of the fact that, as quite often happens, an application for discharge is granted only to the extent of variation to enable a particular development to proceed. Objection which has led to such, sometimes very considerable, reduction in the extent of curtailment of the benefited proprietor's rights, clearly has resulted in some success for the objector.

The second qualification – also present in the general law of expenses – is for cases where some aspect of the applicant's conduct is disapproved. The Tribunal

---

1 1 Sept 2006, Lands Tribunal, *Conveyancing 2006* Case (25). The same points were made, often in the same language, in *West Coast Property Developments Ltd v Clarke* 6 Oct 2006, Lands Tribunal.
2 *Donnelly and Regan v Mullen* at p 6 of the transcript.

suggests two examples: failure or delay in setting out clearly the case for the application, and failure to seek agreement, especially before the application is made. In relation to the latter, the Tribunal notes that:[1]

> No hard and fast rules can be laid down as to steps which parties should take in this direction, each case being dependent on its own circumstances. The Tribunal, however, would expect parties to give reasonable consideration to this question, including reasonable consideration of any suggestions by other parties that matters should be discussed.

These principles are exemplified in the main cases so far decided, which are digested in the following table:[2]

Expenses awarded to applicant

Name of case	% of expenses awarded	Reason for reduction
Church of Scotland General Trs v McLaren 10 May 2005	0	Proceedings commenced under the former legislation.
Ord v Mashford 24 Aug 2005	100, but only in respect of the period after which respondents had been made aware that the 2003 Act applied and not the former legislation.	
Donnelly and Regan v Mullen 1 Sept 2006	50	Time spent at hearing on an unconvincing argument.
West Coast Property Developments Ltd v Clarke 6 Oct 2006	70	Awarded variation not discharge; failure to negotiate; late introduction of one argument; unfamiliarity of objectors with new rules.
At.Home Nationwide Ltd v Morris 2007 GWD 31–535	0	Novel and difficult question under new legislation; failure to negotiate prior to application; some of applicant's arguments unsuccessful.
Smith v Prior 2007 GWD 30–523	60	Awarded variation not discharge; failure to discuss with neighbours prior to application.
Brown v Richardson 2007 GWD 38–666	33	Awarded variation not discharge; failure on the question of title to sue.

---

1 At p 7 of the transcript.
2 Mention should also be made of *J & L Leisure Ltd v Shaw* 30 Oct 2006, Lands Tribunal, *Conveyancing 2006* Case (27), in which expenses were sought only by the unsuccessful objector. He was awarded £750 on the basis that (i) he was successful in his claim for compensation, and (ii) a further hearing had been made necessary only because of a late amendment by the applicant.

From these early cases it is possible to draw out three practical points for clients who wish to maximise awards of expenses. First, try to negotiate with likely objectors before filling in an application to the Lands Tribunal. Secondly, make a full and careful application, giving potential objectors proper notice of the arguments which are to be made. And thirdly, ask for variation to the extent of the proposed development rather than a complete discharge. In all probability a complete discharge will be refused,[1] and in asking for more than is eventually received, the recoverable expenses will be reduced.[2]

Compensation

Sometimes the Lands Tribunal is only willing to grant an application for variation or discharge on the basis that the applicant pays compensation to an objector or objectors. The applicant then has a choice between agreeing to pay the compensation fixed by the Tribunal or having the application refused.[3]

Basis

The basis of compensation is unchanged from the former legislation.[4] The two potential heads are:[5]

(a) a sum to compensate for any substantial loss or disadvantage suffered by, as the case may be –
  (i) the owner, as owner of the benefited property; or
  (ii) the holder of the title condition,
in consequence of the discharge;
(b a sum to make up for any effect which the title condition produced, at the time when it was created, in reducing the consideration then paid or made payable for the burdened property.

A potential problem with head (a) is causation. There are two issues, at least. First, there is the question of whether, if the title condition prevented a particular development on the burdened property, the compensation for its discharge should be computed by reference to the loss caused by the whole development. In other words, is the development caused by the discharge? Quite often the answer will be yes. If a real burden prevents the commercial use of the burdened property, and its discharge leads to the construction of, say, a shopping centre, it may reasonably be argued that the loss of amenity due to the shopping centre was 'in consequence of the discharge'. But sometimes the causal connection may be less clear.

---

1 See eg *Smith v Prior* 2007 GWD 30-523 at p 23 of the transcript.
2 As the Lands Tribunal emphasised in *West Coast Property Developments Ltd v Clarke* 6 Oct 2006, at p 16 of the transcript: 'applicants would be well advised to consider carefully exactly how much to ask for in applications'.
3 Title Conditions (Scotland) Act 2003 s 90(9).
4 Conveyancing and Feudal Reform (Scotland) Act 1970 s 1(4). For a discussion, see Sir Crispin Agnew of Lochnaw, *Variation and Discharge of Land Obligations* (1999).
5 TC(S)A 2003 s 90(7).

An example is *George Wimpey East Scotland Ltd v Fleming*.[1] Here the Lands Tribunal allowed the variation of a servitude of way so that the access road was re-routed.[2] As a result, the applicants were able to build 115 houses on their land. The objectors, who owned neighbouring houses, claimed compensation. In the Tribunal's view, however, compensation could not be measured by the loss caused by the 115 new houses. Rather, the only direct consequence of the variation was the, rather minor, re-routing of the access road, and for that no compensation was due. The Tribunal's discussion on this point is worth quoting:[3]

> The respondents contended both in writing and orally that the development itself, because it faced a planning impasse if the access route was not altered, was a consequence of the variation. Although we appreciate the logic, we very much doubt whether this is correct. To compensate a benefited proprietor in respect of enabling the whole development, or even the temporary effect of the construction of the whole development, because the title condition actually impeded the development, seems to us to come close to compensating for loss of a ransom value. It seems to us that the statute provides for compensation for the effect on the benefited proprietor of the discharge or variation itself, not for the effect on him of the development made possible.

Rather puzzlingly, the Tribunal added that:

> The extent of the effect of the discharge or variation will, however, depend on the intention or purpose of the burden.

George Wimpey East Scotland Ltd was a case involving servitudes. As the Tribunal noted, '[t]he situation in relation to discharge, for example, of a building restriction might be different: as soon as the building commences, all the works … might be a consequence of the discharge'.[4] But that, of course, would depend on the terms of the burden which is being discharged. For example, the discharge of a burden which prevented building only on part of the property could not be said to cause any development which took place on other parts of the same property.

Causation also raises a second issue, on which there is as yet no authority. In practice, applications for variation and discharge are often accompanied by a parallel application for planning permission. Does the order in which these consents are obtained affect the measure of compensation which the Tribunal is likely to order? If planning permission is obtained first, it becomes easy to argue that the eventual development takes place 'in consequence of the discharge' of the title condition. But if the discharge comes first, the argument is harder to make. For the discharge, of itself, has no immediate consequences. Nothing is built on the land for the time being, and nothing can be built without planning permission. At the time when the Tribunal is asked to rule on compensation it cannot know whether planning permission will be granted or not, or, if granted, on what terms. The causal connection between discharge and potential development is thus

---

1 2006 SLT (Lands Tr) 59. And see also *West Coast Properties Ltd v Clark* 2007 GWD 29-511.
2 The decision on its merits is reported at 2006 SLT (Lands Tr) 2, and digested as *Conveyancing 2005* Case (12).
3 2006 SLT (Lands Tr) 59 at 64B–D.
4 At 64F.

fairly weak. Of course, in practice developers will often wish to obtain planning permission first – and indeed they are more likely to succeed before the Lands Tribunal if they do so.[1] Nonetheless, a developer who is anxious to reduce liability for compensation might be sensible to delay the planning application.

Temporary loss

Is merely temporary loss recoverable? In many cases the development on the burdened property, once completed, will have little or no effect on the value or enjoyment of the benefited properties; yet during the construction period there may be considerable inconvenience, and indeed a temporary loss in value as represented by rental income. In *George Wimpey East Scotland Ltd v Fleming*[2] it was held that temporary loss was recoverable in principle,[3] but that in practice it would rarely amount to the '*substantial* loss or disadvantage' which the statutory test requires.[4] In that case the owners of 15 houses claimed £4,000 each as compensation for the temporary disruption caused by the works necessary to divert an access road. Unsurprisingly, the Tribunal refused the claim:[5]

> The respondents are clearly going to be 'put upon' to some degree by the construction works affecting the access road. We have no difficulty in describing this as a form of 'disadvantage' which they will suffer as a result of the alteration to the access route. It would be attractive to award them some compensation.... However, on the evidence, and treating the matter simply as a question of degree, we are unable to accept that this disadvantage is 'substantial'. In our judgment, it can really only be regarded as an increase, perhaps quite a large increase, for a period of around one year in the number of times they will be inconvenienced in their use of the access road: something they could no doubt well do without, but not something which would normally attract legal consequences and not something which in our view can properly be characterised as 'substantial'.

The position of objectors

Thus far we have examined the position of a person seeking to have a real burden varied or discharged. But one's sympathies may lie instead with – or at least one's client may come from – the close neighbours who want to stop the alteration or development in its tracks. In all likelihood they have already objected to planning permission, without success. Now they want to use private law where public law has failed.

---

1 This is partly because one of the statutory factors which favours an application before the Tribunal is that 'there is the consent, or deemed consent, of a planning authority, or the consent of some other regulatory authority, for a use which the condition prevents' (TC(S)A 2003 s 100(g)), and partly because an application is more likely to be rejected if the proposed project is still up in the air (*Hamilton v Robertson* 2008 GWD 8-149).

2 2006 SLT (Lands Tr) 59.

3 In reaching this conclusion the Tribunal followed the decision of the House of Lords in *Wildtree Hotels Ltd v Harrow London Borough Council* [2001] 2 AC 1, a case which was concerned with compensation for temporary inconvenience in connection with road construction arising out of compulsory purchase.

4 TC(S)A 2003 s 90(7)(a).

5 2006 SLT (Lands Tr) 59 at 63C–D.

Naturally, the advice given to such a client will depend both on the nature of the burden and on the development or other use which is being proposed by the applicant. All too often, however, the best advice will be to give up. On the evidence of the cases so far, opposition is rarely successful; and where it is unsuccessful, there is likely to be substantial liability in respect of expenses. In those circumstances only a determined client – and one, preferably, with deep pockets – will fight to preserve his amenity.

Title conditions other than real burdens

Finally, it seems worth mentioning that – as with the previous legislation – the Lands Tribunal's jurisdiction is not confined to real burdens but extends to other title conditions, most notably servitudes and conditions in long leases.[1] Under the old law, applications in respect of servitudes were rare and those in respect of leasehold conditions – rather surprisingly – unknown or virtually so.

As it happens, there has been quite a brisk start for servitudes under the 2003 Act. Unlike the position for real burdens, even an undefended application in respect of servitudes requires to be considered on its merits. So far, however, the success rate is 100%:

Servitudes

Name of case	Servitude	Applicant's project in breach of burden	Application granted or refused
George Wimpey East Scotland Ltd v Fleming 2006 SLT (Lands Tr) 2 and 59	1988 disposition. Right of way.	Diversion of right of way to allow major development for residential houses.	Granted (opposed). Claim for compensation for temporary disturbance refused.
Ventureline Ltd 2 Aug 2006	1972 disposition. 'Right to use' certain ground.	Possible redevelopment.	Granted (unopposed).
Graham v Parker 2007 GWD 30-524	1990 feu disposition. Right of way from mid-terraced house over garden of end-terraced house to the street.	Small re-routing of right of way, away from the burdened owner's rear wall, so as to allow an extension to be built.	Granted (opposed).
MacNab v McDowall 24 Oct 2007	1994 feu disposition reserved a servitude of way from the back garden to the front street in favour of two neighbouring houses.	Small re-rerouting, onto the land of one of the neighbours, to allow a rear extension to be built.	Granted (opposed).

---

1 TC(S)A 2003 s 90(1)(a)(i) allows the Tribunal to vary or discharge 'title conditions' – a term which is defined in s 122(1).

LEASES

Pro indiviso shares of leases

In *Stephen v Innes Ker*,[1] Simon Stephen was tenant of a pair of farms, Meikle Geddes and Broomhill, both in Nairn. These farms had passed down the family for some generations. The landlords were 'the Most Noble Sir Guy David Innes Ker, Baronet, Tenth Duke of Roxburghe, the Right Honourable Simon Frederick Marquis, Third Earl of Woolton, and Robert Cheyne Turcan WS (the Trustees of the Cawdor English Marriage Settlement Trust and of the Cawdor Scottish Discretionary Trust'. The tenancies were typical agricultural tenancies, carrying on from year to year by tacit relocation, and protected from termination by the legislation on agricultural tenancies, the main statute currently being the Agricultural Holdings (Scotland) Act 1991. Although the law of agricultural tenancies is something that we do not seek to cover, the case raises issues of general interest.

By way of background, the 1991 Act says that where a tenancy has been inherited by someone who is not a 'near relative' the landlord can, subject to certain qualifications, terminate the tenancy by notice to quit.[2] That does not mean that a non-near-relative transfer is invalid: it merely means that the pro-tenant protective system in the Act will not be available to the transferee. A grandson is not a 'near relative' for these purposes.[3]

At the beginning of the story, in 2003, the position was that Mr Stephen held the tenancy in common with his grandmother, Margaret Stephen. She died in August of that year, and her executors validly transferred her share to Mr Stephen – and thus to someone who was not her 'near relative'.

Lord Justice Clerk Gill noted that 'if Margaret Stephen had held the entire tenancy and if the pursuer had succeeded to it, he would have been defenceless to a notice to quit served in accordance with section 25(2)'.[4] But she was not the sole tenant. The half share that Mr Stephen already held at the time of his grandmother's death was not open to challenge by the landlords (he had inherited it from his mother, and so the 'near relative' test was satisfied).

The landlords decided to respond to the transfer to Mr Stephen by serving notices to quit, one for each farm. In framing them, they faced a drafting problem. A notice to quit (or, in the traditional terminology, a warning to remove) says: 'you are required to remove from all and whole ...'. The landlords could hardly require Mr Stephen to remove himself from the farms as such, given that his right to a one-half share of the lease was beyond question. What they came up with was this: 'You are required to remove from ALL and WHOLE the interest of the late Margaret Stephen in the tenancy of ALL and WHOLE....' In other words, they were seeking the termination of a one-half share of each tenancy.

Mr Stephen replied by raising an action of declarator that he was the lawful continuing tenant of both farms and for reduction of the two notices to quit. He

---

1 [2007] CSIH 42, 2007 SLT 625.
2 Section 25.
3 Agricultural Holdings (Scotland) Act 1991 s 25, sch 2 pt III para 1.
4 Paragraph 25.

succeeded in the Outer House,[1] where the Lord Ordinary held that 'the interest of the late Margaret Stephen' no longer existed: Mr Stephen was sole tenant. The landlords appealed to the Inner House. They were unsuccessful.[2] The court agreed with the Lord Ordinary that there was no longer any such thing as 'the interest of the late Margaret Stephen' in the tenancy.

It was also held that a notice to quit necessarily requires the tenant to remove physically. That is what the statutory form calls for.[3] The notices to quit had not done that. Nor was this a mere quirk of the wording of the statutory style. Lord Gill comments that 'if a tenant fails to comply with a valid notice, the landlord's remedy is to sue for removing. A removing consists of the physical removal of the tenant, by judicial decree'.[4]

An interesting variant on the facts would have been if the grandmother's share had passed not to Mr Stephen but to, say, his brother. In that case the two shares would have remained distinct. The brother would not have been a 'near relative'. Could the landlords have served a valid notice to quit on him? 'Physical removal' would indeed be possible in such a case. However, there is evidence in the decision of an even broader ratio. Lord Gill says that 'the procedure of notice to quit is not available to a landlord in respect of a partial interest in a tenancy'.[5] If that is right, then the brother would be protected.

At this point one may ask what the landlords sought to achieve by the notices to quit. One possibility is that they would have argued that they, as owners, would have been entitled to shared possession together with Mr Stephen, a situation he would doubtless not have relished. Another possibility is that they would have then argued that Mr Stephen would have been reduced to a half-tenancy, and that a half-tenancy is an impossibility, with the result that the whole lease would have been extinguished. There is some basis for this latter argument in *I & H Brown (Kirkton) Ltd v Hutton*.[6] Whilst the idea of half a lease existing, without the other half, is an odd one, it is not necessarily inconceivable, and indeed is arguably presupposed by section 16 of the Succession (Scotland) Act 1964.[7]

Another puzzle: suppose that Oliver owns land and leases it to Lorna for 10 years. Later Oliver grants an interposed lease to Iona for 7 years. When the 7 years are up Oliver will wish to serve on Iona a notice to quit, for otherwise tacit relocation will operate. But how can he serve a notice to quit? How can he require 'physical removal of the tenant'? A notice to quit is trying to do two things. It seeks to extinguish the tenant's right; and it calls on the tenant to do a physical act in consequence of that extinction: to flit. But its wording is limited to the latter.

---

1 [2006] CSOH 66, 2006 SLT 1105, *Conveyancing 2006* Case (67).
2 [2007] CSIH 42, 2007 SLT 625. There is only one judgment, by Lord Justice Clerk Gill, with which Lords Osborne and Wheatley concurred.
3 See Ordinary Cause Rules r 34.6 and form H2. The Summary Cause Rules are to the same effect: r 30.6, form 3a. It is a curious and perhaps unsatisfactory fact that some of the central rules about leases are contained in legislation about civil procedure.
4 Paragraph 32.
5 Paragraph 30.
6 2005 SLT 885. See *Conveyancing 2005* p 100.
7 See *Conveyancing 2005* p 102, doubting one aspect of *I & H Brown (Kirkton) Ltd v Hutton*.

Usually those two things go together like hand and glove but in unusual cases they do not: in unusual cases the landlord wishes to serve a notice terminating the tenancy without necessarily requiring the tenant to do anything. Compare the case of irritancy, where the notice of irritancy keeps the two issues separate: it says both that the lease is at an end and that the lessee is to remove.

When does irritancy terminate a lease?

If a lease is irritated, when does it come to an end? *Maris v Banchory Squash Racquets Club Ltd*[1] clarifies some but not all of the issues.

The lease was for 99 years from Whitsunday 1979 and was recorded in the Register of Sasines on 19 February 1980. The leased area was within hotel grounds owned by the landlords. The lease required the tenant to erect and maintain squash courts and associated buildings. The rent was only £5 per annum, but the tenant had to allow hotel guests to use the squash courts and facilities on the same basis as the members of the club operated by the tenant, whilst the landlords were required to provide facilities within the hotel for booking squash courts and arranging times of play.[2] The lease had an irritancy clause:

> In the event of the Tenants being in breach of any material condition of this lease or failing to pay rent or comply with any material condition of this Lease the same shall be terminated and the subjects shall revert to the Landlords.

In the 1990s it became apparent that the buildings were not being maintained properly. The landlords complained but little was done. Eventually, on 4 November 2003, the landlords served an irritancy notice with schedule of dilapidations. The notice said that if the necessary works were not carried out within three months, the lease would be irritated. The necessary works were not carried out and on 12 February 2004 the landlords raised the present action of declarator and removing. The case went to proof and in January 2006 decree was pronounced in favour of the pursuers. Thus far it seems a humdrum case. But there is a twist. *After* the action had begun, the tenant began to carry out repairs, finishing them in July 2005. Whether the repairs were sufficient is an issue that was not explored, because the landlords argued that whether the repairs were sufficient or not, they were too late, for the lease had already come to an end, in February 2004.

The defender's argument was based on section 5 of the Law Reform (Miscellaneous Provisions) (Scotland) Act 1985, which says that in the case of a non-monetary breach, a landlord can irritate only if 'a fair and reasonable landlord' would irritate in the circumstances in question. The defender argued that 'the time for application of the fair and reasonable landlord test – the *tempus inspiciendum* – is … the time at which the court seised of an action of declarator of irritancy has to decide, at the conclusion of the court procedures, whether

---

1 [2007] CSIH 30, 2007 SC 501, 2007 SLT 447, 2007 Hous LR 54. The opinion of the court was delivered by Lord Eassie.
2 Whether this provision could bind successors of the landlords would be an interesting question. The point did not arise in the case.

declarator of irritancy should be granted or refused'.[1] This argument had been put to the sheriff, who had rejected it, and it fared no better in the Inner House. 'The action of declarator of irritancy is simply a means of establishing judicially that at an earlier date the lease was validly terminated', the court noted.[2] The lease had come to an end in February 2004. The 1985 Act provisions made sense only in the context of a lease which was still in being, for a decision to irritate or not to irritate can be made only in relation to an existent lease.[3] Turning from the technical issue to broader issues of policy, the court noted that any other result would be inconvenient and even unworkable in practice:[4]

> The interpretation advanced by counsel for the defenders and appellants is productive of considerable practical difficulties. It would mean that no one could confidently advise a landlord as to whether he might validly and conclusively terminate a lease on the basis of his tenant's breach of obligations. The respective rights of parties to a lease would not be tested at the moment of termination but would be dependent upon inter alia the vagaries of the length of proceedings in the subsequent action of declarator of irritancy and the potential ability of the tenant to take steps to remedy the breach.

If, on reading this decision, one has the impression that the law in this area is clear and settled, that impression would be a tribute to the clarity and coherence of the court's opinion, but it would nevertheless be – alas – a false impression.

In the first place, although the general rule is that irritancies are not purgeable,[5] that is true only of conventional irritancies, ie those expressly provided for in the lease. Where the landlord invokes a legal irritancy – ie a right to irritate implied by law rather than by the lease – the rule is that the irritancy is purgeable. If it is purgeable that must mean that it cannot take effect from its date. Take an example. Suppose that a valid irritancy notice, founding on a legal irritancy, is served to take effect on 11 November. The tenant refuses to flit and the landlord raises an action of declarator and removing. While that action is proceeding, the tenant purges the irritancy. The lease continues in force. So presumably a legal irritancy takes effect (in the sense of bringing the lease to an end) only on either (a) acceptance by the tenant, whether by flitting or otherwise, or (b) decree. The unworkability factor mentioned by the court in *Maris* would seem to exist here.

In the second place, there is authority that an irritancy can be waived by the landlord. The implications of this fact are more remarkable than may appear at first sight. Suppose that on 1 May a landlord serves a valid irritancy notice to take effect at 11 November. Clearly the landlord could waive the irritancy during that period. But it seems that the landlord can also waive the irritancy *after* 11 November and if that happens the rule is that the lease does not come to an end.

1 Paragraph 9, summarising the case of the defender's counsel.
2 Paragraph 8.
3 Lord Macfadyen, in the unreported case of *Euro Properties Scotland Limited v Alam* 20 June 2000, CSOH, *Conveyancing 2000* Case (41), had said, *obiter*, that post-irritancy events could be relevant for s 5 of the 1985 Act. *Maris* thus disapproves those *dicta*.
4 Paragraph 23.
5 *McDouall's Trs v MacLeod* 1949 SC 593. The rules about feudal irritancies were different.

Thus in *Dean v Freeman*[1] a landlord irritated, seemingly validly. The tenant did not flit and eventually it was agreed that the lease would carry on. It was held that the continuing lease was the original lease, not a novated lease, so that the third party who had guaranteed the rent continued to be bound. That seems to imply that a valid irritancy does not of itself extinguish a lease. That is not easy to reconcile with *Maris*.

In the third place, the leading case in this area, *McDouall's Trs v MacLeod*,[2] is not as clear as might appear. At the end of his opinion Lord Jamieson says that 'the weight of authority is to the effect that a conventional irritancy such as the present cannot be purged by payment, *at least after an action of removing has been raised'*. Thus *McDouall's Trs* in fact offers two possible dates for termination on irritancy: the date specified in the irritancy notice and the date of raising the action of declarator and removing. In the example above, suppose the tenant does not flit and the landlord raises an action of declarator and removing on 15 December. Does the lease end on 11 November or on 15 December? If the tenant can still purge the irritancy on, say, 1 December, that implies that the lease still subsists as at that date, for it is difficult to see how one could purge an irritancy on a non-existent lease.

Fourthly and finally, section 8(1) of the Leasehold Casualties (Scotland) Act 2001 seems to presuppose that where an action for declarator and removing in relation to a conventional irritancy is raised, the lease does not come to an end until 'final decree is pronounced'.

SERVITUDES

Car parking in paradise

Overview

The decision of the House of Lords in *Moncrieff v Jamieson*[3] provides a remarkable end to a remarkable litigation – one which began, in Lerwick Sheriff Court, as long ago as 1998. In the eyes of their Lordships, this was an 'unfortunate case'[4] with a 'prolonged and highly regrettable history',[5] and evidencing 'a regrettable and surely unnecessary falling out between neighbours who had lived as neighbours in apparent amity for very many years'.[6] Only Lord Rodger was unmoved:[7]

---

1 *Dean v Freeman* 2005 CSOH 3, 2005 GWD 9-137; 2005 CSOH 75, *Conveyancing 2005* Case (23). See also A McAllister, *Scottish Law of Leases* (3rd edn 2002) para 5.7.
2 1949 SC 593.
3 [2007] UKHL 42, 2007 SCLR 790, 2007 SLT 989. For first reactions, see D Bartos, 'Advance to free parking? – *Moncrieff v Jamieson*' (2007) 75 *Scottish Law Gazette* 203; R Paisley, 'Clear view' (2007) 52 *Journal of the Law Society of Scotland* Dec / 50.
4 Paragraph 19 *per* Lord Hope.
5 Paragraph 42 *per* Lord Hope.
6 Paragraph 45 *per* Lord Scott.
7 Paragraph 66.

Your Lordships have variously described it as an 'unfortunate case', as a 'sad one' and as an 'unfortunate matter'. The parties are, however, adults and the dispute between them is genuine. Since the point at issue is difficult, it is not surprising that they have been unable to resolve it for themselves. In these circumstances they have simply chosen to exercise their right to have it resolved by the courts. Those on one side have decided to spend their own money on doing so; the Legal Aid Board has financed the other side. As a judge, I would not describe the resulting situation as sad or unfortunate: after all, courts exist and judges are paid to resolve such disputes, which are indeed the life blood of the common law.

The facts cannot be better introduced than by the sheriff who heard the original ten-day proof:[1]

In brief, this case involves a situation which has bitterly divided two sets of neighbours. The physical or geographical situation (ignoring the problems associated with access) can (in fair weather at least) be described as almost idyllic. The pursuers and the first and second defenders are young, nice-looking, married couples each with a young family. Both couples appear pleasant and intelligent and all were for long enough on reasonably good neighbourly terms with one another. The peace of that demi-Eden was shattered when almost out of the blue the defenders started to build a wall which intruded upon the access route to Da (ie 'the' in the Shetland dialect) Store and a turning place where the pursuers had been in the habit of turning or parking their cars. From that all else has followed.

The dispute was between neighbours in Sandsound in Shetland. The pursuers had a number of craves, including declarator, interdict and damages. Property ('Da Store') owned by the pursuers faced the sea and could be reached from the landward side only by a private road running through the third defenders' land.[2] At one time both properties had belonged to the same person, but the pursuers' property was broken off by a disposition in 1973. This conferred 'a right of access from the branch public road through Sandsound'. There was no dispute as to the pursuers' right to use the road itself, for it was accepted that the words were sufficient to create a servitude of vehicular access. Due to a steep fall in the land, it was not possible to take a car from the end of the road on to the pursuers' property, and the road was too narrow for a vehicle to turn. Accordingly, the pursuers' practice was to use part of the defenders' land for turning and parking. For that purpose the pursuers added hardstanding. Matters proceeded amicably until 1998 when, as the sheriff mentioned, the defenders decided to build a wall taking in most of the turning area.

In the end, the dispute between the parties was a narrow one. It was accepted that the pursuers had a servitude of way over the road. It was further accepted that such a servitude was capable of carrying, by implication, certain ancillary rights, and that those rights included, in the present case, a right to use the defenders' land to load and unload and to turn. But what was disputed was

---

1 Sheriff Colin Mackenzie. See 2004 SCLR 135 at 164–165.
2 However, since the case was before the sheriff a new public road has in fact been built to within metres of the pursuers' property, with a turning circle at its terminus.

whether there was also an ancillary right to park. At first instance, the sheriff held that there was such a right and granted decree in favour of the pursuers,[1] and in 2005 this was affirmed by an Extra Division of the Court of Session (Lord Hamilton dissenting).[2] Now the House of Lords has come to the same conclusion, although with more hesitation than might be indicated by a decision which, in the end, was reached unanimously.[3] Along the way, much was said about the creation of ancillary rights, thus giving the case a significance which goes well beyond servitudes of parking. By the time the case reached the House of Lords, the first and second defenders had sold up and so ceased to be the pursuers' neighbours.[4]

As the House of Lords recognised, Scots and English law are close in this area, both drawing on the same Roman law roots.[5] No doubt partly for this reason, the English members of the court showed greater interest than would normally be expected in an appeal on a matter of Scots property law. From a Scottish viewpoint the result is not entirely welcome. The speeches of Lords Scott and Neuberger are replete with English case law, and the former lapses into English terminology and, on occasion, into English law presented as Scots.[6] Lord Scott cites as many cases from Nigeria – one[7] – as from Scotland.[8] By contrast, the two Scottish judges, Lords Hope and Rodger, rely largely on Scottish authority, and at times seem almost to be deciding a different case.[9]

Can parking be a servitude?

Moncrieff v Jamieson faces squarely an issue which, in recent years, has troubled the courts both in Scotland and in England. Is a right to park a car capable of being constituted as a servitude? So far as Scotland is concerned, there are two possible reasons why the answer might be no. One is the problem of the 'fixed' list of permitted servitudes. The other reason – which applies in England also, but under a different name[10] – is the rule that a servitude must not be 'repugnant with ownership'. We consider these in turn.

Traditionally, a right did not qualify as a servitude in Scotland unless it was included in the list of 'known' servitudes, or was reasonably analogous to a servitude on that list. Whilst this rule has now been displaced by section 76 of the

---

1 2004 SCLR 135, discussed in *Conveyancing 2003* pp 68–70.
2 [2005] CSIH 14, 2005 SC 281, 2005 SLT 225, 2005 SCLR 463, discussed in *Conveyancing 2005* pp 93–96.
3 [2007] UKHL 42, 2007 SLT 989.
4 Paragraph 4 *per* Lord Hope.
5 See paras 45 *per* Lord Scott; paras 111, 136 *per* Lord Neuberger. Compare the view of Lord Hamilton when the case was in the Inner House: 2005 SC 281 at para 79.
6 Eg 'appurtenant' (paras 47, 62, 63) and 'in gross' (para 62). For English law, see below.
7 The Nigerian case is a decision of the Judicial Committee of the Privy Council and the Scots a decision of the House of Lords – respectively *Attorney General of Southern Nigeria v John Holt & Co (Liverpool) Ltd* [1915] AC 599 and *Dyce v Hay* (1852) 1 Macq 305. By contrast Lord Scott cited 11 English cases.
8 We owe this thought to Scott Wortley and Roddy Paisley.
9 The final judge, Lord Mance, gave a brief concurring speech (paras 100–104).
10 'Ouster'.

Title Conditions (Scotland) Act 2003 this is only in respect of servitudes created in writing and after 28 November 2004. For other servitudes, including post–2004 servitudes created by prescription, the old rule continues to govern. It governed the servitude created in *Moncrieff*, which dated from 1973. Lord Scott, it seems, was untroubled by this difficulty:[1]

> I can see no reason in principle, subject to a few qualifications, why *any* right of limited use of the land of a neighbour that is of its nature of benefit to the dominant land and its owners from time to time should not be capable of being created as a servitudal right *in rem* appurtenant to the dominant land (see Gale on *Easements*, 17th ed, para 1–35).

But, as the terminology and reference might suggest, this is English law, or at any rate not Scots.[2] It was left to Lord Rodger to investigate the fixed list rule, and to indicate that it will be applied with flexibility and in the light of the needs of modern times.[3]

The issue of 'repugnancy with ownership' troubled the court more. Although the doctrine's name is new – it derives from section 76(2) of the Title Conditions Act, and before that from the law of real burdens – the idea is old and familiar. Necessarily, a servitude restricts the servient owner in the use of his property, but such restriction must not be so severe as to remove most or all of the rights of ownership itself. If a servitude is to be merely a subordinate real right, something must be left to the owner of the affected property. Further, a servitude must retain its own distinctive characteristics and not mutate into a lease or liferent or a real right of some unknown kind. Among the characteristics of a servitude is the characteristic of non-exclusive use: a servitude does not involve 100% occupation of the servient tenement or, at least in the normal case, of any part of that tenement.

On this whole issue there is recent and highly relevant Scottish authority. In *Nationwide Building Society v Walter D Allan*[4] the alleged servitude was a right to park two cars in an area which could accommodate six. The servitude was rejected by Lady Smith as repugnant with ownership. Yet this decision (unlike authorities that, being English, were less relevant) was overlooked by the court in *Moncrieff*.[5] In fact it seems that all or most of the judges in the House of Lords would have taken a different view from Lady Smith. In *Moncrieff* it was common ground that rights of parking would often be perfectly consistent with the residual rights of the owner in the affected area. The most difficult case was where there was a right to park in a dedicated space – as opposed to at any place

---

1 Paragraph 47, our emphasis.
2 Why this should be presented in a Scottish appeal as a statement of Scots law is puzzling and disquieting.
3 Paragraphs 73, 74.
4 2004 GWD 25-539, discussed in *Conveyancing 2004* pp 85–90.
5 *Nationwide* was indeed mentioned, by Lord Hope at para 21, but in a different context. The main English cases considered were: *Wright v Macadam* [1949] 2 KB 744; *Copeland v Greenhalf* [1952] Ch 488; *London & Blenheim Estates Ltd v Ladbroke Retail Parks Ltd* [1992] 1 WLR 1278; *Batchelor v Marlow* [2003] 1 WLR 764. Reference was also made (at para 61) to A Hill-Smith, 'Rights of parking and the ouster principle after *Batchelor v Marlow*' [2007] *Conveyancer* 223.

within a larger area.[1] Admittedly the former would sometimes be less intrusive than the latter, for if the servient proprietor owned a significant area of land, he might often find it more convenient that the right to park should be confined to one small part of it.[2] The difficulty, however, would be that for that one small part, the rights of the servitude holder would greatly exceed those of the owner. Would that matter? Not necessarily, thought the court. Lord Rodger pointed out that certain existing servitudes can involve precisely such 100% occupation – for example, a dam in aquaehaustus or pipes in aquaeductus.[3] Lord Hope said that 'the fact that the servient proprietor is excluded from part of his property is not necessarily inimical to the existence of a servitude'.[4] Lord Scott was impatient that there should be any restriction at all:[5]

> It is impossible to assert that there would be no use that could be made by an owner of land over which he had granted parking rights. He could, for example, build above or under the parking area. He could place advertising hoardings on the walls. Other possible uses can be conjured up. And by what yardstick is it to be decided whether the residual uses of the servient land available to its owner are 'reasonable' or sufficient to save his ownership from being 'illusory'? It is not the uncertainty of the test that, in my opinion, is the main problem. It is the test itself. I do not see why a landowner should not grant rights of a servitudal character over his land to any extent that he wishes.[6]

The other judges would not go so far as Lord Scott. On the facts in *Moncrieff*, the right to park was not confined to a particular space. The court had not been fully addressed on the issue as a whole. A decision was best left for another day.[7] But the overall approach suggests an expansive view of the law of servitudes.

It is time to return to the question with which this section began: is the right to park a car capable of being constituted as a servitude? It must follow from the decision ultimately reached in *Moncrieff* that car parking can be *ancillary* to a servitude right of way. But can car parking also exist as a servitude *on its own*, as where, for example, the parking area is reached by a public road?[8] A majority of their Lordships – Lords Scott, Rodger and Neuberger[9] – considered the answer

---

1 In such a case the dedicated space alone would be the servient tenement: see Lord Scott at para 57.
2 The fact, however, that the unburdened land could be sold separately suggests that this example should not be treated differently from the case where the dedicated space is all that the servient proprietor owns. See *Conveyancing 2004* pp 88–89.
3 Paragraph 76. It had been the same in Roman law: see para 75.
4 Paragraph 24.
5 Paragraph 59.
6 Lord Scott went on to suggest a replacement test, which may possibly make sense in English law but which makes none in Scots: 'I would, for my part, reject the test that asks whether the servient owner is left with any reasonable use of his land, and substitute for it a test which asks whether the servient owner retains possession and, subject to the reasonable exercise of the right in question, control of the servient land.'
7 See in particular Lord Neuberger at paras 143–145.
8 Lord Scott took for granted (at para 49) that, once a road is public, it can be used by anyone without the need for a servitude. On this issue see further *Conveyancing 2006* p 30.
9 Paragraphs 47, 72, 75 and 137.

to be yes; and while the remaining judges (Lords Hope and Mance)[1] thought it unnecessary to reach a view, they too were supportive of the principle of a servitude. In the light of this decision, it must now be accepted that car parking joins the dozen or so rights which comprise the 'known' servitudes in Scots law.[2] Accordingly, a freestanding servitude of parking can be established by any means by which a servitude may be created, and could be so established even before 28 November 2004. This is a welcome clarification.

Two tests for ancillary rights

In the event, *Moncrieff* did not turn on the existence of a freestanding servitude. The main argument of the pursuers, as it had been all along, was that parking was implied into the (express) grant of servitude made in 1973.

Long before *Moncrieff* it had been accepted that ancillary rights could be implied as part of a servitude. But the law was so little developed that there was no agreed test as to the circumstances in which such an implication might arise. Professor Gordon, for example, offers the cautious view that 'it may be possible to imply rights necessary to make the main grant effectual'.[3] Sheriff Cusine and Professor Paisley are more expansive, preferring *'reasonably* necessary' to plain 'necessary' – a qualification derived from a leading decision in England, *Jones v Pritchard*[4] – and even speculating as to whether ancillary rights might sometimes extend to allow works which are no more than 'desirable'.[5]

To some extent this division of views is reflected in the discussion in *Moncrieff*. For Lord Rodger, 'only such rights as are "essential" to its effective operation are to be implied into an express grant of servitude'[6] – a formulation which is drawn, by way of an earlier decision of the House of Lords, *Chalmers Property Investment Co Ltd v Robson*,[7] from Ferguson on the *Law of Water*.[8] It did not find favour with the rest of their Lordships,[9] whose own formulations are notably more generous. According to Lord Hope, ancillary rights are implied wherever they are 'necessary for the convenient and comfortable use and enjoyment of the servitude'.[10] Lord Neuberger thought that ancillary rights were implied if they are 'reasonably necessary' to the servitude's exercise and enjoyment.[11] These formulations come from different sources – Lord Neuberger's from the English case of *Jones v Pritchard*

1 Paragraphs 22, 24 and 102.
2 For an authoritative account, see D J Cusine and R R M Paisley, *Servitudes and Rights of Way* (1998) ch 3.
3 W M Gordon, *Scottish Land Law* (2nd edn 1999) para 24–60.
4 [1908] 1 Ch 630.
5 D J Cusine and R R M Paisley, *Servitudes and Rights of Way* paras 12.124–12.127.
6 Paragraph 86, and see also para 82.
7 Astonishingly, this case has hitherto been known only at the Outer House stage, where it is reported in 1965 SLT 381. But the case later went to the First Division (20 May 1966) and then to the House of Lords (20 June 1967). Neither of the appellate stages was reported.
8 J Ferguson, *The Law of Water and Water Rights in Scotland* (1907) p 264, cited in *Chalmers Property Investment Co* by Lord Guest.
9 Although there was no express disapproval.
10 Paragraph 29.
11 Paragraph 110.

(see above)[1] and Lord Hope's from an adaptation of a well-known passage by Lord Campbell LC in *Cochrane v Ewart*,[2] a case about implied servitudes. Yet they are virtually indistinguishable, the stark requirement of 'necessary' being qualified by 'convenient and comfortable' in one case and by 'reasonably' in the other.[3] In both cases, the qualification is expressly justified in the interests of balance. Lord Neuberger, for example, explained that:[4]

> [I]t seems to me important to focus on the dual nature of the requirement that the alleged implied right be 'reasonably necessary'. Without the necessity, there would be the danger of imposing an uncovenanted burden on the servient owner, based on little more than sympathy for the dominant owner; without the reasonableness, there would be a danger of imposing an unrealistically high hurdle for the dominant owner.

But this is not all. Both Lord Hope and Lord Neuberger would supplement this first test with a second. And, once again, different formulations are used for what is in essence the same thing. Although there is no sign of direct influence, Lord Hope's formulation is the same as that normally used to delimit the scope of a servitude.[5] According to Lord Hope[6] it is necessary that the ancillary rights which are being claimed

> may be considered to have been in contemplation at the time of the grant, having regard to what the dominant proprietor might reasonably be expected to do in the exercise of his right to convenient and comfortable use of the property.... Activities that may reasonably be expected to take place in the future may be taken into account as well as those that were taking place at the time of the grant. So the fact that very little, if any, use was being made of the servient tenement at that time for the parking of vehicles cannot be taken as an indication that the need to park vehicles there when Da Store became habitable cannot have been in contemplation.[7]

In part this was a response to the argument, based on *Cochrane v Ewart*, that a right cannot be implied unless it is being exercised at the time of severance of the properties.[8] But, as Lord Neuberger seems to suggest in his own version of the test, a test along these lines is the scarcely avoidable result of taking implied rights seriously. For if the ancillary rights are to be explained as being implied

---

1 Although acknowledging that this was English law, Lord Neuberger noted that it had been approved by Cusine and Paisley, and continued (para 111): 'It would be surprising if that were not the law of Scotland. It accords with good sense, and it is a point on which one would not expect Scots and English law to differ.' If the reasoning employed here has more than a whiff of the nineteenth century, the result, at least, is perfectly acceptable.
2 (1861) 4 Macq 117 at 122–123. In addition, Lord Hope cites *Jones v Pritchard* with approval (at para 29).
3 Paragraph 112 *per* Lord Neuberger.
4 Paragraph 112. And see also Lord Hope at para 29.
5 Ie the base line from which any increase in the burden is to be measured. See Cusine and Paisley, *Servitudes and Rights of Way* para 12.187.
6 Paragraph 30.
7 See also Lord Scott at para 52: 'what the parties must, if they had thought about it, have had in mind ...'.
8 Paragraph 30.

into the original grant of servitude, then they must have been within the sights of the parties at that time:[1]

> In fact, it appears to me that these two types of case[2] are no more than examples of the application of a general and well established principle which applies to contracts, whether relating to grants of land or other arrangements. That principle is that the law will imply a term into a contract, where, in the light of the terms of the contract and the facts known to the parties at the time of the contract, such a term would have been regarded as reasonably necessary or obvious to the parties.

It seems unlikely that this second test was properly established in the previous law. If that is correct, *Moncrieff* has changed the law. In effect it means that reasonable necessity (the first test) is to be judged, not by current circumstances, but by the circumstances which obtained at the time the servitude was created. On the whole the change is unwelcome. On the one hand, the justification for the test – that parties should not be signed up to things which they could not have predicted or wished – does not seem particularly strong in the case of rights which are merely ancillary in nature. On the other hand, the test is undeniably awkward in practice. The older a servitude, the more difficult it will be to say what rights the parties might have had in contemplation, or to admit rights of a kind which are made necessary only by modern technological developments.[3] As Cusine and Paisley note, 'a party can anticipate only what is reasonably foreseeable and he is not endowed with a faculty of clairvoyance'.[4] The effect of the second test is to rein in the first, and in a manner which is not especially desirable. In our view it would have been better to break altogether with the attribution of intention to the original parties and to provide a neutral rule to the effect that a servitude, once created (and however created), carries such ancillary rights as are, *at any given point in time*, reasonably necessary for its exercise.[5] This approach would carry other advantages as well. It would provide a means of adding ancillary rights to servitudes created by prescription, where there is no grant (or reservation) into which such rights could be implied.[6] And it would avoid the possibility, considered below, that less can be implied where a servitude was created by reservation rather than by grant.

The analysis in *Moncrieff* is, however, to be welcomed. It provides, for the first time, a stable and reasonably clear set of rules for deciding when ancillary rights can be added to servitudes. And these rules are not confined to the highly unusual facts of *Moncrieff* but apply to all types of servitude and to all types of ancillary right. They will be of particular assistance in determining the legality

---

1 Paragraph 113.
2 The other type was the creation of a servitude by implication.
3 Lord Neuberger (at para 128) offers the uncertain thought that, in deciding what was implied, it might be permissible to take account of events occurring *after* the grant.
4 Cusine and Paisley, *Servitudes and Rights of Way* para 12.187.
5 That may have been Bell's approach: see *Principles* s 985.
6 It is, however, possible that prescriptive servitudes also contain ancillary rights, although on what legal principle is unclear.

of improvements to roads by the holder of a servitude of way. The rules will also help with drafting. Of course, in drawing up a servitude, conveyancers will continue to make express mention of such ancillary rights as seem likely to be needed, for in that way future argument is avoided. But there will now be the comfort that things which have been overlooked, or not anticipated, may yet be considered to be part of the servitude.

The House of Lords' decision on this point may be put into a broader context. As the law has developed, implied terms are now resorted to in three different ways in relation to servitudes. First, a servitude may be impliedly granted or reserved as part of the deed which effects the separation of two properties. That is the principle of *Cochrane v Ewart*[1] and cases like it.[2] Secondly, the scope of a servitude once created – the question whether, for example, a servitude allows vehicular access as well as pedestrian, or whether it places limitations on the volume of traffic to be carried – is determined by whatever terms can be implied into the original grant or reservation.[3] And thirdly, and following the decision in *Moncrieff*, the grant or reservation of the principal right may be supplemented by rights which are ancillary in nature. As the table which follows shows, however, the rules are far from being the same:

Implied rights in relation to servitudes

Type of implication	Requirements	Reservation treated less favourably than grant?
Existence of servitude	(1) Use at time of severance. (2) Necessary for convenient enjoyment of dominant tenement.	Yes
Scope of servitude	(1) Use at time of severance or ordinary and reasonable.[4] (2) Reasonable contemplation of the parties at time of creation of servitude.	?
Ancillary rights	(1) Necessary for convenient enjoyment of servitude. (2) Reasonable contemplation of the parties at time of creation of servitude.	?

---

1 (1861) 4 Macq 117.
2 In *Moncrieff* this was suggested as an alternative basis for the creation of parking rights, given that such rights (unlike the rights which are typically ancillary to a servitude) could themselves exist as a freestanding servitude. See in particular para 52 *per* Lord Scott. A difficulty not mentioned by Lord Scott is that there was no prior use, as was said to be necessary in *Cochrane*.
3 Obviously, this rule and the next cannot apply to servitudes created by prescription.
4 This is the formulation found in Hume, *Lectures* III, 272. But Bell would push the bar higher, requiring that the scope be for the 'necessary use' of the dominant tenement: see *Principles* s 986. As Cusine and Paisley observe (*Servitudes and Rights of Way* para 12.187), the proper test 'remains strangely unstated in the relevant authorities'.

The impression given is of three sets of rules which, while close in both subject matter and theoretical underpinning, have grown up with little reference to one another. Of course, the differences can often be justified. For example, the test for ancillary rights is what is necessary for the convenient enjoyment of the *servitude* and not, as with the creation of the servitude itself, for the convenient enjoyment of the *dominant tenement*.[1] But not everything is so easily explained. Why, for example, does the ancillary right include things not yet done but within the reasonable contemplation of the parties while the principal right insists on actual use at the time of severance?[2] And why must an ancillary right be necessary for the convenient enjoyment of the servitude whereas the equivalent test in respect of scope focuses on use which is ordinary and reasonable? This whole area is in need of re-thinking.

One other matter is worthy of mention. In the *creation* of servitudes it is a long-established rule that it is harder to imply servitudes by reservation (ie in favour of the granter of the deed) than by grant (ie in favour of the grantee). This is because of the principle that a granter is not to derogate from his grant by withholding rights.[3] We have no wish to see this unattractive rule extended.[4] Nonetheless, if it applies in relation to one implied term of a deed, it is hard to see why it should not apply to others.[5] *Moncrieff* was a case in which a servitude was *granted* in the disposition; but had the servitude been created by *reservation* rather than by grant, it is possible that the result would have been different – that, in other words, the House of Lords' willingness to find an implied *grant* of a right to park would have evaporated if the issue had been one of implied *reservation*.

Applying the tests: was parking an ancillary right?

Having identified the appropriate tests for ancillary rights, the House of Lords then proceeded to apply them to the facts as found by the sheriff. From the same set of facts, different members of the court drew strikingly different conclusions. For Lord Hope, as for the courts below, the physical circumstances were such that it was inevitable that a right of parking should be implied:[6]

> For the owners, use of their own vehicles would involve walking a distance of about 150 yards, in all weathers and in times of darkness as well as in daylight, over what the sheriff has described as a significantly steep descent or climb in open and exposed country. In the case of a mother with very young children, for example, this would mean leaving them unattended and unsupervised in the house while parking or collecting her vehicle, or alternatively taking her children with her on foot in such conditions to and from the place where she had to park her vehicle. Owners who had no

---

1 Sometimes these will amount to much the same thing: see para 52 *per* Lord Scott.
2 As to whether use at severance is always implied in the creation of servitudes, see Cusine and Paisley, *Servitudes and Rights of Way* para 8.18.
3 Cusine and Paisley, *Servitudes and Rights of Way* para 8.19.
4 For a discussion, see *Conveyancing 2005* pp 89–92.
5 In the passage from para 113 quoted earlier, Lord Scott emphasises the unity of the doctrine of implied rights.
6 Paragraph 34.

difficulty in driving but found walking difficult because they were disabled or elderly would have to do this too, as the restriction on parking for which the defenders argue applies to everyone.... In my opinion it is impossible to reconcile such hardships with the use that might reasonably have been expected to be made of the servitude right of vehicular access for the convenient and comfortable use of the property. It would mean, as Lord Philip said in the Extra Division, para 90, that the proprietor's right of vehicular access would effectively be defeated.

In a judgment which in places came close to a dissent, Lord Rodger – whose own test for implying rights was, it will be recalled, notably severe – took a quite different view of the facts. The pursuers' position, in his opinion, was no different from that of countless other people:[1]

Especially in cities, there are many flats or houses without any adjacent land on which cars can be parked. That feature is often a significant factor for people when deciding whether to buy the flats or houses and, if so, at what price. Those who own such properties can get to them by car, but are very familiar with the need to drop off their shopping and passengers before trekking off to search for a resident's parking space some streets away. Those with young children and no one to watch them have to take the children to the parking place and then trail them back home, whether up or down a steep hill, whether through icy rain or in blistering sun. These are simply the inevitable everyday consequences of the owners' decision to buy the house or flat in question.... Unlike your Lordships, I am, accordingly, utterly unmoved by the supposedly intolerable sufferings of owners of Da Store who might face that dire modern dilemma of leaving their children unsupervised or taking them on foot, back and forward, up or down a significant slope in open and exposed country.[2]

If a property was unsuitable, its owners had only themselves to blame for buying it. That was no basis for demanding additional rights from the sellers:[3]

[U]nless by specific agreement, the seller of a house does not warrant that it is suitable for occupation by any particular type of person who he foresees may want to buy the property. If, for instance, he is selling a flat at the top of a four storey block with no lift, he gives no warranty that it will suit a couple with young children. So parents of young children have only themselves to blame if they buy the flat and then find that they cannot stand the hassle of hauling a baby, a buggy, a fractious older child, a dog and shopping up four flights of stairs. Similarly, an elderly couple cannot complain if they buy a house at the top of a steep hill and then find that they cannot manage the walk up from the bus stop. Houses or flats which are suitable at one stage in our lives may be quite unsuitable at a different stage. If a house turns out to be unsuitable,

---

1 Paragraphs 85, 86.
2 To this Lord Hope countered (at para 34) that: 'The situation in this case ... is far removed from the urban situation to which Lord Rodger refers where people who buy flats or houses without adjacent car parking just have to put up with it.'
3 Paragraph 68. And see also para 86: 'Even if, when granting the servitude of access to Mrs Stuart back in 1973, Mr Georgeson foresaw the tribulations of future car owners with elderly parents and young children, he was no more obliged to provide an access that would be suitable for them than he was obliged to provide a house that would be suitable for them. Purchasers, who know their own requirements, have to think for themselves.'

we cannot blame the seller. It is no business of his. Our only remedy is to move to somewhere that is suitable.

Lord Neuberger, too, was sceptical:[1]

I have real doubts as to whether the sheriff was correct to hold that the expressly granted servitude in this case could not reasonably be enjoyed without there being a right to park. It seems to me that there is force in the argument that the servitude could be fully enjoyed without there being such a right: its enjoyment would merely be of more limited value to the owner and occupier of Da Store.

But he was prepared to accept that the combination of factors found in the present case might be sufficient for parking rights to be implied.[2] For his part, Lord Rodger was also 'prepared to yield' to the sheriff's view of the facts.[3] Thus it was that the right to park cars was finally won. There are unlikely to be many other such cases. Throughout the speeches, it was emphasised that the circumstances in *Moncrieff* were 'particular and unusual'[4] being based on 'unusual topography'[5] and amounting to 'unusual facts';[6] and while one result of the decision will be to raise the profile of ancillary rights in general, their use for matters such as car parking is likely, in Lord Neuberger's words, to be viewed as 'a questionable extension'.[7]

Avoiding extinction: *res merae facultatis*

The general idea

Neglect leads to extinction: a servitude which lies unexercised for 20 years is brought to an end by the long negative prescription.[8] The doctrine of negative prescription is, however, subject to an exception for 'any right exercisable as a *res merae facultatis*'.[9] This statutory lapse into Latin is instructive. On the one hand, rights *res merae facultatis*[10] were exempt from prescription under the law which the 1973 Prescription Act replaced. On the other hand, no one was – or is – sure what, precisely, is encompassed within the term. Leaving the term untranslated was thus a convenient way of leaving the law unchanged without confronting the problem of what that law actually was.

---

1 Paragraph 125.
2 Paragraph 127. Lord Neuberger saw these as 'hybrid' rights – rights which were justified partly as reasonably necessary for the enjoyment of the servitude and partly as reasonably necessary for the enjoyment of the dominant tenement itself. No indication is given as to which of the six factors that Lord Neuberger identified can be attributed to one rather than the other, or why.
3 Paragraph 98.
4 Paragraph 36 *per* Lord Hope.
5 Paragraph 101 *per* Lord Mance.
6 Paragraph 124 *per* Lord Neuberger.
7 Paragraph 125.
8 Prescription and Limitation (Scotland) Act 1973 s 8.
9 PL(S)A 1973 sch 3 para (c).
10 The usage is convenient as long as one recognises that, as a matter of literal translation from the Latin, 'right' and '*res*' cannot be placed side by side without intervening words. Thus it is that the statute talks of rights 'exercisable' as a *res merae facultatis*.

In his book on *Prescription and Limitation* (1999), David Johnston gives a detailed analysis of the authorities on rights *res merae facultatis* before concluding that:[1]

> a *res merae facultatis* is a property right which cannot be lost by negative prescription either (1) because it is a right whose exercise implies no claim on anyone else or against their rights or (2) because it is a (normal) incident of ownership which can be lost only as a consequence of the fortification in some other person of a right inconsistent with it.

Since a servitude does not fall into either of these categories, it is tempting to conclude that the exception does not apply to servitudes. Admittedly, that conclusion is at odds with the decision of the First Division in *Smith v Stewart*,[2] but this rather obscure case is usually thought of as having been wrongly decided or, to say the same thing more politely, special on its facts. Rankine, for example, describes *Smith* as 'a narrow case',[3] while Johnston states bluntly that servitudes 'clearly prescribe and so cannot be *res merae facultatis*, although sometimes the borderline between a servitude right and a right *res merae facultatis* may be difficult to draw'.[4] Johnston adds, in a footnote, that *Smith* is 'better regarded as servitude since it relates to another's property', thus implying that the case is mis-classified and wrongly decided.

Peart v Legge

A new case, *Peart v Legge*,[5] has now brought *Smith v Stewart* into unexpected prominence. And although the court in *Peart* was unenthusiastic about the *res merae facultatis* exception, and found the means of distinguishing *Smith*, the method of reasoning which it adopted seems more likely to promote the exception than to keep it in check.

Peart v Legge concerned land at Newbattle in Midlothian. By a disposition recorded in 1981 the Marquis of Lothian conveyed a plot of land together with

> a right of access to said piece of ground by the lane or track leading from the Eskbank/ Newtongrange road to the northwest side of the said piece of ground as the same is shown coloured blue on said plan but subject to the provisions that the disponee shall be entitled to breach the existing wall on the northwest boundary of the said piece of ground only subject to the approval of me and my successors as adjoining proprietors of making good the wall where necessary and inserting gates or doors of a form and type satisfactory to me and my foresaids all of which and the maintenance of the same shall be done at the sole expense of the disponee and his foresaids.

Subsequently this plot came to belong to the defender. By a disposition recorded in the Register of Sasines in 1997 the Marquis of Lothian disponed a different plot to the pursuers. Included in that plot was the lane over which

---

1 Paragraph 3.16.
2 (1884) 11 R 921.
3 J Rankine, *Landownership* (4th edn 1909) p 440.
4 D Johnston, *Prescription and Limitation* (1999) para 3.18(3).
5 [2007] CSIH 70, 2007 SLT 982.

access rights had been created in 1981. As the 1981 deed indicates, the defender's plot was separated from the lane by a wall so that the lane could not be used for access unless or until a gap in the wall had been created. No gap was made, and the right over the lane went unexercised for a period which exceeded 20 years. In these circumstances the pursuers sought a declarator that the servitude over the lane had been extinguished by negative prescription.

These facts were uncannily close to those of *Smith v Stewart*. In *Smith*, too, a wall prevented the use of the road, and the grant of servitude likewise provided for the wall to be breached. At first instance in *Peart*, the sheriff concluded that *Smith* was binding on him and found for the defender.[1] As in *Smith*, prescription was held to be excluded by the doctrine of *res merae facultatis*. On appeal, the sheriff principal reached the same view, although 'not without hesitation'.[2] On further appeal, an Extra Division of the Court of Session has now decided that *Smith* can be distinguished and that the pursuers should prevail.[3]

The Extra Division began by seeking to define a *res merae facultatis*. This was 'a right which may be asserted whenever the proprietor pleases without the risk of losing it through prescription'.[4] Such a definition, the court conceded, did little to identify which rights fell within its scope. For that, further criteria must be found:[5]

> The true scope of the category[6] encompasses any right the inherent nature of which is that it is intended to continue to subsist whether its possessor chooses to exercise it or not. The ordinary incidents of ownership are an example of that category. Their nature, as rights intended to subsist whether exercised or not, derives from the general law of property. Another example of the category can be found, however, in rights which acquire their nature not from the general law, but from the terms of the instrument by which they are constituted. *Smith* can be seen as an illustration of that example; the factors on which Lord President Inglis founded in characterising the right in that case as a *res merae facultatis* were to be found 'contemplated and implied in the words of the bond'.

Armed with this explanation, the court proceeded to compare the facts of *Peart* with those of *Smith*. Although there were obvious similarities, there were also, the court said, important differences. The servitude in *Smith*, read carefully, contained a number of pointers to the fact that the right was not to be exercised at once. In *Peart*, however, there was only the requirement to breach the wall. In the opinion of the Extra Division, that was not enough to qualify as *res merae facultatis*:[7]

---

1 2006 GWD 18-377.
2 2007 SCLR 86 at para 21 per Sheriff Principal Edward F Bowen QC. For a discussion of this decision, see: *Conveyancing 2006* pp 128–131; R R M Paisley, 'Right to make roads and *res merae facultatis*' (2007) 11 *Edinburgh Law Review* 95.
3 [2007] CSIH 70, 2007 SLT 982. The opinion of the court was given by Lord Macfadyen.
4 Paragraph 25.
5 Paragraph 26.
6 Perhaps surprisingly, the court saw this as an expansion of the second of the two categories identified by David Johnston and quoted above.
7 Paragraph 27.

We do not think that the mere fact that the creation of the access required the breaking open of a gap in the wall by itself supported the implication that the right of access was only to be exercised at some indeterminate date in the future. If that were so, any new right of access which involved work to make it useable (whether the making of a gap in an existing wall, or the laying of a suitable surface to bear the contemplated traffic) would convert a servitude into a *res merae facultatis.*

It is possible to question how different the facts of the two cases really were. But the court was evidently intent on reining in the *res merae facultatis* exception:[1]

In interpreting the terms of the grant, it is in our opinion right in principle to construe the exception to the general rule in s 8 constituted by para (c) of Sch 3 narrowly. We are not prepared to hold that every servitude which, in order to be exercised, requires work to be done to open a gap in a wall or other boundary structure, or otherwise to render the servient tenement fit for the exercise of the right, is on that account to be regarded as indicating that the right is intended to subsist whether exercised or not until such indefinite future time as the dominant proprietor may choose to carry out the works.

We have considerable sympathy with this approach. Exemption from prescription requires strong justification. The decision, in our view, is correct and to be welcomed. But the court's reasoning may give rise to unwelcome consequences.

Contracting out of prescription

Insofar as there was previously an agreed interpretation of *Smith v Stewart*, it was that the *res merae facultatis* exception applied only where the dominant proprietor had significant building work to perform before the servitude could be used. Such a requirement was no doubt illogical, but it had the merit of keeping the exception in check. That requirement has now been removed. Instead it appears that everything depends on the words used to create the servitude. The result is a shift towards party autonomy in an area of law where such autonomy would not be expected. It is a fundamental principle, enshrined in section 13 of the Prescription and Limitation (Scotland) Act 1973, that parties cannot contract out of prescription. Yet the decision in *Peart* seems to allow the same result by other means. For if parties wish to ensure that a servitude lasts for ever, all they have to do, it seems, is to provide that 'the right is intended to subsist whether exercised or not'. After all, an *express* statement to that effect could hardly be less effective than its *implied* cousin which the Extra Division managed to tease out of the clause in *Smith*. Further, there is nothing in *Peart* to suggest that this new liberality is confined to servitudes. On the contrary, the Extra Division would apply the same rule to all 'rights which acquire their nature ... from the terms of the instrument by which they are constituted'.[2] So to prescription-free servitudes can potentially be added prescription-free contracts, leases, and securities. In attempting to limit the *res merae facultatis* exception, the Extra Division may have greatly increased its scope. The prospect is not attractive.

---

237 Paragraph 28.
238 Paragraph 26.

Postponing starts

There is a difference between a servitude which is *res merae facultatis* and an 'ordinary' servitude in which the start happens to be postponed. The first is a right which can be exercised, or not exercised, as the dominant proprietor chooses. The second is a right which cannot be exercised at all until the moment for commencement arrives. The consequences for prescription are different too: while the former can never prescribe,[1] prescription for the latter will potentially begin on the date when the servitude becomes live.[2] This distinction, clear enough in principle, is muddied by the approach taken in *Peart v Legge*. Although a right *res merae facultatis* was described by the court as one 'which may be asserted whenever the proprietor pleases',[3] in practice the emphasis was on the postponing of its start. In order for the servitude in *Peart* to be *res merae facultatis*, the court said, the deed must indicate 'that the right was not to be exercised at once, but was to subsist until exercised at an indefinite future date to be chosen by the proprietor of the dominant tenement'.[4] What, then, is the difference between a servitude *res merae facultatis* and one which merely has a postponed start? The answer, it is suggested, lies in who has power to do the starting. As the words just quoted indicate, a servitude is *res merae facultatis* if the power to begin lies with the dominant proprietor. Conversely, if commencement is determined in some other way – for example, at the election of the servient proprietor or on a fixed date – this is merely an ordinary servitude, which is subject to the ordinary rules of prescription.

The emphasis on postponed starts in *Peart* invites one final question. What happens when the dominant proprietor starts using the servitude? Does it remain a servitude *res merae facultatis*, forever exempt from the ravages of prescription? Or does it become an 'ordinary' servitude which will be lost if not exercised for 20 years. The logic of *res merae facultatis* would suggest the former; the discussion in *Peart* seems to hint at the latter.[5] If the latter is correct, there is little difference between a servitude *res merae facultatis* (at least of this kind) and an 'ordinary' servitude in which the start is postponed.

Servitudes in the land registration system

Introduction

Yaxley v Glen[6] is the latest case on a disputed question about how servitudes work in the Land Register. Before we get to *Yaxley* itself, some background is needed.

---

1 Subject to what is said in the next paragraph.
2 Under s 8(1) of the Prescription and Limitation (Scotland) Act 1973, prescription begins to run 'after the date when any right to which this section applies has become exercisable or enforceable'.
3 Paragraph 25.
4 Paragraph 28.
5 Thus at para 28 it is said that, to qualify as *res merae facultatis*, the servitude must indicate 'that the right is intended to subsist whether exercised or not *until* such indefinite future time as the dominant proprietor may choose to carry out the works'. This suggests that, once the works are carried out, the dominant proprietor needs to exercise the servitude.
6 [2007] CSOH 90, 2007 SLT 756, 2007 Hous LR 59.

How does the Land Register deal with servitudes? As far as the dominant property is concerned, a servitude is a benefit, a pertinent, and so it will appear (if it appears at all) in the A Section (Property Section) of the title sheet. As far as the servient property is concerned, a servitude is not a benefit but an encumbrance, and so it will appear (if it appears at all) in the D Section (Burdens Section). Because servitudes are classified by the legislation as 'overriding interests',[1] their validity does not depend on whether they do or do not appear in the D Section of the servient property.

There are thus four types of case, all of which are possible under the current legislation. (1) The first is that the servitude appears in the dominant title sheet but not in the servient one. (2) The second is that it appears in the servient title sheet but not in the dominant one. (3) The third is that it appears in both. (4) The fourth is that it appears in neither. A chart shows the four cases.

	Dominant Title Sheet	Servient Title Sheet
1	Appears (as an A Section pertinent)	Does not appear
2	Does not appear	Appears (as a D Section encumbrance)
3	Appears (as an A Section pertinent)	Appears (as a D Section encumbrance)
4	Does not appear	Does not appear

Evidently, the ideal is (3), and for servitudes that are created consensually after Martinmas 2004, (3) is compulsory.[2] But servitudes created before Martinmas 2004 – which is to say the large majority – can fall under (1), (2), (3) or (4). And even since Martinmas 2004, (3) does not apply to pipe/cable servitudes[3] or to servitudes constituted by prescription.

Actually, this chart is only the beginning of the difficulties. There are further dimensions. One is that a servitude can appear in the Land Register as a result of (i) registration, or (ii) entering or (iii) noting, and these can have different preconditions and different consequences.[4] A second is that there can be more than one servient property, as where a servitude of way crosses two or three distinct plots of land, with some of the servient title sheets disclosing the servitude but not others. A third is that one or other of the properties may not yet be in the Land Register.

Suppose a property comes in to the Keeper for first registration, and that in the pertinents clause of the Sasine title there is the following:

---

1 Land Registration (Scotland) Act 1979 s 28(1).
2 Title Conditions (Scotland) Act 2003 s 75.
3 TC(S)A 2003 s 75(3)(b).
4 See the analysis in the Scottish Law Commission's Discussion Paper on *Land Registration: Miscellaneous Issues* (Scot Law Com DP 130, 2005; available at www.scotlawcom.gov.uk) part 4. 'Noting' is competent only in relation to the servient title sheet, while 'entering' is competent only in relation to the dominant title sheet.

together with a servitude of way for all necessary purposes from the said subjects to the Kirkcudbright/Thurso road, along the south margin of the field known as Murder Acre.

On first registration this clause will tend to be carried forward into the A Section of the title sheet – even, sometimes, where the servitude to which it refers is not valid. And in practice this will be case (1), ie there will be no matching entry on the servient title sheet.

While invalid servitudes can enter the Land Register for more than one reason, the commonest, as in the above example, is on the first registration of the (allegedly) dominant property. Of course, if a servitude appears as a pertinent in the Sasine titles, it will in most cases be a valid servitude anyway. But not always. Conveyancers do sometimes try to upgrade their client's position by slipping in a wished-for pertinent. Often such an addition merely reflects a servitude that in fact already exists, eg because of prescription. But if it does not, it is invalid: a neighbour cannot boot-strap a servitude into existence.

What happens if an invalid servitude appears in the Register?

What happens if the Keeper enters an invalid servitude in the A Section of the allegedly dominant property? In the Sasine system a void servitude is a void servitude, and the fact that it appears in a recorded deed makes no difference. But in the Land Register, the Keeper has the 'Midas touch'. Everything (or almost everything) that he touches turns to gold. Title flows from the Register. If the Blackmains title sheet says that Blackmains enjoys a servitude right of way over Whitemains, then such a right necessarily exists.[1] Thus take this story: in 1990 Ruth dispones Blackmains to Serafina, and the disposition is recorded in the Register of Sasines. At that time no servitude exists over Whitemains, but nevertheless in this 1990 deed words are slipped into the pertinents clause asserting (falsely) the existence of such a servitude. In 2008 Serafina dispones to Tom. This is a first registration. If the Keeper fails to pick up its suspect history, the servitude will be entered in the A Section, and the Midas touch does the rest: a void servitude has been converted into a subsisting servitude.

The result, of course, is an 'inaccuracy' on the Register. If it can be rectified, then the owner of Whitemains will not suffer in the long run, though in the short run there is likely to be some unpleasantness. Equally, if it is rectified, Tom is likely to be unhappy. He bought Blackmains in good faith, and if the benefit of the servitude vanishes, that may be a real problem for him. The same would be true of anyone who bought from Tom in reliance on a servitude which, after all, was entered on the Register. In principle (i) if Tom keeps the servitude, the owner of Whitemains will be compensated by the Keeper,[2] and (ii) if Tom does not keep

---

1 Land Registration (Scotland) Act 1979 s 3(1)(a). The converse is not true. If the Whitemains title sheet says that Whitemains is encumbered by a servitude in favour of Blackmains, but the Blackmains title sheet is silent, the servitude may be good or it may not.

2 LR(S)A 1979 s 12(1)(b).

the servitude, he will be compensated by the Keeper.[1] So whichever party loses the 'mud' will end up with the 'money'. Land registration is a fairy tale in which there are only happy endings. That, at least, is the theory. In practice there can still be cases where someone ends up with neither mud nor money. And anyway, in real life people usually prefer mud to money. But here we will say no more about indemnity.

Can there be rectification?

The Land Registration (Scotland) Act 1979 says that, where there is an inaccuracy, there should be rectification, except where there should not be.[2] An inaccuracy cannot normally[3] be rectified if such rectification would be to the prejudice of a 'proprietor in possession'. The idea that the Keeper can know that his Register is inaccurate but be compelled by law to ensure that it remains inaccurate seems odd to the layperson – and not just to the layperson – but that is an issue that will not be pursued here.[4]

The 1979 Act does not explain what it means by a 'proprietor in possession'. Uncertainty has existed about both nouns. Is 'proprietor' to be taken literally, to mean someone who owns the land, thus excluding those with subordinate real rights? Or can it extend to the holders of such lesser rights? If so, which? And what does 'possession' mean? In particular, does it mean only natural possession, or does it take in civil possession as well? The main case on these issues, *Kaur v Singh*,[5] decided that 'proprietor' does not include a heritable creditor, and therefore, by implication, the holders of subordinate real rights.[6]

Now consider the Blackmains case. If the owner of Whitemains seeks rectification, by deleting the servitude from the A Section of Tom's title sheet, what will happen? There is no doubt that the entry is an inaccuracy. But can Tom successfully argue that he is a 'proprietor in possession'? He is probably not 'proprietor' *of the servitude*, given what was said in *Kaur*. Does that mean that he has no defence against rectification? Not necessarily. As proprietor in possession *of Blackmains*, he can argue that the statutory protection of the 'proprietor in possession' extends to the pertinents of that property, at least if they are possessed. Pertinents such as servitudes are not independent rights. They are accessory rights which cannot exist without their principal – here, Blackmains. A property and its pertinents are, it may be argued, a *unum quid*. On that view, to remove a pertinent by rectification would be to prejudice a proprietor in possession.

---

1 LR(S)A 1979 s 12(1)(a).
2 LR(S)A 1979 s 9.
3 There are exceptions, such as where the inaccuracy was caused by the fault of the person in question.
4 The Scottish Law Commission has proposed that *all* inaccuracies should be rectifiable, but that in some cases an inaccurate entry should be deemed to become an accurate one. See Discussion Paper on *Registration, Rectification and Indemnity* (Scot Law Com DP No 128, 2005) proposal 24.
5 1999 SC 180.
6 Other than long leases, which are treated by the 1979 Act as being similar to ownership. See G L Gretton and K G C Reid, *Conveyancing* (3rd edn 2004) paras 8–08, 8–15.

There are thus two conflicting arguments. One is that Tom's servitude is unprotected by the 'proprietor in possession' defence, because Tom is not proprietor of the servitude. The other is that Tom's servitude is protected by the 'proprietor in possession' defence, because the servitude is merely an accessory of the property itself, and Tom is proprietor of the property. Which is right?

The earlier case law

Before 2007, the issue had been considered twice. The first case was *Mutch v Mavisbank Properties Ltd*,[1] where, although the sheriff did not have to decide the point, the view was expressed that in our example Tom would have the 'proprietor in possession' defence. The second was *Griffiths v The Keeper of the Registers*[2] in which the Lands Tribunal reached the opposite conclusion.

Yaxley v Glen

There is now a new case. The events of *Yaxley v Glen*[3] were fairly similar to the story of Blackmains and Whitemains. A property in Fife, a former mill, was developed, and sold off in four units. Mr Yaxley was the buyer of two units, acquiring them in 1993 and 1994. His units were collectively called 'The Mill'. Since Fife became an operational county only in 1995, his two titles were recorded in the Register of Sasines. The other two units were 'The Stables' and 'The Granary'. They were sold off later, the titles being registered in the Land Register. One or other or both (the report is not easy to follow in this connection) dispositions contained, in the pertinents clause, a servitude of way. The route of this servitude included ground that was part of The Mill. The Keeper inserted the servitude in the A Section. Mr Yaxley did not give his consent, nor was there any mention of such a servitude in the 1993 and 1994 dispositions in favour of Mr Yaxley.

Eventually Mr Yaxley raised an action seeking reduction of the disposition of the other property, insofar as it purported to grant a servitude over his land, and rectification of the title sheet to remove the servitude from the A Section.[4] The defenders argued that they were proprietors in possession and that accordingly the servitude could not be deleted from the title sheet.

The Lord Ordinary[5] considered both *Mutch* and *Griffiths*, and came to the conclusion that the former was the better approach:[6]

> The servitude appears in the property section of that title sheet and it is that title sheet the pursuers seek to have rectified, by deletion of the servitude. In my view the second defender is a proprietor within the meaning used in *Kaur v Singh* as 'an owner of land

---

1 2002 SLT (Sh Ct) 91 See *Conveyancing 2002* pp 85–86.
2 20 Dec 2002, Lands Tribunal, unreported but available at www.lands-tribunal-scotland.org.uk/register.html. See *Conveyancing 2003* pp 88–91.
3 [2007] CSOH 90, 2007 SLT 756.
4 Of The Stables or of The Granary or both; this is unclear but it makes no difference to the point of law.
5 Lady Dorrian.
6 Paragraphs 46, 47.

who is in possession'. The fact that a servitude is capable of forming a separate interest in land is beside the point: it is the second defender's ownership of the benefited land which is the critical issue. As the owner in possession of land which is benefited by a servitude she is a person who may be prejudiced by its removal and in my opinion she comes within the category of a 'proprietor in possession' for the purposes of s 9(3). Such an interpretation is consistent with the principle behind s 9(3) that an innocent registered proprietor who is in possession should not be disturbed in that enjoyment save in very limited circumstances.

As the person registered as entitled to the interest in 'The Stables' there is vested in her, by virtue of s 3(1)(a) of the [Land Registration (Scotland)] Act, a real right in and to that interest and in and to any right, pertinent or servitude forming part of that interest. The servitude is part of that interest in land. She is proprietor of her whole right and for these purposes that includes the servitude. The servitude is not in any real sense separate from the main interest. The concept of a servitude of this kind as intrinsic to the rights of the proprietor of the dominant tenement clearly does not apply to a heritable security which does not run with the land in the same way. A heritable security is a separate interest which does not depend to any extent on possession of the land in question. The second defender cannot in my view simply be considered to be someone who possesses the servitude as a separate interest in land in the way of the holder of a heritable security. Possession of the dominant tenement, along with use of the servitude adhering to it, is sufficient possession for the purpose of s 9. It seems entirely in keeping with the policy of the Act that a servitude necessary for the enjoyment of the land should attract the protection of s 9(3).

This is a reasonable approach. But it can also be said that the position of the Lands Tribunal in *Griffiths* was also reasonable. In truth, this is a question that the 1979 Act neither answers nor gives the means of answering. Whether the question is approached as a technical one, or as one of policy, one gets no clear answer.[1]

But *Yaxley*, though reasonable, has the unfortunate effect of leaving the law in doubt. Had the Lord Ordinary taken the same approach as the Lands Tribunal in *Griffiths*, the law could have been regarded as fairly settled, and the remarks of the sheriff in *Mutch* ignored as mere *obiter dicta*. But now there is a conflict between two first-instance courts.

The Scottish Law Commission project

A review of land registration law is being undertaken by the Scottish Law Commission. Three discussion papers have appeared,[2] and the final report is due either late in 2008 or early in 2009. It is expected that the report will recommend that the 1979 Act should be repealed and replaced. That is, however, less dramatic than it sounds. As far as users are concerned – and as far as the staff at the Registers of Scotland are concerned – the system will continue very much as

---

1 For a discussion, see C Anderson, 'Servitudes, the Land Register and the proprietor in possession' 2007 SLT (News) 275. The Scottish Law Commission, in its review of the law of land registration, inclines to an approach that is comparable to that taken by the Lord Ordinary in *Yaxley*: see Discussion Paper No 128, proposal 11.
2 *Void and Voidable Titles* (DP No 125, 2004); *Registration, Rectification and Indemnity* (DP No 128, 2005); *Miscellaneous Issues* (DP No 130, 2005). All are available at www.scotlawcom.gov.uk.

at present. The Land Register will continue to exist. Its form will continue to be the present form, with title sheets divided into four sections. There will still be first registrations and thus a continued gradual expansion of the extent of registered land. Titles will still be guaranteed. Where there is an inaccuracy, innocent parties will still be protected by the Keeper's indemnity. Relatively speaking, practitioners will be little affected, although there will of course be some changes of significance. The Law Commission sees the exercise as one of taking out a prototype engine (the 1979 Act) and inserting a more developed one which should deliver better performance and enhanced reliability, while leaving the driver's controls almost wholly unchanged. The benefits of the modern land registration system will thus be preserved.

ACCESS RIGHTS

Mrs Gloag's garden

Overview

Ann Gloag, well-known as the 'Stagecoach tycoon',[1] is the owner of Kinfauns Castle in Perthshire. This is a large mansion, built in the 1820s, and set in 23 acres of grounds. In the summer of 2005 Mrs Gloag erected a wire fence, some six feet in height and topped with barbed wire, round a part of her property comprising (i) the Castle itself (ii) the immediate garden, and (iii) an area of woodland. The total area involved appears to have been about 11 acres. One effect of erecting the fence was to prevent members of the public from walking in the areas in question.

Mrs Gloag's action met with opposition. For example, on 9 February 2006 – the anniversary of the statutory access rights coming into force – the Ramblers' Association held a press conference at the gates of Kinfauns Castle with the purpose of challenging the fence. Chic Nash, the chairman of Ramblers' Scotland, was quoting as saying:[2]

> Ann Gloag is trying to stop public access to a superb area of native woodland and specimen conifers of national significance. Here is the best location in Scotland to see swamp cypress and to see the giant sequoia and coast redwood growing side by side. These are national assets to be enjoyed by the public, not hidden away in a private kingdom. We want to know why the new land reform legislation has allowed Ann Gloag to get away with this insensitive action.

The land reform legislation in question was of course part 1 of the Land Reform (Scotland) Act 2003 which confers access rights on the public in respect of most land in Scotland.[3]

Section 28(1)(a) of that Act allows a summary application to be made to the sheriff for a declaration that certain land is not land in respect of which access

---

1 At least according to the BBC News on 12 June 2007.
2 www.ramblers.org.uk/scotland/accessN/press/kinfauns-righttoroaml-feb06.html.
3 Land Reform (Scotland) Act 2003 s 1. For an account of the legislation, by Alan Barr and Andrew J M Steven, see *Conveyancing 2003* pp 131–141.

rights are exercisable, and in June 2006 Mrs Gloag made an application under this provision. The application was opposed both by Perth and Kinross Council and by the Ramblers' Association. At issue was the meaning of what may be termed the 'privacy exemption' in the 2003 Act. While in principle access rights are exercisable over *all* land, certain types of land, listed in section 6, are exempt. The privacy exemption is set out in section 6(1)(b)(iv), and makes provision for houses, caravans, tents and other places affording a person privacy or shelter. As to houses the provision reads:[1]

> The land in respect of which access rights are not exercisable is land which comprises in relation to a house sufficient adjacent land to enable persons living there to have reasonable measures of privacy in that house and to ensure that their enjoyment of that house is not unreasonably disturbed.

The question to be determined by the court was, how much land was needed to provide reasonable privacy for and undisturbed enjoyment of Kinfauns Castle. Mrs Gloag argued for the full extent of the area within the new fence. The Council and the Ramblers' Association were, it seems, willing to concede the whole of the garden proper (an area of several acres) but none of the woodland. In effect, the sheriff[2] was being invited to choose between two rival lines on the map – lines that were often 5 to 7 metres apart.[3] On 12 June 2007, after a proof which included a site visit, the sheriff issued a decision finding in favour of the lines drawn by Mrs Gloag: see *Gloag v Perth & Kinross Council*.[4]

The case attracted a great deal of press interest and, as might be expected, the sheriff's decision was controversial. Sarah Boyack, a Labour MSP, obtained a parliamentary debate on a motion which was strongly critical of the decision:

> That the Parliament is concerned about the decision by Perth Sheriff Court to grant a declarator to Ann Gloag, owner of the Kinfauns Castle estate, which has the effect of denying the statutory right to roam over parts of the estate that was previously allowed under the Land Reform (Scotland) Act 2003; notes that Perth and Kinross Council and the Ramblers' Association opposed the declarator and gave evidence to the court that such a declarator would be contrary to the intention of the Act; believes that this decision undermines the clear will of the Parliament which legislated for the widest possible access to the countryside and that the court judgment ignores the significance of the Scottish Outdoor Access Code approved by MSPs to accompany and inform the operation of the Land Reform (Scotland) Act 2003, and considers that the judgment should be examined and appropriate action taken to give proper effect to the land reform legislation and, if necessary, guidance issued to the courts on the status of the access code.

The debate, on 12 September 2007,[5] gave rise to the expression of a range of views on a range of subjects. The sheriff's decision was attacked, but also defended

---

1 For ease of understanding we have removed the words which apply only to caravans and other like places.
2 Sheriff Michael John Fletcher.
3 2007 SCLR 530 at para 59.
4 2007 SCLR 530.
5 Scottish Parliament, *Official Report* cols 1653 ff (12 Sept 2007).

as in the following passage from Murdo Fraser, a solicitor and Conservative MSP:[1]

> In a parliamentary democracy such as ours, we in the legislature pass laws, and we rely on the courts to interpret them. To do that, we must have faith in the ability of the courts. Other members have already made the point that we have a mechanism for appeals to higher courts, to try to reach judgment on difficult circumstances.
>
> I accept that it is quite proper for a Parliament to look again at legislation if it feels that a pattern of court judgments is developing that goes against the intention of legislators at the time the Act was passed, but I find it ludicrous that we should propose a review of the situation after one judgment – which, for that matter, was made in a sheriff court, sets no precedent and against which no appeal has been made. It is far too early for such a move.

In view of the controversy, an appeal might have been expected, but in the event there was none, and on 7 July 2008 expenses – a hardly believable £200,000 according to some reports – were awarded against Perth and Kinross Council and the Ramblers' Association. Mrs Gloag immediately announced that the sum would be given to charity.

The Access Code

So far as public comment was concerned, the most controversial aspect of the decision was its treatment of the Scottish Outdoor Access Code.[2] The Access Code has this to say about the privacy exemption:

> 3.14 [T]he Land Reform (Scotland) Act 2003 states that you cannot exercise access rights on 'sufficient adjacent land' next to a house (this also includes a caravan, tent or other place affording a person privacy or shelter). This means land sufficient to allow those living there to have reasonable measures of privacy and to ensure that their enjoyment of their house is not unreasonably disturbed. There are two important things to remember:
>
> - you cannot exercise access rights in this area of 'sufficient adjacent land' and so you need to be able to identify such areas; and
> - when exercising access rights close to a house or a garden, you need to respect the privacy and peace of people living there.
>
> 3.15 'Sufficient adjacent land' is defined in this Code as normally being the garden around someone's house. For most houses, this should be reasonably obvious on the ground: a formal garden next to the house and surrounded by a wall, hedge or fence. Some houses might have no garden at all or be located right next to a road, track or path. In some cases, the garden might be near to the house but not adjoining it or it might be more difficult to identify, perhaps because there is no obvious boundary such as a wall, fence or hedge. Things to look out for in judging whether an area of land close to a house is a garden or not include:
>
> - a clear boundary, such as a wall, fence, hedge or constructed bank, or a natural boundary like a river, stream or loch;

---

1 Column 1670.
2 Available at www.outdooraccess-scotland.com/default.asp?nPageID=26.

- a lawn or other area of short mown grass;
- flowerbeds and tended shrubs, paving and water features;
- sheds, glasshouses and summer houses;
- vegetable and fruit gardens (often walled but sometimes well away from houses).

3.16 Some larger houses are surrounded by quite large areas of land referred to as the 'policies' of the house. These are usually areas of grassland, parkland or woodland. Here, too, you will need to make a judgment in the light of the particular circumstances. Parts of the policies may be intensively managed for the domestic enjoyment of the house and include lawns, flowerbeds, paths, seats, sheds, water features and summer houses. Access rights would not extend to these intensively managed areas. The wider, less intensively managed parts of the policies, such as grassland and woodlands, whether enclosed or not, would not be classed as a garden and so access rights can be exercised. In these areas of grassland, parkland or woodland, you can also exercise access rights along driveways, except where the ground becomes a garden, and pass by gatehouses and other buildings.

This account of the exemption neatly encapsulates the dispute between the parties. Mrs Gloag argued for garden plus some of the woodland. The Council and the Ramblers' Association argued for garden only. Admittedly, in what seemed to the sheriff an artificial means of strengthening her position, Mrs Gloag had erected swings and other garden toys in a corner of one of the woods.[1] The woodland paths were also being restored. Nonetheless, if the Access Code's definition was binding, it was difficult to see how Mrs Gloag could succeed.

The sheriff decided that the Code was not binding. He was right to do so. The Land Reform Act is clear that the Code is for 'guidance' only.[2] Although the Code required the approval of Scottish Ministers and of Parliament, it is not itself legislation. As the Code makes clear:[3]

> Although the Code provides guidance on access rights and responsibilities, it is not an authoritative statement of the law. Only the courts can provide this.

Furthermore, as the sheriff pointed out, the Act[4] confines the Code's ambit to advice as to *how* – and not *where* – access rights can be exercised:[5]

> On examination it is clear that the Code is to give help and guidance on the one hand to the people taking access and on the other hand to those over whose land access is to be taken as to how to act responsibly in relation to the rights given by the Act. Importantly, in this context, there is no mention of the Code being a tool for

---

1 Suspicion was particularly aroused due to the fact that they were out of sight of both the house and the garden. At para 6 the sheriff said: 'I came to the conclusion that it was more likely than not that the children's play equipment had been sited where it was purely for the purposes of this action, to make it appear that more privacy was required in the woodland area than might otherwise have been expected.'
2 Land Reform (Scotland) Act 2003 s 10(1).
3 Paragraph 1.5.
4 LR(S)A 2003 s 10(1).
5 Paragraph 35.

the interpretation of any other part of the Act and in particular of section 6. Indeed, looking at the terms of the Code it is clear that it is prepared as a practical guide to the taking or giving of access rather than an aid to interpretation of one of the exceptions to the rights given in the Act.

That is just as well, for the account in the Code of the privacy exemption is inaccurate and bears little relation to the relevant legislative provision. No doubt there are sound practical reasons for the Code's emphasis on whether or not land is 'intensively managed'. A good citizen will not walk over someone else's lawn, and the Code would like to make good citizens of us all. But that is not the approach of the legislation. As the sheriff observed: 'Any suggestion that the nature of the ground itself should be decisive as to whether the land should be excluded from the rights of access is in my view misconceived.'[1] Under the Act, land is exempt from access rights to the extent reasonably necessary for privacy and lack of disturbance.[2] Current or future use of that land is irrelevant. If it were otherwise, Mrs Gloag could exclude members of the public from the entire estate of 23 acres – and not merely from the 11 acres requested – by the simple (if expensive) expedient of maintaining it as lawn.

Large gardens for large houses

Although a number of factors contributed to the ultimate result,[3] the heart of the sheriff's reasoning seems to lie in the following passage from his opinion:[4]

> I agree with counsel for the pursuer that the evidence in this case shows that persons living in a house of this kind located as it is in the country, would consider that their enjoyment of that house would be considerably reduced if the house was not located in reasonably large grounds which were private. I think one can take from the evidence and applying judicial knowledge and common sense, that persons capable of and interested in purchasing a house of the kind which is the subject of these proceedings as their own private house would not consider doing so if the house itself and its grounds, and by that I mean a substantial area round the house, were not able to be used by them privately.

In other words: the owners of large houses want large, and private, gardens. And so, no doubt, they do. There may be much to be said for allowing this wish to be fulfilled. But what this has to do with section 6(1)(b)(iv) of the Land Reform Act is perhaps less clear.

It is true that in the sentence which immediately follows, the sheriff links up these sentiments with the wording of that provision:

> The reasonable person would consider that reasonable measures of privacy for that house and sufficient adjacent land to secure that the enjoyment of the house was not unreasonably disturbed would require a reasonably substantial area of ground.

---

1 Paragraph 36.
2 LR(S)A 2003 s 6(1)(b)(iv) quoted earlier.
3 And are discussed later.
4 Paragraph 47.

But the linkage seems forced, for enjoyment reasonably free from disturbance is not at all the same thing as enjoyment in the abstract.[1]

There is also a more fundamental difficulty. The sentence just quoted is as close as the sheriff comes to explaining the proposition that large houses should have large gardens which are free from access rights. Yet this is assertion rather than justification, and the case for conceding greater privacy to large houses than to small seems not to be made.

Of course, it is possible to think of arguments which might tend in that direction. As the sheriff says elsewhere in his judgment, the owners of large houses tend to have possessions of value and hence to be an attractive target for thieves.[2] They may also be prominent people – like Mrs Gloag – and so subject to unwelcome interest from the public and the mass media. One might add that comparisons with suburban houses are apt to mislead. If the garden of a mansion house is many times the size of a suburban garden, it should not be assumed that the latter affords sufficient privacy and freedom from disturbance. It is simply the best that can be obtained in the circumstances, and if owners of mansion houses can do better, that does not mean that they have more land than they need for the purposes of reasonable privacy. Finally, 11 acres is perhaps a less extensive area than might at first appear. A perfect circle whose area is 11 acres has a radius of only about 119 metres, which is less privacy than many would wish for. Since the fenced-off area was not a perfect circle with the house in the middle, it follows that the distance from house to fence will often have been less than 119 metres. It is noteworthy that, as already mentioned, the disagreement between the parties concerned a distance of only 5 to 7 metres. These different factors have a certain cumulative power; but whether they are sufficient to justify the 11 acres allowed in *Gloag* is a matter on which further discussion seems needed.

Mr Morris' ramble

A key witness on behalf of the Ramblers' Association was its Scottish Director, Dave Morris. Mr Morris was one of a number of witnesses to give 'effusive evidence' as to the success of the Land Reform Act so far, and in particular to the fact that '95 per cent of those taking access did so in a responsible way'.[3] By implication, Mrs Gloag would have nothing to fear from the presence of members of the public in her woods. At the same time, Mr Morris gave a detailed account of his own ramble within the fenced-off area at Kinfauns Castle. The sheriff takes up the story:[4]

---

1 In the next paragraph, the sheriff returns to his original theme: 'Applying that judicial knowledge generally to this case one, I think, can come to the conclusion that the average reasonable person purchasing a house of this kind would consider that quite a large area of ground would be required to be sufficient for the enjoyment of the house, and that would include such things as the lawns and the gardens of the house as well as, in my opinion, areas of the woodland immediately surrounding the gardens, especially when these woodlands are developed in a way to allow paths to crisscross them and steps to be built in them, and considering that they can be used according to the evidence for children to play in.' See also para 58.
2 Paragraphs 52–55.
3 Paragraph 17.
4 Paragraphs 19, 20.

He described an episode in which he attended at Kinfauns Castle to investigate the suggestion that rights of access were being obstructed by the erection of a fence put up by the pursuer. He explained that he attended at that Castle and made his way round the fence for some distance until he arrived at the main gate. As he did so the gate opened, probably not to facilitate his entry, but he took the opportunity to go in. At that point the ground consists of a tarmac driveway bounded on both sides by short cultivated grassland which could, I think, reasonably be described as a lawn. As he made his way into the gate a Land Rover could be seen coming from the direction of the Castle and the driver of that vehicle stopped and spoke to him. He explained his purpose in being there and indicated that he was intending to walk through the grounds for the purpose of trying to come to a conclusion as to whether rights of access were being impeded. The driver of the Land Rover asked him to leave the premises, probably more than once, but the conversation between them was entirely civilised with no raised voices and was conducted in a polite manner. Mr Morris indicated that he firmly but politely indicated that, despite being asked to leave the premises, he was going to continue with his walk through the grounds and the driver of the Land Rover indicated something along the lines he would have to do something about that and drove off back to the Castle.

Mr Morris then set off on his expedition walking round the edge of the lawn as demonstrated on the plan by him and round what has been described in the evidence as the horseshoe area to the south west and then at some stage noticed a police car arriving in the back gate of the Castle, so he immediately began to traverse the garden area near where there is an ornamental stream, a small bridge and some cultivated flowerbeds towards the police officers. The car contained two police officers who spoke to Mr Morris. He explained his purpose in being in the premises. He claimed to be operating in terms of the new legislation. The police officers indicated they were aware of the existence of the legislation but did not claim to have a detailed knowledge of its terms. At some stage Mr Morris asked if they had a copy of the Code and when they explained that they did not he proffered one for their future use, explaining he had plenty of them. He informed the police officers that he was of the view that any dispute between him and the land manager was a civil dispute, implying, if not specifically saying, that it had nothing to do with them, which dispute arose in terms of the new legislation. In the meantime another police car arrived at the scene with two further police officers who joined in the discussion. It was agreed by the police officers that the matter was a civil dispute and they intended to take no action in relation to Mr Morris other than to request him to give them his full name and address and other details, and then they made their way to the Castle itself. Mr Morris of course was not aware of what the police officers told those in the Castle but he assumed that they told them that the matter was a civil dispute which did not concern them (the police officers). He then finished his business at the Castle and made his way back across the edge of the lawn and when he arrived back at the main gate, coincidentally, the gate opened to allow others to pass through and he made his exit.

That there was a certain tension between this story and the assertions of responsible walking was not lost on the sheriff:[1]

In some ways that evidence was rather surprising considering what Mr Morris had said about the majority of access takers. He had indicated that 95 per cent of such people

---

1 Paragraph 21.

follow the Code. Yet he himself had taken access across land in the teeth of opposition by the land manager which he was acutely aware was land excluded from the right of access by the legislation, and very certainly by the very document which he had handed over to police officers. Not only was he not exercising access responsibly in terms of the Code he was exercising access over land which he knew was excluded from the right of access contained in the legislation in circumstances when he had specifically been requested to leave. Matters become worse, however, because when the police officers arrived, in circumstances where prior to the legislation no doubt they would have simply asked him to leave, they were informed by him that it was not a criminal matter for them but a civil matter and they fell for it, when in truth he was probably creating a breach of the peace by refusing to leave when requested to do so in circumstances where he was exercising a right of access which he knew did not exist. In short he had chosen to ignore the very legislation that he was complimenting because it suited his purpose.

'If', the sheriff added, 'that were the way the Act is put into effect by a person such as the Director of the Ramblers' Association what can one expect of others whose experience of the Code and workings of the Act is much less developed?'[1] In those circumstances the sheriff 'found the evidence of those who indicated that it was appropriate to assume that the high ideals of the Act would be followed by the vast majority of persons who took access to land to be rather naïve'.[2]

Some further matters

Apart from what has already been said, three further aspects of the sheriff's approach seem worth mentioning. In the first place, the sheriff saw his task as being to fix the boundaries of an area sufficient to afford reasonable privacy and to ensure that enjoyment was not unreasonably disturbed. This meant rejecting any attempt to balance the interests of owner and general public, even if that might be the correct approach in respect of other parts of the Act.[3] Equally, it meant ignoring article 8 of the European Convention on Human Rights and so eschewing the artificiality of trying to read the statutory provision in a way which favoured the owner; for as it was conceded that the Act was ECHR-compliant, all that remained to be done was to apply it properly.[4]

Secondly, while a certain amount of evidence was led about Mrs Gloag (although she did not herself give evidence), it was accepted that the extent of exempt land must be viewed objectively, without reference to the needs of particular owners. Otherwise the size of the exempt land would change from owner to owner. The correct test, the sheriff said, was the needs of a fictitious reasonable occupant – 'the man (or woman) with the Chelsea tractor'.[5]

Finally, though less convincingly, the sheriff gave some weight to the fact that the new fence followed the line of an earlier wall or fence:[6]

---

1 Paragraph 22.
2 Paragraph 23.
3 Paragraphs 39–42.
4 Paragraph 65.
5 Paragraph 45.
6 Paragraph 56.

When one is trying to assess what is sufficient land adjacent to the house to afford reasonable measures of privacy in the house, and to ensure the enjoyment of the persons living there is not unreasonably disturbed, it seems to me to be not unreasonable to take into account the boundaries established by persons not influenced in any way by the new rights created by Parliament in relation to access across private property, at least as an adminicle of evidence.

Yet it is not clear why evidence of what a predecessor wanted, and achieved, by way of a private enclosure should be a guide as to what an owner is now entitled to under the Land Reform Act. One of the purposes of that Act was precisely to disturb the *status quo*.

Conclusion

It is not necessary to agree with everything which was said by the sheriff in *Gloag v Perth & Kinross Council* to regard the decision as a thorough and accomplished first attempt at applying vague and difficult provisions to a particular set of facts. Much in the sheriff's approach is likely to be accepted without question in later cases. But on the most important question of all – whether privacy can really be used to justify excluding the public from the 11 acres fenced off at Kinfauns Castle – there seem grounds for questioning the sheriff's reasoning.

In the immediate aftermath of the decision, Dave Morris (whose solo ramble was recounted earlier) commented that:[1]

> This gives the green light to landowners to go around the countryside erecting fences without planning permission. This is a very serious adverse judgment and may in fact undermine all of the intentions of the land reform legislation.

This verdict seems unduly pessimistic. Whether it turns out to have any truth in it will depend on the course of future litigation. The next case on the privacy exception is indeed already with us: at the time of writing, *Snowie v Stirling Council* had been at avizandum in Stirling Sheriff Court since 5 November 2007.[2] It will be covered in the annual volume for 2008.

Feddonhill Wood and the horse riders

The *Tuley* case

Tuley v Highland Council[3] is, like the *Gloag* case, about the right to roam, and at first glance it seems, like the *Gloag* case, to be a 'where' case. In fact it is a 'how' case, and, as will be seen, differs from the *Gloag* case quite dramatically in its facts. We quote from the sheriff's[4] fifth finding in fact:

---

1 http://news.bbc.co.uk/1/hi/scotland/tayside_and_central/6746067.stm. The reference to planning permission is because Mrs Gloag originally erected the fence without obtaining such permission, an omission which was subsequently rectified. It need hardly be stated that the sheriff's decision does *not* give 'the green light' to erecting fences without planning permission.
2 See www.scotways.com/news/detail.php?newsid=115.
3 2007 SLT (Sh Ct) 97.
4 Sheriff A L Macfadyen.

Since acquiring Feddonhill Wood the pursuers[1] have developed it as an amenity and recreational area. They have created an area for use by mountain bikers within the woodland. They have actively encouraged walkers, including walkers with dogs both on and off the lead to use the woodland. The woodland is used by members of the public for recreational walking. The pursuers have incurred time and expense in making various tracks in the woodland suitable for walkers. They have kept the tracks clear and well drained. They have cultivated flora and provided seats for walkers.

A sense of unreality settles over the reader. Here are landowners who seem to be doing everything they can to encourage access to their woodland, at considerable and apparently uncompensated expense to themselves. One imagines that not many landowners have acted in such a remarkably altruistic and public-spirited manner. Nor was this a last-minute conversion. The Tuleys had owned the woodland – Feddonhill Wood, near Fortrose in Ross-shire – since 1992 and had always had this commendable outlook. One might have thought that if any landowners would be the targets of right-to-roam litigation it would not be the Tuleys. Their mistake was to decide that one particular path was unsuitable for horse riding.

Next door there was a riding establishment (Broomhill Farm) with between 60 and 70 horses. The Tuleys welcomed horse riders to the southern part of their woodland, but not to the northern part, and they padlocked the two gates at each end of the main path there, called the 'red path'.[2] At the side of the padlocked gates, between the gates and the fence, was a gap wide enough for walkers but too narrow for horses. It was this path, the red path, that was in dispute. It seems that nobody was proposing horse-riding on other tracks within the northern part of the wood. The Tuleys wished to keep horses out of the red path because they thought it unsuitable: riding would cause the path to deteriorate, churning it into mud and causing erosion, and thus, among other things, making it difficult or impassable for all but the most robust walkers.

Under the Land Reform (Scotland) Act 2003 local authorities have both the power and the duty to enforce access rights.[3] Highland Council took the view that riding should be allowed along the red path, and served an order on the Tuleys requiring them to unlock the gates. The present action was an application to the court for a recall of the Council's order.

'The right to exercise access', said the sheriff, 'is in respect of all land in Scotland unless the right cannot be exercised responsibly or the land in question is excepted from the application of the Act. In the present case, the pursuers' argument was based only on the first of those exceptions.'[4] In other words, the Tuleys were not seeking to exclude the red path on the basis that it was not within the scope of the right to roam (which had been the point at issue in the *Gloag* case). They accepted

---

1 The owners, Mr and Mrs Tuley, were appealing against the order made by the local authority that they should unlock certain gates.
2 The wood was divided by a private roadway called the 'black track' and it seems that this had a fence on each side. Broomhill Farm had a servitude along the black track.
3 Land Reform (Scotland) Act 2003 s 13.
4 Paragraph 107.

– more than accepted, positively asserted – that it was indeed within the scope of public access rights, but argued that the physical nature of the ground meant that 'responsible' access could be satisfied on two legs but not on four. Thus this was a case not on the *existence* of access rights in a particular place (the 'where' question, that is the concern of section 1 of the Act) but on the *mode of exercise* of such rights in a particular place (the 'how' question that is the concern of section 2). It is the first such decision to be given by the courts.

The Tuleys were unsuccessful.[1] The sheriff heard extensive evidence as to the likely effect of horse riding on the red track. His main findings in fact were:

27. In the event of regular exposure of the red path to horse traffic throughout the year the following consequences will ensue. Horse traffic on the red path will cause a progressive deterioration on the steepest sections of the path primarily by cutting of the surface, reduced water infiltration and ultimately soil erosion. On other parts of the red path where the gradient is effectively flat, the present fragile (ie barely surviving under human foot traffic at present) cover of grass (which exists in some places) will be damaged and lost from the path. In other flat areas where no grass is present, the surface will become more compact and very likely to suffer from reduced water infiltration and hence soil erosion will occur. The presence of grass on parts of the path makes it very suitable for walkers and horses alike, but the presence of horses will cause a progressive degradation of the path to the detriment of its long-term suitability as a woodland path.

28. The use of the red track by about ten horses on several days each week would occasion those consequences.

29. Those consequences will not ensue in the event of light horse traffic on the red path.

In short, very light usage would not be a problem, but medium or heavy usage would be. Since very light usage would not be a problem, it would be 'responsible' and hence the pursuers could not lawfully prevent it. And yet by excluding *all* riding, they *were* preventing it. Hence they were preventing responsible access. That was unlawful. The sheriff commented:[2]

The pursuers have a genuine apprehension. However, in my view, their remedy lies in co-operation with the defenders in the erection of signs warning horse riders not to enter the network of paths to the north of the red path at any time and warning against riding in weather or soil conditions when the creation of mud is an obvious risk of the presence of horses on the red path.

How reassuring that will be to the Tuleys one may wonder. If, despite notices, the condition of the path deteriorates as a result of excessive use, precisely who is it who is exercising the access rights irresponsibly? Are the early-morning riders guiltless and the evening riders irresponsible? Or the other way round? And would the Tuleys be entitled at *that* stage to padlock the gates?

---

1 However, on 9 August 2007 the sheriff decided that the defender was only entitled to two thirds of the taxed expenses. He explained: '[T]he testing of the effect of the legislation is likely to be of more general use to the defenders that the pursuers. The pursuers were acting in good faith.'
2 Paragraph 126.

Aftermath

An appeal has been lodged and has, we understand, been set down for hearing by the Court of Session in December 2008. After the sheriff's decision, the *Inverness Courier*[1] quoted Mr Tuley as saying: 'I have already stopped maintaining the paths and if they get blocked, tough, so be it.... In future, fallen trees will be allowed to provide a more attractive woodland for the wildlife including red squirrels and woodpeckers.' He had previously intended creating more paths for walkers and mountain bikers but now he had 'no intention of wasting my time and money' on new paths. The end result may be that horse riding, hitherto possible in part of the wood, will become impossible throughout it, that access for cyclists will end, and that even walkers will suffer. For whilst the Tuleys can be ordered to unlock two gates, it is difficult to see any basis in the legislation for ordering them to keep paths clear of natural growth, or from fallen timber.

Would the Council have the right to make and maintain paths instead? Section 15(4) of the 2003 Act says:

> The local authority may install and maintain, in any land in respect of which access rights are exercisable, gates, stiles, moorings, launching sites or other means of facilitating the exercise of these rights, and seats, lavatories and other means of contributing to the comfort and convenience of persons exercising them.

Perhaps paths might be made and maintained on the basis of 'other means of facilitating the exercise of these rights'. While that view could be defended, it runs counter to the *ejusdem generis* principle of statutory interpretation. The provision in question is all about the installation of physical objects: 'gates, stiles, moorings, launching sites[2] ... seats, lavatories'. Even so, the argument that this includes power to make and maintain paths is stateable, at least if the provision is taken in isolation. But looking at the Act as a whole, it seems likely that paths are exclusively dealt with in the special provisions about 'path agreements' and compulsory 'path orders' in sections 21 and 22. So if Mr Tuley carries out his threat the council could probably make and maintain paths by virtue of a path order – at some cost to itself.

Postscript

As the Access Code says, '"recreational purposes" is not defined in the legislation. It is taken to include ... horse riding'.[3] That view was accepted without question by the parties in the *Tuley* case. The Act itself lacks any specific provision about riding. The core provision, section 1, confers access rights on human beings. The nearest the Act gets is in section 9, where it is provided that 'being on or crossing

---

1 13 July 2007.

2 This is specially welcomed by one of the authors who since boyhood has wished to send up a missile powered by a bipropellant rocket engine.

3 Access Code para 2.7. The expression 'recreational purposes' is found in s 1. It is the first of three purposes for which access may be taken. The Code seems to mention riding only for this first purpose. Arguably the third purpose (s 1(3)(c)) was the most relevant to the *Tuley* case.

land while responsible for a dog or other animal which is not under proper control' is not allowed. So by implication, the access taker may be accompanied by a properly controlled animal. That the 'dog or other animal' may be ridden is a further step in the inferential chain. The inference is perhaps a reasonable one, though the fact that the only animal mentioned is a dog suggests that the question of riding was perhaps not in the minds of the legislators. Assuming that the inference is correct, it raises questions about how the right to take access on horseback relates to public rights of way. A public 'footpath' cannot be used for riding, but a 'bridleway' is available for both walking and riding.[1] Had the red track been a public footpath, what then? Would that have meant that the Tuleys would have won? Or does the 2003 Act upgrade all footpaths to bridleways? If a public footpath crosses land, can riders go along the path, or can they go everywhere *except* along the path? Indeed, the relationship of access rights to public rights of way may have many ramifications.[2]

TENEMENTS

Counting flats

Under the Tenements (Scotland) Act 2004 every tenement must have a management scheme. If such a scheme is provided for by the titles, well and good. But if or to the extent that the titles are silent, a default management scheme is provided by the Act.[3] This is the Tenement Management Scheme ('TMS'), and it is set out in schedule 1 of the Act.

One of the main purposes of the Act, and of the TMS, is to make it easier for owners to agree on repairs. On this topic, the provisions of the TMS are straightforward. Repairs to 'scheme property'[4] – the essential fabric of the building – will be carried out if the owners of a majority of the flats so decide.[5] Such a 'scheme decision' can be reached by whatever means are convenient – typically, by an owners' meeting, or by letter, or by going round and knocking on people's doors.[6] Once the repair is carried out, liability is divided in accordance with the titles or, if the titles are silent, in accordance with the TMS, where the usual rule is that each pays the same amount.[7]

As already mentioned, a scheme decision is one which is agreed to by the owners of a majority of flats. But what is a 'flat' for this purpose? That issue

---

1 D J Cusine and R R M Paisley, *Servitudes and Rights of Way* (1998) paras 21.03 ff. As the authors observe (para 21.10): 'If a route is proved, or accepted, to be one for use by those on foot, that will not allow use by those on horseback.'
2 Section 5(3) says that 'the existence or exercise of access rights does not diminish or displace any other rights (whether public or private) of entry, way, passage or access.' The implications of that provision may be open to discussion.
3 Tenements (Scotland) Act 2004 s 4.
4 Tenement Management Scheme (hereafter referred to as 'TMS') r 1.2.
5 TMS r 2.2, 2.5. But if the titles provide a different rule, that is the rule which governs: see Tenements (Scotland) Act 2004 s 4(4).
6 TMS r 2.6–2.8.
7 TMS r 4.2.

arose starkly in *PS Properties (2) Ltd v Callaway Homes Ltd*.[1] This concerned 49–53 Murray Place in Stirling. On the ground floor there were two shops, one of which – occupied by Poundstretcher – extended to the whole of the first floor. There were two flats on the second floor and a further two on the third or top floor. The pursuer owned the shops and the defender the two flats on the top floor. They were at loggerheads in relation to repairs to the common stair. Repairs were proposed by the defender but opposed by the pursuer. The defender enlisted the support of the owner of one of the second floor flats but, with only three flats in favour, fell short of the majority necessary for a scheme decision. Accordingly, when the defender went ahead with the work anyway, the pursuer sought, and obtained, an interim interdict against the work proceeding.

That was in August 2006. In the current phase of the litigation the defender sought to have the interdict recalled. Matters had indeed changed in one crucial respect, for the defender had now acquired both flats on the second floor, with the result that the decision to carry out repairs was now supported by four flats. But was that a majority? Simple arithmetic suggested that it was, for the tenement comprised four flats and two shops – six 'flats' altogether (because under the Act shops are treated as flats)[2] – and four is a majority of six. But the pursuer argued that 'one had to look at the original purpose for which the building was designed, not the way in which it was now divided up'.[3] The original design, the pursuer said, was of a traditional tenement of eight flats. It therefore followed that Poundstretcher, which stretched to the whole of the first floor, must be regarded as three flats. Four out of eight is not a majority.

This argument was rejected by Lady Dorrian, and the interim interdict recalled:[4]

> I did not accept the pursuers' submission that the building required to be looked at as a building of eight units. I did not accept that one had to look at the historical design of the building for the purpose of determining how many votes were to be allocated in terms of rule 4 of schedule 1 [ie the TMS]. In my view, the building was properly to be considered, having regard to the titles and section 29, as a building of six units. It follows that the defenders have a majority in favour of the Scheme Decision.

This must surely be right. Over the years, flats within a tenement may be divided or combined. Even if it was practical to determine the internal organisation of the building at the time it was first erected, it is hard to see the point in doing so. The TMS is concerned with tenements as they are and not with tenements as they were. And counting flats is a matter of numbers and not of history, or indeed of size, for a flat which is three times the size of any other still has only one vote. It is worth adding that, under the Act, the fact that a shop or apartment extends to two floors – as was the case with Poundstretcher – does not prevent it from being a single flat.[5]

---

1 [2007] CSOH 162, 2007 GWD 31-526.
2 T(S)A 2004 s 29(1) (para (a) of the definition of 'flat').
3 Paragraph 7.
4 Paragraph 9.
5 T(S)A 2004 s 29(1) (para (b) of the definition of 'flat').

In considering whether the interim interdict should be recalled, counsel, and the court, paid some attention to whether the repairs in question were really needed. They need not have bothered. Under the Act a scheme decision, once taken, 'is binding on the owners and their successors as owners' and 'may be enforced by any owner'.[1] If a decision is to be challenged on its merits, this must be done in the sheriff court within 28 days.[2] In the absence of such a challenge, the decision is binding and can be insisted upon.

Compulsory insurance

Section 18 of the Tenements (Scotland) Act 2004 came into force on 24 January 2007,[3] and imposes an obligation on owners to insure their flats. Like the rest of the Act, the provision originates with a report of the Scottish Law Commission, which explains that:[4]

> Within a tenement each owner is uniquely vulnerable to the physical condition of the property of his neighbours. Since a flat is no more than a single unit in a larger building, an owner may often be affected by damage to parts of the building which are not his. Hence he has an interest not merely in the insurance of his own flat but in the insurance of the other flats in the building. In the most extreme case, where a tenement is badly damaged or destroyed, the fact that even one of the flats is uninsured, or underinsured, may be enough to prevent the building from being restored. In summary, in a tenement an owner is not adequately insured unless his neighbours are insured also.

Under section 18, insurance must be for reinstatement value and in respect of the 'prescribed risks'. Following consultation with the Association of British Insurers and the Council of Mortgage Lenders, the following risks have now been prescribed:[5]

> The risk of damage to a flat or any part of a tenement building attaching to that flat as a pertinent caused by:
>
> (a) fire, smoke, lightning, explosion, earthquake;
> (b) storm or flood;
> (c) theft or attempted theft;
> (d) riot, civil commotion, labour or political disturbance;
> (e) malicious persons or vandals;
> (f) subsidence, heave or landslip;
> (g) escape of water from water tanks, pipes, apparatus and domestic appliances;
> (h) collision with the building caused by any moving object originating outside the building;

---

1 TMS r 8.2, 8.3.
2 T(S)A 2004 s 5.
3 Tenements (Scotland) Act 2004 (Commencement No 2) Order 2007, SSI 2007/17.
4 Scottish Law Commission, *Report on the Law of the Tenement* (Scot Law Com No 162 (1998); available on www.scotlawcom.gov.uk) para 9.1.
5 The Tenements (Scotland) Act 2004 (Prescribed Risks) Order 2007, SSI 2007/16. Oddly, this came into force only on 1 May 2007, some three months after s 18.

(i) leakage of oil from fixed heating installations; and

(j) accidental damage to underground services.

These are much the same as the risks listed in part 1 of the *CML Lenders' Handbook for Scotland* as potentially being required by individual lenders,[1] although the latter also includes

- professional fees, demolition and site clearing costs
- public liability to anyone else
- falling trees and branches and aerials
- aircraft.

Insurance is not required to the extent that it is unavailable, or only available at a cost which is unreasonably high.[2] This recognises the difficulty of obtaining cover for certain properties or for certain owners.

In a tenement, insurance can be taken out either for the building as a whole or, piecemeal, for individual flats. Section 18 makes no choice between these methods and either is allowed. However, under the Tenement Management Scheme owners are able to make a scheme decision to move to a common policy of insurance for the whole building, and to determine on an equitable basis the liability of each owner to contribute to the premium.[3] In addition, common insurance is sometimes required by a real burden in the titles, although, at least in older tenements, the level of cover stipulated may be inadequate.

The impact of section 18 is likely to be relatively modest. It is thought that at least 90% of flats were insured already, often no doubt because there was a secured loan and hence a requirement to insure by the lender. Presumably this percentage will now rise, but there will continue to be an irreducible minimum of uninsured flats.

One problem, of course, is enforcement. Failure to insure is not a criminal offence under the Act, and no public body is charged with monitoring compliance. Instead power lies with the individual owners. Section 18(5) encourages letter-writing among neighbours:

> Any owner may by notice in writing require the owner of any other flat in the tenement to produce evidence of –
>
> > (a) the policy in respect of any contract of insurance which the owner of that other flat is required to have or to effect; and
> >
> > (b) payment of the premium for any such policy,
>
> and not later than 14 days after that notice is given the recipient shall produce to the owner giving the notice the evidence requested.

In a case where insurance has not been taken out, the owners of other flats in the tenement have power to enforce the statutory obligation.[4]

---

1 Available at www.cml.org.uk/handbook/Overview.aspx. See para 6.13.6.

2 Tenements (Scotland) Act 2004 s 18(4).

3 Tenement Management Scheme r 3.1(e). The TMS is contained in sch 1 of the Act.

4 Tenements (Scotland) Act 2004 s 18(6).

Further commencement

Section 18 was the last provision in the Tenements (Scotland) Act 2004 which had not been commenced, with the result that the whole Act is now in force. However, section 19, which allows the installation of pipes and other equipment in 'any part' of the tenement, is in force only in a technical sense because it depends on a statutory instrument – of which there is no sign – to list the services to which it applies.

PROFESSIONAL CLAIMS

Q: What's the cost of a wrong fax number? A: £412,380 plus interest at 8%

The closing date is set for high noon. Your client tells you on the phone the amount to offer. Your carefully-crafted offer is faxed off well before noon, with the paper version going out that afternoon. All is well?

In *Watts v Bell & Scott WS*,[1] a property in Abercromby Place in Edinburgh's New Town was on the market. The selling agents, D M Hall, set a closing date for noon on Friday 21 June 2002. That morning, Mr Watts instructed his solicitors to submit an offer of £1,100,000. The solicitors faxed the offer, but the number that was keyed into the fax machine was not D M Hall's number but that of Mr Watts. He was away from his office at the time and did not immediately notice what had happened. The property was sold to someone else at a price of £1,057,000. Mr Watts sued his solicitors for damages. They admitted fault. The issue was whether any actual damages were due, and if so, how much.

Mr Watts argued that he would have developed the property and resold it at a profit of several hundred thousand pounds. The defenders argued that the property was worth roughly what he had offered for it, and so the fact that he did not acquire it was balanced by the fact that he still had an asset of approximately equal value, namely the money he would have paid. He could have used that money to buy and develop other property. Indeed, they said, he had done so, for not long afterwards he had bought a property in nearby Albany Street for £1,739,000 and had developed that instead.

The defenders also argued that Mr Watts' testimony had to be taken with caution. At an earlier stage he had made a lower offer (£1,050,000) for Abercromby Place. To persuade the owners to accept this offer, he had written to them: 'Based upon current information and my research my offer represents in excess of a 20% premium on this valuation.' That had been untrue: the figure of £1,050,000 was below the valuation figure. He had also written: 'I have two other development opportunities in consideration at this time for my development funds and again these opportunities have timescales which require early decisions.' That had been untrue. His counsel 'argued that the pursuer's conduct simply reflected commercial reality in the world of property development'.[2] If that is true, it is

---

1 [2007] CSOH 108, 2007 SLT 665.
2 See the Lord Ordinary's opinion at para 18.

disturbing. The Lord Ordinary[1] agreed that all this was 'a factor that I have to consider in assessing his credibility and reliability'[2] but in the event it did not affect the outcome.

The solicitors had known that Mr Watts wanted the property for development. He was able to establish that the Albany Street development was one that he would have proceeded with anyway, and in this connection he was able to present evidence from his bank that it would have been prepared to lend for both projects. Thus the Albany Street development was not a substitute for the Abercromby Place development. Mr Watts was further able to satisfy the court that, apart from Albany Street, there was no other suitable development project available at that time. The Lord Ordinary, after an extensive review of the authorities, agreed that the defenders were liable for the loss of profit, but accepted the defenders' method of calculation, which was based on the average profit that Mr Watts achieved in such developments. This figure was 17.4% of sale proceeds. The expected gross sales proceeds were £2,370,000 (this figure seems to have been accepted by both sides), so that the lost profit figure was £412,380, with interest running from the likely date that Mr Watts would have been able to resell. The pursuer had contended for a much higher projected profit, so on this point at least the defenders were successful.

Liability for consequential loss remains a controversial issue in professional negligence cases. The usual measure of damages is that of 'diminution in value', which is what the defenders argued for in *Watts*. Another case from 2007 in which the court went the other way, rejecting a claim for consequential loss, was *Murray v J & E Shepherd*.[3] The law in this area cannot be regarded as settled.

Q: What's the cost of misreading a title condition?
A: £381,500 (perhaps)

Conveyancing is a business in which minor inadvertencies can result in large claims. *Watts* was not the only such case in 2007; another was *Henderson v Sayer*.[4] The pursuers bought a property at Torphichen, West Lothian. They later raised an action seeking damages against their solicitor on the ground that he had failed to explain to them a title condition encumbering the property:

> The occupier undertakes that the planning permission subjects shall be constructed all in terms of the consent. The planning permission subjects, once constructed shall be used as a single dwelling house in all time coming solely for the occupation of one person and his or her family or dependants and for no other purpose whatsoever and said person must be solely or mainly employed in the management and/or running of the fish hatchery and sport fishery operated on the planning unit.

---

1 Temporary Judge C J Macaulay QC.
2 Paragraph 19.
3 2007 GWD 7-108, Sh Ct.
4 [2007] CSOH 183, 2007 GWD 37-655.

The source of this title condition is unclear, but it seems likely that it was created under section 75 of the Town and Country Planning (Scotland) Act 1997, and so could not be varied or discharged by the Lands Tribunal.[1]

The title condition's importance is not apparent at first sight. Whilst we do not know what happened in this case, we can all too easily imagine reading the first few lines and quickly coming to the conclusion that it was of only limited significance. The sting is in the tail.

The sum claimed by way of damages was £381,500. The case turned on whether the pursuers' approach to the calculation of damages was a sound one. Proof before answer was allowed.

Can a law firm be liable for the estate agent's commission?
Or: Are solicitors deemed to read every piece of paper sent to them?

Christie Owen & Davies plc v Campbell[2] concerned the marketing of a leasehold property in Cambridge Street, Glasgow, known as 'the Waldorf Bar'. The seller, a Mrs Campbell, signed an agency agreement with the pursuers, an estate agency company. One of the terms was the following:

> We hereby authorise the vendor's solicitors STATE NAME AND ADDRESS OF SOLICITOR Valance Kliner, Cambridge House, Cambridge Street, Glasgow G2 3B1 or any other solicitor acting on behalf of the vendor in connection with the disposal of the business to pay out of money received by such solicitors the fees requested by you in any invoice submitted by you to such solicitors pursuant to this agreement and not to release any proceeds arising from such disposal of the business to any person up to the amount of the invoice, until it has been paid, except for payment of mortgages and charges and the legal costs of sale.

The property sold for £46,000. The commission charged by the estate agents was £9,360.05. They then wrote the following letter to the seller's law agents:

> Dear Mr Vallance
>
> We understand that missives have now been concluded in respect of the assignation of the Waldorf Bar. On speaking with Mrs Anne Campbell she advises that the purchase price has been placed in joint deposit until a letter is issued confirming the assignation of the lease.
>
> In this instance, we remit to you our fee note in respect of the assignation in advance of the consideration being released. We understand that receipt of the assignation letter from the landlord is imminent and therefore look forward to receiving payment in early course.
>
> We look forward to hearing from you in due course.

---

1 The Lands Tribunal jurisdiction only extends to 'title conditions' in the strict sense, ie as defined in the Title Conditions (Scotland) Act 2003: see ss 90(1), 122(1). In the text we use 'title condition' loosely.
2 2007 GWD 24-397, affd December 2007, Glasgow Sheriff Court.

It will be noted that the letter did not refer to the agency agreement. A copy of that agreement was, however, included in the same envelope.

The seller's law agents did not pay the estate agency company the sum requested, but remitted the whole net proceeds to their client. The company did not receive the money from Mrs Campbell either. It then raised an action against both Mrs Campbell and the law agents for £9,360.05. In relation to the law agents' alleged liability,[1] the pursuers argued (i) that the quoted clause in the agency agreement constituted an assignation of the future proceeds of sale, and (ii) that the fact that a copy of the agreement was enclosed with the letter to the law agents constituted intimation of that assignation. It was held, both by the sheriff[2] and by the sheriff principal[3] that (i) was correct but that (ii) was not.

Whether the views concerning the first point expressed by the sheriff and sheriff principal are sound in all respects may perhaps be debated.[4] But the decision on the second point, at any rate, is surely correct. Intimation is a juridical act. As the sheriff principal said:[5]

[T]he letter is silent with regard to any intimation of assignation. Furthermore there is nothing in its terms to hint that the first defender had granted an assignation. For example if, to meet the second stage of Lord Kincraig's test,[6] the pursuers had referred to them having an entitlement to receive payment, that might have been sufficient to put the pursuers on notice of a potential assignation. In such circumstances it might be said that they were then under an obligation to read the Sole Selling Rights Agreement enclosed. But the letter of 20 December 2006 ... is the equivalent to only a request for payment. Thus the letter does not even meet the second stage of Lord Kincraig's test. There is no assertion of the pursuers' entitlement to payment.

The pursuers argued that solicitors are deemed to read every word of every document sent to them. The sheriff principal did not agree. 'I am not prepared to hold that a solicitor is under an obligation to read every document sent to him or that a solicitor is deemed to have read all such documents.'[7] That is a welcome comment.

What is not wholly clear is whether the court would have held in favour of the pursuers if the defenders had in fact read the agency agreement. As Professor

---

1 It is not clear to us from the opinions issued what happened to the crave as directed against Mrs Campbell.

2 2007 GWD 24-397 (Sheriff Anthony Deutsch).

3 December 2007, Glasgow Sheriff Court (Sheriff Principal James Taylor).

4 On the whole subject of assignation and intimation, see R G Anderson, *Assignation* (forthcoming, 2008).

5 Paragraph 7.

6 The reference is to Lord Kincraig's opinion in *Libertas-Kommerz GmbH v Johnson* 1977 SC 191. The passage referred to is this: 'It seems to be that both cases show that if there has been a written intimation to the debtor of the fact that an assignation has been granted, the terms of that intimation must be considered, and if they are such, on a reasonable interpretation, as to convey to the debtor that the debt has been transferred, and that the transferee is asserting his claim to the debt from the debtor, intimation will be held to be effectual.'

7 Paragraph 6. There is a link here with another 2007 case, *Credential Bath Street Ltd v Venture Investment Placement Ltd* [2007] CSOH 208, where Lord Reed said: 'the question is whether the reasonable recipient of the letter would have said to himself, "I am being called on to do the work specified in the schedule".'

McBryde has commented, 'one of the long, slow-burning questions in the law is whether a debtor's *mere knowledge* of an assignation is sufficient intimation to him'.[1]

PRESERVATION NOTICES

The age of preservation notices is past and also still to come. It is past because the bewildering variety of notices allowing feudal superiors to preserve real burdens had all to be registered before 28 November 2004. And it is still to come because the deadline for the second wave of notices – notices preserving rights to enforce real burdens of neighbours which were created, by implication, under the rule in *J A Mactaggart & Co v Harrower*[2] – is not until 28 November 2014. But one should not forget such notice skills as one has: not only will they be needed in the future but they may be needed now, to evaluate the effectiveness of a notice registered in the first wave. Section 44(1) of the Abolition of Feudal Tenure etc (Scotland) Act 2000 provides that: 'Any dispute arising in relation to a notice registered under this Act may be referred to the Lands Tribunal.' *SQ1 Ltd v Earl of Hopetoun*[3] is the first dispute to be so referred.

Toilet troubles

The notice in *SQ1 Ltd v Earl of Hopetoun* was one of only 1,960 notices to be registered under section 18 of the Abolition of Feudal Tenure etc (Scotland) Act 2000,[4] and, like most such notices, it was registered right at the last minute, on 26 November 2004. The burdens which the notice sought to preserve had been created in a 1985 feu disposition.

In order to use section 18 the superior had to own (the *dominium utile* of) other land in the same area as the feu. The idea was that, following registration of the notice and the subsequent abolition of the feudal system, the benefited property would switch from the superiority (now abolished) to the neighbouring land. But there was a catch. In order to keep the preservation of burdens within reasonable bounds, section 18 required that one of three conditions set out in section 18(7) be met. And the only one that was likely to be met in practice was the first: that the nominated land 'has on it a permanent building which is in use wholly or mainly as a place of human (i) habitation or (ii) resort' within 100 metres of the feu. This was the '100 metres rule', and it could not be satisfied by land which was empty.

The land nominated in the notice under consideration in *SQ1 Ltd* was not empty. On the contrary, it contained a toilet block which had been constructed in

---

1 W W McBryde, *The Law of Contract in Scotland* (3rd edn 2007) para 12–93. Emphasis added.
2 (1906) 8 F 1101. See further *Conveyancing 2004* pp 97–103. The main statutory provision is s 50 of the Title Conditions (Scotland) Act 2003.
3 2 Oct 2007, Lands Tribunal. The Tribunal comprised Lord McGhie and K M Barclay FRICS.
4 Yet this was by far the most common type of notice. For the figures of notices registered, see *Conveyancing 2004* pp 95–96.

about 1994 for the convenience of persons using an adjacent sports ground, also owned by the superiors, for archery. By the time that the notice was registered, however, the sports ground had been vacant for more than two years, and the superiors were trying to attract new tenants. Indisputably, the toilet block was a place of human 'resort' (though presumably not of human 'habitation'). But, if the sports ground was unlet, could the toilet be said to be 'in use' at the time when the notice was being drawn up and registered? In other words, how much human resort to the toilet was needed for section 18(7) to be satisfied? In short, when, in the eyes of the law, is a toilet in use?

The Lands Tribunal decided, surely correctly, that 'in use' was a flexible term:[1]

> [T]he words 'in use' do not, in normal English usage, have a single proper and exact meaning. They can have a range of meanings depending on context. The present case happens to provide a clear example. A toilet might be said to be 'in use' when the 'engaged' sign was displayed and not 'in use' when the 'vacant' sign was seen. At the other end of the range, a toilet block might be said to be 'in use' in the sense that it was not 'disused' or 'out of use'. It was not suggested that the former meaning was required. In practical terms, it was not contended that there need be evidence of running water at or about the time of the notice.

In the absence of any better place to draw the line, the Tribunal thought that 'in use' could probably be taken as meaning 'not disused'. Admittedly, the distinction between use and disuse might be hard to draw in some cases. The Tribunal continued:[2]

> However, in relation to a dwellinghouse, we think that if it was maintained wind and water tight and not put to use for any other purpose, then in the absence of contrary intention, it would normally fall to be regarded as a building being used as a dwellinghouse and, accordingly, one which was in use as a place of human habitation for the purposes of section 18(7).
>
> We see no reason to apply a different approach to the question when it arises in relation to a place of human resort. Inevitably, the range of circumstances to be considered will be wider and the difficulties of finding a useful practical test or set of tests, may be greater. We need not attempt that exercise. It is sufficient to say that where subjects have been in active use for human resort and there is no actual change or intention to change the use, it can be taken to continue unless there are circumstances which point to a different conclusion.

Whether such circumstances existed in the present case would have to be a matter of proof. But the Tribunal concluded that the challenge by the applicant (the owner of the former feu) must fail insofar as based on relevancy.

Notice troubles

The applicant had a second argument. Section 18 notices must follow the statutory style, which is set out in schedule 5 of the Abolition of Feudal Tenure Act. Among

---

1 At p 11 of the transcript.
2 At p 13 of the transcript.

the information which the style requires to be given is 'Specification of the condition met', by which is meant the condition under section 18(7). Where, as in the present case, that condition is the 100 metres rule, the notes for completion, also in schedule 5, suggest the following wording:

> The dominant tenement has on it a [specify type of building] at [specify address of building] which is within 100 metres of the servient tenement.

The notice used in the present case read:

> The dominant tenement has on it a building capable of human resort in East Shore Wood, Hopetoun, South Queensferry, West Lothian which building is within 100 metres of the servient tenement.

The applicant challenged the fill-in for 'specify the type of building' as incorrect. By 'type of building' was meant whether the building was in use as a place of human habitation or a place of human resort.[1] The superior had provided neither. Instead the building was merely stated as being *capable of* human resort'. The effect of this mistake was to make the notice void.

In considering this argument, the Tribunal pointed out that section 18 imposed two quite separate requirements in relation to notices. First, in respect of *form*, the notice must be 'in, or nearly as may be in, the form contained in schedule 5'.[2] Secondly, in respect of *content*, the notice must contain the information set out in section 18(2). It seems worth adding that the structure of section 50 of the Title Conditions (Scotland) Act 2003 – which provides for the notices still to come mentioned earlier – is exactly the same.

The Tribunal was satisfied that there was no difficulty in respect of form. The notice followed the statutory style, and it was 'unnecessary to consider whether it follows, precisely, the guidance given by the notes because these are expressly said to have no legal effect'.[3]

The position as to content was perhaps less clear. The requirement of section 18(2), in this respect, was that the notice 'specify which of the conditions set out in subsection (7) is (or are) met'. It was true, as the applicant argued, that there was a difference between saying that something was 'in use' for some purpose and saying – as in the notice – that it was merely 'capable of' being in use. But, in the Tribunal's view – with which we would agree – all that section 18(2) required was 'a tolerably clear intimation to the recipient as to which condition the sender says is met'. 'The statutory obligation was not to set out why a particular condition was met but simply to specify which of the conditions was met.'[4] Although 'not

---

1 Although the Tribunal accepted this as correct (p 17), the recollection of Professor Reid (who devised the notices) is that all that was intended was to describe the building in order that it could be identified (eg 'toilet block').
2 Abolition of Feudal Tenure etc (Scotland) Act 2000 s 18(1).
3 At p 15 of the transcript. The statement that 'These notes have no legal effect' appears at the start of the notes in sch 5.
4 At p 16.

happily worded',[1] the notice had at least provided the information which was required.

The Tribunal's decision is the subject of an appeal.

POSITIVE PRESCRIPTION: VIOLATING YOUR HUMAN RIGHTS?

Introduction

For some years now there has been grinding through the English and European courts a case in which it was argued that positive prescription (to use Scots terminology) violates human rights, in that it deprives owners of their property without compensation. This may sound surprising. The European Convention on Human Rights emerged after the Second World War and was intended as a safeguard against the abuses of state power. It set forth guarantees against torture, guarantees of family life, guarantees of fair trial and so on. The idea that it could have anything to say about the usually humdrum business of private law would have seemed absurd. But that was then. In time so restrictive an interpretation came to be rejected by those who saw in the Convention the opportunity to remodel law – not just public law – in accordance with their own ideals. The silence of the Convention about private law was no obstacle, for the Convention was declared to be a 'living instrument'. The actual text of the Convention is thus of limited significance, which is perhaps just as well, considering how poorly much of it is drafted. Whether one likes the results depends on one's own ideals.

Article 1 of Protocol 1 is the provision that protects property rights. The Convention is authentic in two languages, English and French. The two texts often diverge markedly. Only the English text was enacted by the Human Rights Act 1998, and so it is not clear that it is correct to say that the Convention has been 'incorporated' into UK law.[2] Here is Article 1:

French	English
Toute personne physique ou morale a droit au respect de ses *biens*. Nul ne peut être privé de sa *propriété* que pour cause d'utilité publique et dans les conditions prévues par la loi et les principes généraux du droit international.	Every natural or legal person is entitled to the peaceful enjoyment of his *possessions*. No one shall be deprived of his *possessions* except in the public interest and subject to the conditions provided for by law and by the general principles of international law.
Les dispositions précédentes ne portent pas atteinte au droit que possèdent les Etats de mettre en vigueur les lois qu'ils jugent nécessaires pour réglementer l'usage des *biens* conformément à l'intérêt général ou d'autres contributions ou des amendes.	The preceding provisions shall not, however, in any way impair the right of a State to enforce such laws as it deems necessary to control the use of *property* in accordance with the general interest or to secure the payment of taxes or other contributions or penalties.

---

1 At p 17.
2 The same point applies to the way that the Convention interacts with the devolution settlement: Scotland Act 1998 s 29(2)(d) read with s 126(1).

Each text uses two terms. The French text uses 'biens' and 'propriété', whilst the English text uses 'possessions' and 'property'. But they do not match up.

Usage number	French		English
1	Biens	=	Possessions
2	Propriété	=	Possessions
3	Biens	=	Property

This example (others could be given) illustrates why one cannot treat the Convention as one would treat a genuine legislative text. It is an expression of general ideas, rather like a letter to the editor of a newspaper.

The facts

J A Pye (Oxford) Ltd – we will refer to the company as 'Pye' – had a land bank and in this land bank was an area in rural Berkshire extending to about 50 acres. Pye's title was in HM Land Registry. The company was not interested in the land except for its development potential and so it allowed neighbouring farmers Mr and Mrs Graham to graze their beasts on it. After some years this grazing let was terminated. The Grahams carried on as before, but no longer paying a grazing rent, and Pye seems not to have noticed, for after all the current use of the land was of little interest to it. In England, at least as the law then was,[1] an adverse possessor could acquire land simply by possession for the relevant period, then 12 years, without first registering anything. So after 12 years had passed the Grahams claimed the land as their own.

The home fixtures: Grahams 2, Pye 1

Pye fought hard, taking the case all the way up to the House of Lords. Pye did not base its case on the ECHR because the events in question took place before the Human Rights Act 1998. Instead, Pye argued that the Grahams had not had the right type of possession. Pye lost at first instance,[2] won in the Court of Appeal,[3] and lost finally in the House of Lords.[4] As far as English law was concerned, that was the end of the road. The Grahams had won: the land was theirs.

The first away match: Pye 4, UK 3

Now Pye sued the UK Government in the European Court of Human Rights at Strasbourg for breach of the ECHR. For although the ECHR has been part of English domestic law only since the Human Rights Act 1998, the UK Government had previously been bound by the Convention. Pye sought damages of £10,000,000

---

1 The English law about what we would call positive prescription was radically altered by the Land Registration Act 2002. The *Pye* case turned on the law as it was before that Act.
2 *J A Pye (Oxford) Ltd v Graham* [2000] Ch 676.
3 *J A Pye (Oxford) Ltd v Graham* [2001] Ch 804.
4 *J A Pye (Oxford) Ltd v Graham* [2002] UKHL 30, [2003] 1 AC 419.

for loss of the land plus £800,000 being its costs in the English litigation. Pye argued that, by allowing the existence of legislation that caused its loss of property, the UK Government was violating its human rights in terms of Article 1 of Protocol 1. Pye won, by a four-to-three majority.[1] (The question of damages was reserved.) We dealt with that decision in *Conveyancing 2005*.[2]

The second away match: Pye 7, UK 10

A party who loses in the seven-member court can petition a five-member panel to refer the case to the seventeen-member Grand Chamber. Such a referral is a re-hearing rather than an appeal. Given the narrowness of the Chamber decision (four to three) and given the importance of the issue it is not surprising that the UK petitioned for a re-hearing and that that petition was granted. And as already mentioned, the result was another close one, but this time in favour of the UK.[3] The majority was ten to seven.

In the Chamber decision, both the majority and the minority had agreed that Pye had been deprived of its property. The difference between them was whether that deprivation (without compensation) was justifiable or not. But in the Grand Chamber a mysterious change took place. Both majority and minority agreed that, after all, Pye had *not* been deprived of the property.[4] What had happened was not a 'deprivation' but a 'control of use'. This is impossible to explain, other than to say that over the years Strasbourg case law has developed this distinction. Even given the distinction, why the *Pye* case should be classified as the one rather than the other goes unexplained. The re-characterisation was not in itself decisive, for 'control of use' must be justified as well as 'deprivation',[5] but it was enough to tip the balance, so that the view that what had happened was an unjustifiable control of use was held by fewer judges than the view that it was a justifiable control of use. The majority view is captured by the following two remarks:[6]

> Even where title to real property is registered, it must be open to the legislature to attach more weight to lengthy, unchallenged possession than to the formal fact of registration.

> Such arrangements fall within the State's margin of appreciation, unless they give rise to results which are so anomalous as to render the legislation unacceptable.

---

1 *J A Pye (Oxford) Ltd v UK* (2006) 43 EHRR 3.
2 *Conveyancing 2005* pp 65–72. For further Scottish reactions, see D Johnston, '*J A Pye (Oxford) Limited v United Kingdom*: deprivation of property rights and prescription' (2006) 10 *Edinburgh Law Review* 277; K Swinton, 'Prescription, human rights and the Land Register: *Pye v UK*' (2005) 73 *Scottish Law Gazette* 179; G L Gretton, '*Pye*: a Scottish view' (2007) 15 *European Review of Private Law* 281.
3 *J A Pye (Oxford) Ltd v UK*, 30 Aug 2007, European Court of Human Rights (Grand Chamber). For commentary on the Grand Chamber decision from a Scottish perspective, see G L Gretton, 'Private law and human rights' (2008) 12 *Edinburgh Law Review* 109; F McCarthy, 'Positive prescription in the human rights era' 2008 SLT (News) 15.
4 With the partial exception of Judge Loucaides and Judge Kovler. The separate dissent of Judge Loucaides, though not one with which we would agree, is better argued than either the majority or the main minority opinions, both of which are weak.
5 Article 1 does not say that, but never mind.
6 Respectively paras 74 and 83.

The more obvious solution to the case, namely that the purpose of Article 1 is to protect property rights against invasion by the state and by state bodies, and is not to alter private law, was not adopted. It had been put forward by the UK's counsel, and whilst the court does not expressly reject it, it does so by implication.

So where does this leave us?

Had the Grand Chamber voting been slightly different, the implications – including the implications for Scots law – could have been dramatic. Even now, there is no room for complacency. There is no doctrine of *stare decisis* at Strasbourg. Because the Convention is a 'living instrument',[1] its provisions cannot have an objective and fixed meaning, and so the Court is always free to depart from its own previous decisions, even decisions of the Grand Chamber. One cannot therefore say, at the end of 2007, that 'the law of positive prescription is ECHR-compliant'. One can only say that 'the law of positive prescription of the type in the particular statute under consideration is ECHR-compliant in the view of a majority of the Grand Chamber as it was constituted in 2006/7'.[2] So whilst the decision means that the Scottish Parliament is not going to have to rush through a Prescription Amendment (Scotland) Act, the narrowness of the decision means that as and when the law of positive prescription is examined in future, whether by the Scottish Law Commission or others, the risk of a Convention-based challenge will have to be borne in mind.

Postscript

From the Grand Chamber in Strasbourg to Glasgow Sheriff Court: attempts to refashion private law on the basis of the ECHR continue. In *MacLeod's Tr v MacLeod*[3] Mr and Mrs MacLeod were co-owners of their home in Newlands, Glasgow. Mr MacLeod was sequestrated. His trustee in sequestration raised an action of division and sale. Mrs MacLeod had two lines of defence. The first was that an action of division and sale contravenes Article 1 of Protocol 1 of the European Convention on Human Rights (protection of property rights) and also, where the property is a dwellinghouse, Article 8 (protection of family life). The sheriff[4] rejected this argument, holding that 'the remedy of division and sale is Convention-compliant'.[5]

STAMP DUTY LAND TAX[6]

It is probably fair to say that the regime for stamp duty land tax ('SDLT'), largely contained in Finance Act 2003 part 4 as very extensively amended, has begun to

---

1 As with so much else, this principle is not to be found in the Convention itself.
2 The case was heard in 2006 but the decision was not issued until 30 August 2007. The delay may mean that the final outcome was in doubt until a very late stage.
3 2007 Hous LR 34.
4 Sheriff A W Noble.
5 Paragraph 13.
6 This part is contributed by Alan Barr of the University of Edinburgh.

settle down. In 2007 there were further changes in the law, but the most important change of all was the growing effectiveness of electronic submission of SDLT returns, allowing registration of deeds to proceed without undue delay. It is significant (not least to its own costs and administration) that HMRC is pushing practitioners towards electronic submission. HMRC emphasises the speed of the service, the fact that a great deal of validation takes place automatically, and that enquiries (in either direction) will be less common, leading to savings of time and money. But while this may be so in relation to relatively simple transactions, it remains extremely difficult to get substantive assistance in more difficult cases. However, the range of transactions for which electronic submission is now possible is extending all the time – an announcement made it clear that leases running from a future date could now be reported electronically, as could leases with commencement dates as early as 1 January 1500 (*sic*).[1]

There were a number of administrative changes to the SDLT regime. It is now possible for an agent to complete a self-certificate (SDLT 60), to the effect that no land transaction return is required in respect of qualifying transactions.[2] The payment of tax was also formally separated from submission of the SDLT return, facilitating not only electronic compliance with the SDLT rules, but also electronic conveyancing more generally.[3] Further, it has been announced that the need to notify virtually all purchases (even within the 0% threshold, where no SDLT is payable) will be relaxed following Finance Act 2008. The notification requirements will also be relaxed for a greater number of leases.

On a more esoteric administrative front, legislation was introduced to replace the anti-avoidance rules previously contained in section 75A of the Finance Act 2003,[4] although one section has now become three.[5] The idea of these rules is that if a number of 'scheme transactions' are involved in the acquisition and disposal of a chargeable interest, and the result is that less SDLT would be payable than on a notional transaction of a direct transfer from vendor to purchaser, then SDLT will be chargeable as if on the notional transaction. It will be payable on the largest amount of consideration paid in any of the scheme transactions, or, if different, received by the vendor. It is to be noted that there is no motive test and the rules are perfectly capable of catching arrangements where there was no intention of avoiding SDLT. There are, however, a number of limitations on this potentially wide-reaching measure, for example in relation to any relief that would be available on the incidental transaction (where for example the ultimate purchaser was a charity). Certain incidental transactions are also ignored, such as some (but by no means all) transfers of shares and securities; sales of things other than land; and genuinely free-standing building contracts. These provisions require careful attention for any sequence of transactions involving land interests.

---

1 The penalty regime will be interesting.
2 Finance Act 2003 sch 11 para 2A, inserted by Finance Act 2007 s 81(2).
3 See the various amendments made by Finance Act 2007 s 80.
4 As inserted by the Stamp Duty Land Tax (Variation of the Finance Act 2003) Regulations 2006, SI 2006 / 3237.
5 Finance Act 2003 ss 75A–75C, inserted by the Finance Act 2007 s 71.

There is a distinct danger of paying *more* tax than would be payable in a simple transaction to achieve the same results.

A consultation has been announced on the use of companies as vehicles for the purchase of high-value *residential* property. Can similar interest in commercial special purpose vehicles be far behind?

If sequential transactions and possible avoidance have troubled HMRC since the introduction of SDLT, it is true to say that there has been particular concern with transactions involving partnerships. These can be structured so that interests change hands without there being an actual transfer of a chargeable interest in land; and complex provisions in Finance Act 2003 schedule 15 are designed to prevent avoidance by this means. Schedule 15 has been subject to incessant tinkering, no doubt caused by incessant avoidance deriving from earlier versions of it. New changes limit the use of companies in transfer to and from partnerships (although group relief is generally preserved for transfers into partnerships involving companies). Other changes ensure that charges will arise where a partner comes into a property-investment partnership, even where the interests of the other partners do not change (because of assets brought in by the new partner), and on other changes within a property-investment partnership.[1]

The result of the partnership regime in its current form is that changes in family trading partnerships (including farming partnerships) will often escape the special charging regime. But any movements in partnerships where property investment is the main partnership activity are likely to require careful attention, as once more there is no motive test to prevent unexpected charges arising – even where no actual land changes hands. And the complications in this area can be seen by the fact that it has already been announced that changes will be made in Finance Act 2008 to *prevent* charges arising where certain changes occur within property-investment partnerships, for instance where no consideration is involved and the partners are connected other than as partners. The interaction between partnership law and SDLT is a story with more chapters to come.

There is an extension to the special provisions for *sharia*-compliant security arrangements, allowing trading in such arrangements by financial institutions without SDLT cost in the same way as would apply to actual transfers of interest-bearing land securities.[2]

Section 19 of the Finance Act 2007 inserts new sections 58B and 58C into the Finance Act 2003, which in turn laid the basis for the Stamp Duty Land Tax (Zero-Carbon Homes Relief) Regulations 2007, SI 2007/3437. Subject to very detailed and demanding conditions, these provide (from 1 October 2007) for SDLT exemption for land transactions with a consideration up to £500,000, where they relate to the first acquisition of a new 'zero-carbon home'. There is a relief of £15,000 where the consideration exceeds that amount. An accredited assessor will have to issue a certificate that the new home meets requirements in relation to the 'heat loss parameter', the 'dwelling co2 emission rate', and (naturally) the 'net co2 emissions'. The effects of this incentive to reduce hot air are eagerly awaited.

---

1 Finance Act 2007 s 72.
2 Finance Act 2007 s 75.

Finally, section 76 of the Finance Act 2007 provides that the two land transactions involved in an excambion (exchange) are not linked transactions for the purposes of section 108 of the Finance Act 2003. This is a useful reminder that excambions of land, even where little or no money changes hands, are transactions on which SDLT could arise (for both parties) by virtue of Finance Act 2003, section 47. But now such transactions can be regarded as two independent transactions, even where the parties are individuals connected with each other (such as parent and child or brother and sister). This means that the various thresholds will only be relevant where the market value of an individual property exchanged exceeds the relevant figure, rather than where combined market value exceeds that figure.

❧ PART V ❧
TABLES

TABLES

CUMULATIVE TABLE OF APPEALS 2007

This lists all cases digested in *Conveyancing 1999* and subsequent annual volumes in respect of which an appeal was subsequently heard, and gives the result of the appeal.

Adams v Thorntons
2003 GWD 27-771, OH, 2003 Case (46) *affd* 2004 SCLR 1016, 2005 SLT 594, IH, 2004 Case (44)

Aerpac UK Ltd v NOI Scotland Ltd
31 March 2004, OH, 2004 Case (1) *affd* [2006] CSIH 20, 2006 GWD 18-365, 2006 Case (7)

Anderson v Express Investment Co Ltd
2002 GWD 28-977, OH, 2002 Case (5) *affd* 11 Dec 2003, IH, 2003 Case (13)

Armstrong v G Dunlop & Sons' JF
2004 SLT 155, OH, 2002 Case (48) *affd* 2004 SLT 295, IH, 2003 Case (39)

Bank of Scotland v Forman
25 July 2005, Peterhead Sheriff Court, A59/99, 2005 Case (36) *affd* [2007] CSIH 46, 2007 Case (48)

Bell v Fiddes
2004 GWD 3-50, OH, 2004 Case (8) *affd* [2006] CSIH 15, 2006 Case (13)

Bell v Inkersall Investments Ltd
[2005] CSOH 50, 2005 Case (28) *affd* [2006] CSIH 16, 2006 SC 507, 2006 SLT 626, 2006 Case (59)

Ben Cleuch Estates Ltd v Scottish Enterpise
[2006] CSOH 35, 2006 GWD 8-154, 2006 Case (61) *rev* [2008] CSIH 1, 2008 GWD 7-135, 2007 Case (47)

Burnett v Menzies Dougal
2004 SCLR 133 (Notes), OH, 2004 Case (42) *rev* [2005] CSIH 67, 2005 SLT 929, 2005 Case (40)

Burnett's Tr v Grainger
2000 SLT (Sh Ct) 116, 2000 Case (21) *rev* 2002 SLT 699, IH, 2002 Case (19) *affd* 2004 SC (HL) 19, 2004 SLT 513, 2004 SCLR 433, HL, 2004 Case (24)

Cahill's Judicial Factor v Cahill
2 March 2005, Glasgow Sheriff Court, A2680/94, 2005 Case (49) *affd* [2006] CSIH 26, 2006 GWD 19-409, 2006 Case (88)

Caledonian Heritable Ltd v Canyon Investments Ltd
2001 GWD 1-62, OH, 2000 Case (69) *rev* 2002 GWD 5-149, IH, 2002 Case (61)

Candleberry Ltd v West End Homeowners Association
12 October 2005, Lanark Sheriff Court, A492/5 *affd* 2006 GWD 21-457, Sh Ct, 2005 Case (9) *rev* [2006] CSIH 28, 2006 Hous LR 45, 2006 Case (15)

Caterleisure Ltd v Glasgow Prestwick International Airport Ltd
2005 SCLR 306, OH, 2004 Case (21) *rev* [2005] CSIH 53, 2005 SLT 1083, 2005 SCLR 943, 2005 Case (15)

Cheltenham & Gloucester plc v Sun Alliance and London Insurance plc
2001 SLT 347, OH, 2000 Case (63) *rev* 2001 SLT 1151, IH, 2001 Case (73)

City Wall Properties (Scotland) Ltd v Pearl Assurance plc
[2005] CSOH 139, 2005 GWD 35-666, 2005 Case (32) *affd* [2007] CSIH 79, 2008 GWD 5-93, 2007 Case (43)

Conway v Glasgow City Council
1999 SCLR 248, 1999 Hous LR 20 (Sh Ct) *rev* 1999 SLT (Sh Ct) 102, 1999 SCLR 1058, 1999 Hous LR 67, 1999 Case (44) *rev* 2001 SLT 1472, 2001 SCLR 546, IH, 2001 Case (51).

Glasgow City Council v Caststop Ltd
2002 SLT 47, OH, 2001 Case (6) *affd* 2003 SLT 526, 2004 SCLR 283, IH, 2003 Case (6)

Grampian Joint Police Board v Pearson
2000 SLT 90, OH, 2000 Case (18) *affd* 2001 SC 772, 2001 SLT 734, IH, 2001 Case (17)

Hamilton v Mundell; Hamilton v J & J Currie Ltd
20 November 2002, Dumfries Sheriff Court, 2002 Case (13) *rev* 7 October 2004, IH, 2004 Case (11)

Harbinson v McTaggart 2006 SLT (Lands Tr) 42, 2006 Case (69) *affd* under the name of *Allen v McTaggart* [2007] CSIH 24, 2007 SC 482, 2007 SLT 387, 2007 Hous LR 29, 2007 Case (40)

Henderson v 3052775 Nova Scotia Ltd
2003 GWD 40-1080, OH, 2003 Case (58) *affd* [2005] CSIH 20, 2005 1 SC 325, 2005 Case (47) *rev* [2006] UKHL 21, 2006 SC (HL) 85, 2006 SLT 489, 2006 SCLR 626, 2006 Case (86)

Inverness Seafield Co Ltd v Mackintosh
1999 GWD 31-1497, OH, 1999 Case (19) *rev* 2001 SC 406, 2001 SLT 118, IH, 2000 Case (13)

Jones v Wood
27 October 2003, Dumfries Sheriff Court, 2003 Case (52) *affd* [2005] CSIH 31, 2005 SLT 655, 2005 Case (42)

Kaur v Singh (No 2)
1999 Hous LR 76, 2000 SCLR 187, 2000 SLT 1324, OH, 1999 Case (34) *affd* 2000 SLT 1323, 2000 SCLR 944, IH, 2000 Case (26)

Kingston Communications (Hull) plc v Stargas Nominees Ltd
2003 GWD 33-946, OH, 2003 Case (35) *affd* 17 December 2004, IH, 2004 Case (31)

Labinski Ltd v BP Oil Development Co
2002 GWD 1-46, OH, 2001 Case (16) *affd* 2003 GWD 4-93, IH, 2003 Case (17)

Little Cumbrae Estate Ltd v Island of Little Cumbrae Ltd
April 2006, Glasgow Sheriff Court, 2006 Case (73) *rev* [2007] CSIH 35, 2007 SC 525, 2007 SLT 631, 2007 Hous LR 40, 2007 Case (42)

McAllister v Queens Cross Housing Association Ltd
2001 Hous LR 143, 2002 SLT (Lands Tr) 13, 2002 Case (26) *affd* 2003 SC 514, 2003 SLT 971, IH, 2003 Case (28)

Minevco Ltd v Barratt Southern Ltd
1999 GWD 5-266, OH, 1999 Case (41) *affd* 2000 SLT 790, IH, 2000 Case (36)

Moncrieff v Jamieson
2004 SCLR 135, Sh Ct, 2003 Case (20) *affd* [2005] CSIH 14, 2005 SC 281, 2005 SLT 225, 2005 SCLR 463, 2005 Case (6) *affd* [2007] UKHL 42, 2007 SLT 989, 2007 Case (3)

Peart v Legge
2006 GWD 18-377 *affd* 2007 SCLR 86, Sh Ct, 2006 Case (18) *rev* [2007] CSIH 70, 2007 SLT 982, 2007 Case (5)

Robertson v Fife Council
2000 SLT 1226, OH, 2000 Case (84) *affd* 2001 SLT 708, IH, 2001 Case (82) *rev* 2002 SLT 951, HL, 2002 Case (69)

Royal Bank of Scotland plc v Wilson
2001 SLT (Sh Ct) 2, 2000 Case (53) *affd* 2003 SLT 910, 2003 SCLR 716, 2004 SC 153, IH, 2003 Case (40)

Scottish Youth Theatre (Property) Ltd v RSAMD Endowment Trust Trustees
2002 SCLR 945, OH, 2002 Case (3) *affd* 2003 GWD 27-758, IH, 2003 Case (8)

Souter v Kennedy
23 July 1999, Perth Sheriff Court, 1999 Case (69) *rev* 20 March 2001, IH, 2001 Case (81)

Spence v W & R Murray (Alford) Ltd
2001 GWD 7-265, Sh Ct, 2001 Case (9) *affd* 2002 SLT 918, IH, 2002 Case (1)

Stephen v Innes Ker
[2006] CSOH 66, 2006 SLT 1105, 2006 Case (67) *affd* [2007] CSIH 42, 2007 SC 501, 2007 SLT 625, 2007 Case (41)

Stevenson v Roy
2002 SLT 445, OH, 2002 Case (67) *affd* 2003 SC 544, 2003 SCLR 616, IH, 2002 Case (54)

Superdrug Stores plc v Network Rail Infrastructure
2005 SLT (Sh Ct) 105, 2005 Case (35) *rev* [2006] CSIH 4, 2006 SC 365, 2006 SLT 146, 2006 Case (62)

Tesco Stores Ltd v Keeper of the Registers of Scotland
2001 SLT (Lands Tr) 23, 2001 Case (30) *affd* sv *Safeway Stores plc v Tesco Stores Ltd* 2004 SC 29, 2004 SLT 701, IH, 2003 Case (25)

Thomas v Allan
2002 GWD 12-368, Sh Ct, 2002 Case (7) *affd* 2004 SC 393, IH, 2003 Case (22)

Warren James (Jewellers) Ltd v Overgate GP Ltd
[2005] CSOH 142, 2006 GWD 12-235, 2005 Case (26) *affd* [2007] CSIH 14, 2007 GWD 6-94, 2007 Case (35)

Wilson v Inverclyde Council
2001 GWD 3-129, OH, 2001 Case (29) *affd* 2003 SC 366, IH, 2003 Case (27)

TABLE OF CASES DIGESTED IN EARLIER VOLUMES BUT REPORTED IN 2007

A number of cases which were digested in *Conveyancing 2006* or earlier volumes but were at that time unreported have been reported in 2007. A number of other cases have been reported in an additional series of reports. For the convenience of those using earlier volumes all the cases in question are listed below, together with a complete list of citations.

Ashford and Thistle Securities LLP v Kerr
2006 SCLR 873, 2007 SLT (Sh Ct) 60

At.Home Nationwide Ltd v Morris
2007 GWD 31-535

Black v McGregor
 [2006] CSIH 45, 2007 SC 69

Connolly v Brown
[2006] CSOH 187, 2007 SLT 778

Fee v East Renfrewshire Council
2006 Hous LR 99

Holms v Ashford Estates Ltd
2007 SCLR 460

J & L Leisure Ltd v Shaw
2007 GWD 28-489

McPherson v Mackie
[2007] CSIH 7, 2007 SCLR 351

Melfort Pier Holidays Ltd v The Melfort Club
 [2006] CSIH 61, 2007 SC 243

Middlebank Ltd v University of Dundee
[2006] CSOH 202, 2007 GWD 10-190

Sheltered Housing Management Ltd v Jack
2007 GWD 32-553

West Coast Property Developments Ltd v Clarke
2007 GWD 29-511